SMALL GROUPS AS COMPLEX SYSTEMS

SMALL GROUPS AS COMPLEX SYSTEMS

Formation, Coordination, Development, and Adaptation

HOLLY ARROW

JOSEPH E. MCGRATH

JENNIFER L. BERDAHL

Sage Publications, Inc.
International Educational and Professional Publisher
Thousand Oaks ■ London ■ New Delhi

For information:

 Sage Publications, Inc.
2455 Teller Road
Thousand Oaks, California 91320
E-mail: order@sagepub.com

Sage Publications Ltd.
6 Bonhill Street
London EC2A 4PU
United Kingdom

Sage Publications India Pvt. Ltd.
M-32 Market
Greater Kailash I
New Delhi 110 048 India

Printed in the United States of America

Library of Congress Cataloging-in-Publication Data

Arrow, Holly.
  Small groups as complex systems: Formation, coordination, development, and adaptation / by Holly Arrow, Joseph E. McGrath, and Jennifer L. Berdahl.
      p. cm.
Includes bibliographical references and index.
  ISBN 0-8039-7229-6 (cloth: acid-free paper) — ISBN 0-8039-7230-X (pbk.: acid-free paper)
  1. Small groups. 2. Teams in the workplace. I. McGrath, Joseph Edward, 1927- II. Berdahl, Jennifer L. III. Title.
  HM736 .A77 2000
  302.3'4—dc21   99-050490

00   01   02   03   10   9   8   7   6   5   4   3   2   1

Acquiring Editor: C. Deborah Laughton
Editorial Assistant: Eileen Carr
Production Editor: Diana E. Axelsen
Editorial Assistant: Cindy Bear
Typesetter: Danielle Dillahunt
Designer: Marion Warren
Cover Designer: Candice Harman

Contents

PART III: ISSUES AND STRATEGIES

Preface

*W*riting this book has been a challenge, a frustration, and a delight. Our goal of creating a new theory of small groups that would incorporate ideas from fields far removed from our own created constant conceptual challenges. The material we were trying to develop, articulate, and integrate forced us to rethink many of the things we thought we "knew." This in itself was frustrating. The frequently unsuccessful attempts to communicate developing insights to the other two and the stress of constantly hearing (and having to tell each other) that this or that passage "just doesn't make sense" created another level of interpersonal frustration.

Repeatedly, just as we thought we had pinned down some part of the material conceptually, one of us would come up with a "but how about X?" query, and we would have to reconsider what we had just "finalized." Each of us found that explaining ideas clearly enough that the other two authors were willing to accept them proved maddeningly difficult. It also provided an essential "quality control" mechanism that helped get this book over the hurdle from a promising mess to what we feel is a coherent theory.

This project has also been a delight, both in spite of, and perhaps because of, the challenge and frustration. Collaborating on difficult material with serious scholars who are also good friends and demanding critics is one of the main sources of satisfaction in our field.

We had help from many people. We want to acknowledge some of them here: colleagues who read all or part of the book in earlier drafts— Eck Doerry, Richard Hackman, Richard Moreland, M. Scott Poole, Philip Runkel, and two anonymous reviewers; members of Arrow's graduate seminar and of McGrath's graduate seminar, who critiqued some of the material in earlier forms; and our colleagues on the two JEMCO studies, who helped us gain many of the insights incorporated in this work—Kelly Bouas Henry, Kellina Craig, Anne Cummings, Deborah Gruenfeld, Andrea Hollingshead, Linda Lebie, Joselito Lualhati, Kathleen O'Connor, Jon Rhoades, and Ann Schlosser.

We also want to acknowledge the support of both the Social Psychology Section and the Information and Technology in Organizations Section of the National Science Foundation, whose support of our empirical research under Grants BNS 91-06501, IRI 91-07040, and IRI 93-10099 (J. E. McGrath, Principal Investigator) made it possible for us to develop a strong empirical underpinning for our theory. A grant to the first author from the Center for Entrepreneurial Leadership, Inc. and the Ewing Marion Kauffman Foundation provided support during the early stages of work on the book, and NSF Grant SBR-9729320 provided support during the later stages of refining and revising.

We thank C. Deborah Laughton, our editor at Sage, for her patience and encouragement during what proved to be a much lengthier process of creation than we had anticipated.

A special thanks to the director of the Baldwin Research Institute in Baldwin, Michigan, who graciously hosted the three of us during several summer retreats in which we struggled with the book. Thanks also to our respective spouses, Bruce, Marion, and Jim, whose support sustained us through the challenge, frustration, and delight. Finally, we want to thank one another for an inestimably valuable, nonreproducible, many-leveled learning experience.

PART I

ORIENTATION, HISTORY, AND OVERVIEW OF THE THEORY

∞ *1* ∞

Introduction

*T*his book presents a general theory of small groups as complex systems. Our theory addresses what groups are, how they behave, and with what consequences. We treat groups as adaptive, dynamic systems that are driven by interactions both among group members and between the group and its embedding contexts. We do not believe that groups can be adequately understood as collections of independently acting individuals. Instead, we focus our attention on relationships among people, tools, and tasks, activated by a combination of individual and collective purposes and goals that change and evolve as the group interacts over time.

The ideas in the book are both old and new. We build on our own past work (e.g., Argote & McGrath, 1993; Arrow, 1997; Arrow & McGrath, 1995; Berdahl, 1998, 1999; McGrath, 1997; McGrath & Berdahl, 1998; McGrath, Berdahl, & Arrow, 1995; McGrath & O'Connor, 1996) and also draw heavily on the work of many scholars who have made important empirical and theoretical contributions to the century-long history of small group research. This body of work is cited throughout the book, but we draw on past theory and research selectively, highlighting those ideas and data that seem most closely connected to the concepts in our own theory.

∞ GROUPS AS COMPLEX ADAPTIVE SYSTEMS

Although we consulted much past and current work to inform our thinking, we also believe this book offers something new. Our theory of groups is based on concepts borrowed from several other fields—general systems theory, dynamical systems theory, complexity and chaos theory—that study complex, adaptive, dynamic systems. Conceptualizing groups as holistic and dynamic systems is not new (e.g., Altman & Rogoff, 1987; Lewin, 1948). Drawing on concepts from the branch of mathematics known as dynamical systems theory for use in the social sciences is more novel, but we are not alone in our excitement about potential applications (see, e.g., Barton, 1994; Vallacher & Nowak, 1994). What is genuinely new, we believe, is the development of a comprehensive theory of small groups that adapts, transforms, and integrates concepts from dynamical systems theory in a way appropriate to thinking about systems that are themselves composed of complex systems—members whose actions are guided by goals, intentions, perceptions, and preconceptions that also change over time.

Let us specify the boundaries of our discourse. By *small group*, we mean a loosely coupled (Weick, 1995) system of mutually interacting, interdependent members, projects, and technology with a shared collective identity (see McGrath, 1984). Groups have temporal and psychological boundaries; group members are aware of the group as an entity and of their membership in it; and members' behavior is linked and interdependent, with shared consequences. We do not include in our concept of small groups large sets of people who belong to a social category—such as Navajo, or female, or lower-middle-class American—whose members do not all interact directly and interdependently with one another. We also exclude sets of people in physical proximity who do not interact with one another or have a shared identity as a group—for example, people riding in an elevator together, or the students sitting in the first two rows of chairs in a classroom.

Small groups are formed for many different reasons and have different purposes—to provide enjoyable activities, to complete projects, to create political solidarity, to make money, or to enhance the status of members. Our thinking has been shaped most strongly by research on task-oriented groups in organizational settings—a traditional focus of much past research on small groups. However, the scope of our theory and our discussion is not limited to such groups. We intend our theory to apply to a broad range of small groups, including work groups but also friendship groups and sports teams, activity clubs and laboratory groups, expeditions and families.

To illustrate the importance of a complex systems perspective, consider a hypothetical project made up of six people from different departments of an organization: Sally from sales, Ed from engineering, Manuel from manufacturing, Felicia from finance, Mark from marketing, and Richard from R&D. The group has been assembled by top management at Minerva, a software company, to develop a plan for a sophisticated electronic notepad. What would one want to know about this group to predict how well its members will work together, whether one or more of its members will emerge as a group leader, and how creative and viable the product developed by the group will be?

One important feature of the group is the collection of attributes of the six people in it—their age, tenure, gender, race, and cultural background and the array of their individual skills, knowledge, training, values, and many other attributes. Interaction within the group is also affected by group members' relationships with others outside the group—with friends and family, with people in their primary organizational departments, and with other people they know well and work with in the organization. These relationships help determine members' status within the wider organization. But the group is much more than just the collection of individual members with various attributes and social connections. It is also in part defined by its purposes, which include, in this case, developing plans for a sophisticated notepad and by the resources—office and lab space, hardware and software equipment, policies, precedents, and budgets—that the group can acquire to fulfill its purposes. Some of these resources are controlled by the organization in which it is embedded. Group behavior is shaped by many aspects of the organization, including the status of the members' departments (and how much clout group members have within these departments), the organization's age and success within the industry, and organizational norms and culture. The group may also have to work with constraints established directly by the organization, such as an internal deadline for developing the product plan.

Some organizational attributes are in turn defined by the industry in which the organization operates. The competitiveness of the industry, the availability of capital via the stock market, and the organization's history of innovation versus imitation of other companies' products may also affect the ultimate viability of the product plan developed by this group.

Obviously, this cross-functional task force exists and operates at a level of group *qua* group, even though much of the work of the group (researching the marketplace, developing a budget, projecting sales, etc.) is completed by individual members. Members act on behalf of the group, in response to group purposes and shared expectations. Besides developing a successful product plan, the group's purposes may also include serving member needs and maintaining satisfactory interpersonal relationships so that work can proceed.

This group can be viewed as an entity, or unit, or system, but it should not be viewed as an isolated system. Any group must continually coordinate both the varied contributions of its members and their often divergent interests. It must also reckon with various external forces and the environmental contexts within which the group is situated.

When attempting to predict what will happen in this group over time, one should look first to the prevailing conditions when the group formed. Which member(s) took charge and asserted a vision of the product and expertise at fulfilling that vision? Was Manuel still angry at Richard for dating his ex-girlfriend, or had their friendship been repaired? Were the marketing and finance departments at odds? Did Sally see the work of this group as competing with or supporting the mission of her department? What initial resources were provided to the group for developing and testing ideas? These and many other initial conditions could profoundly affect how well the group does whatever it is doing.

The group's internal development—how relations between members change over time, for example, and how various ideas are developed by the group—will also be affected by changes in external conditions that alter the outcomes of group actions. Both initial circumstances and emergent events and conditions affect the group's developmental path. The market for electronic notepads may change; a competitor company may beat Minerva in the race to develop one; the organization may cut the group's budget, change its time line, or fire one of its members. These changes in circumstances will require adjustments by the group; if the group fails to adapt, the widening gap between group goals and an altered reality may generate a host of new stresses on both internal and external relations.

In this book, we argue that to fully understand groups, we need to view them as complex, adaptive, and dynamic systems, as illustrated in this extended example. Moreover, we need to deal not only with the group as a system but also with its interchanges with agents and forces in its embedding contexts and its interchanges with its constituent members. Furthermore, we need to consider not only the group's members and their distribution of attributes but also the group's tasks and technology; and we need to understand how those members, tasks, and tools are intertwined, coordinated, and adjusted. These issues are taken up, in detail, in Part II of the book.

∞ HOW THE BOOK IS ORGANIZED

The book is organized into three parts. Part I has three chapters. After this opening chapter's general orientation, Chapter 2 provides a brief history of small group research, and Chapter 3 presents an overview of the theory.

In Chapter 2, we identify seven bodies or "schools" of early group research whose proponents had different conceptions of what groups are and what they do and who concentrated both theory and research on different focal problems. Three of those schools focus primarily on basic research questions; four focus more on applied issues. We then describe six more recent bodies of theory and research. We note which insights or elements from this "baker's dozen" of research streams we found particularly helpful in developing our theory of groups, and we analyze some limitations of most past and current work, which we attribute to an overreliance on positivist, reductionist notions of research and to methodological features of much research based on these notions.

Chapter 3 presents an overview of the theory, organized around five propositions about (a) the nature of groups, (b) three levels of causal dynamics that characterize group functioning, (c) the multiple functions that groups serve, (d) the elements of groups (members, projects, and technology) and patterns of relations among them, and (e) three modes of a group's life course.

Part II of the book, consisting of Chapters 4 through 8, provides a detailed presentation of the theory organized around three modes of group life (formation, operations, and metamorphosis) and three levels of dynamics (local, global, and contextual dynamics). Chapter 4 discusses the mix of forces that lead to the formation of groups. Newly formed groups differ in the relative emphasis they place on group goals and on member needs and in the relative importance of their members, their projects, and their technology in determining the group structure. On the basis of these distinctions, we identify prototypical kinds of groups.

Chapters 5, 6, and 7 discuss the operations mode of a group's life. Although all three levels of causal dynamics operate simultaneously, continuously, and interdependently, these three chapters examine the three levels of causal dynamics separately as they play out during the group's operations mode. Chapter 5 examines local dynamics: the ongoing interactions among a group's components at the relatively micro level. We use the term *coordination* for the operation of local dynamics and discuss the elaboration, enactment, and modification of the group's pattern of member-task-tool relations, which we call the *coordination network*.

Chapter 6 addresses the global dynamics that emerge from the group's local dynamics over time and that subsequently shape its local dynamics. We use the term *group development* to encompass the operation and outcome of these group-level processes. In Chapter 6, we identify six classes of global variables of interest to group researchers, which correspond to three intrinsic group functions (group production, member needs, and system integrity) and three instrumental functions (information processing, conflict and consensus managing, and coordination of member behavior). Drawing on ideas from dynamical systems and complexity theories, we discuss how global variables may evolve over time in groups under varying conditions and how such trajectories over time may be viewed as movement in an "attractor landscape." We propose that the evolution of different global variables may follow different patterns within the same group, as well as differing across groups.

Chapter 7 addresses change over time that is driven by events that alter a group's relationship with its embedding contexts. This is the level of contextual dynamics; it includes changes in the environment that affect the group and also initiatives by a group to come into better alignment with its environment. We call this bidirectional process *adaptation*. Drawing on ideas from evolutionary theory, we conceptualize adaptation as movement within a fitness landscape. Chapter 7 covers principles of adaptation, barriers to successful adaptation, internal factors affecting adaptation, and features of external change and of group responses to change.

Chapter 8 discusses the processes of transformation that take place as a group either disbands completely or else changes so fundamentally that its members no longer consider it to be the same group. We call this *metamorphosis.*

Part III of the book examines the implications of the theory as a basis for research on groups. The application of our ideas raises some perplexing issues, and we offer some practical suggestions for building a research program that can handle those challenges. Chapter 9 discusses conceptual and methodological issues that arise when one attempts to study groups as complex, adaptive, dynamic systems. Practical challenges include the time and expense of studying groups over time and the difficulties of dealing with multiple levels of analysis. Conceptual challenges include the need to rethink the meaning of time and validity for theory and research, the nature of causality, the proper scope for generalizing from results, and assumptions about measurement and error. Chapter 10 proposes a multiple-strategy program for developing and carrying out a systematic theoretical and empirical examination of groups as complex systems. It illustrates that strategy with recent examples of research that has studied groups over time. It ends with a section that recapitulates the main ideas of the book and outlines a research agenda for the future.

We conclude this opening chapter with a caveat and an invitation. The caveat arises because we find that our ideas are difficult to communicate in a medium that requires us to present the components of our theory sequentially rather than simultaneously. Just as different levels of group dynamics take place simultaneously and interdependently, the components of our theory are tightly interconnected. Some portions of various chapters can be more fully appreciated if they are re-read after reading later chapters. After repeatedly moving material backward and forward as we wrote and rewrote the book, we concluded that there was no best sequence for presenting the ideas. Instead, the very need to present them in a sequence was a root problem. Although we have done our best to create a logical sequence, the result may still frustrate the reader in some places. Thus, we invite the reader to imagine that the product is in hypertext and that our many forward and backward references are "links" leading to information that broadens and deepens the information presented at the link. Unfortunately, the reader cannot just click on those links to have the relevant information displayed but rather must find it by the more primitive means of leafing to another section or chapter. But some such linking back and forth may help the reader attain a fuller understanding.

The convoluted process by which the three of us, a small group, created this book served as a constant and sometimes painful reminder that the dynamics of groups are rarely simple and do not unfold in a straightforward, one-dimensional sequence over time. The past constrains the possible future; seemingly small local actions divert the global course of a group; and changes in context, meaning, and priorities alter both individual and collective plans and actions.

This is how we experience the life of the many small groups to which we belong. We have developed a theory that, we hope, captures this richness while at the same time abstracting it into a framework of ideas that can guide thinking and research on many different kinds of small groups. Our hope is that this book will inspire scholars to develop the framework further and use it in developing their own theories and empirical study designs.

∞ 2 ∞

Small Group Research

The Past and Some Needs for the Future

*I*n this chapter, we offer a brief characterization of a century of small group research, highlighting features of past and current work that we build on in this book. We also note some major limitations of the knowledge base within the field and suggest how some new conceptual tools may help us transcend those limitations.

∞ A BRIEF HISTORY OF PAST RESEARCH ON SMALL GROUPS

Although its roots go back to the end of the 19th century (e.g., Triplett, 1898), small group research first became a distinguishable field within North American social psychology in the early part of the 20th century. It flourished in that domain through the 1940s and 1950s. Then, in the late 1960s, group research suffered a system crash within North American social psychology, more or less coincident with the rise of social cognition as a dominant paradigm for research in that field. Although its centrality diminished within social psychology in the 1970s, the 1980s, and the first part of the 1990s, small group research continued to flourish in related social and behavioral science disciplines such as

11

speech communications, political science, organizational behavior, group psychotherapy, social work, and educational psychology. Accounts of this history can be found in numerous publications (e.g., Cartwright & Zander, 1953, 1960, 1968; McGrath, 1997; McGrath & Altman, 1966; Moreland, Hogg, & Hains, 1994; Sanna & Parks, 1997). In our condensed summary, we note some of the strengths of group theory and research up to the present time and some of its weaknesses. We cite representative work within each tradition discussed, but the reader should note that we do not intend this as an exhaustive review.

Some Main Themes From Past Research

Small group research has always incorporated a diffuse array of research and theory. Much of the earliest research was generated by several relatively distinct "schools" of small group research, each with its own perspective about what groups are, what they do, and how to study them. McGrath (1997) summarized early work in terms of three schools and identified three additional defining metaphors for group research in more recent work. We flesh out that account by adding several additional bodies of research, many of which have a more applied focus than the six reviewed by McGrath.

The first three schools of early research identified by McGrath focused on studying groups as (a) systems for influencing members, (b) systems for patterning interaction, and (c) systems for performing tasks. To these we add (d) the classic work of the National Training Laboratory (NTL) and others on groups as a setting in which individuals grow in self-understanding; (e) the Tavistock Institute's groundbreaking research in work organizations, in which groups were viewed as intact sociotechnical systems with multiple outcomes (e.g., task performance and member satisfaction); (f) the Hawthorne studies plus the work of Katz, French, and others on how informal groups develop within work settings and affect both work effectiveness and member satisfaction; and (g) work by Sherif and others on the dynamic interplay of intergroup and intragroup processes.

Three more recent bodies of research identified by McGrath (1997) explore groups as (h) information-processing systems; (i) systems for managing conflict and attaining consensus; and (j) systems for motivating, regulating, and coordinating the activities of members. We add to that list recent work reflecting some of the earlier applied themes: (k) research on work teams in organizational settings and (l) research in education, clinical psychology, and social work on using groups in classroom, clinical, and community settings to enhance the learning and psychosocial adjustment of members. We also add another stream of basic research: (m) research on cognition and behavior in the minimal group and social categorization tradition. Several of the more recent research traditions integrate or reinterpret themes within one or more of the earlier bodies of work.

Theoretical insights and empirical findings gleaned from these 13 research streams form the substantive underpinnings of our approach to small groups. At the same time, each of those bodies of work contains some serious constraints and limitations—some common to all of them, some shared by most. Many of those constraints arise from inherent features of the conceptual and methodological paradigms that allowed that work to generate so much useful knowledge. These limitations suggest to us that the field of small group research needs to transcend some established assumptions and practices if it is to continue to gain new insights and understandings about groups and how they operate.

The next section covers each of the 13 bodies of past and current research briefly. We then discuss some limitations of the existing knowledge base and identify some conceptual tools we think are needed if the next century of research on small groups is to make the dramatic progress that we feel is possible.

Early Group Research

Groups as Vehicles for Influencing Members

A large body of small group research in its early years viewed groups as *vehicles for influencing members* (e.g., changing their attitudes). That school was built on the work and inspiration of Kurt Lewin (e.g., Lewin, 1948, 1953; Lewin, Lippett, & White, 1939), with many now-famous contributions, such as Festinger's (1954, 1957) social comparison theory and dissonance theory, Thibaut and Kelley's (1959) exchange theory,

Newcomb's (1953, 1961) theory of communication acts and work on the acquaintance process, French and Raven's analysis of power (French, 1956; French & Raven, 1959), and Cartwright and Zander's (1953, 1960, 1968) conceptual framework, which shaped the early organization of the field.

Although this body of work began with the study of natural groups (e.g., Festinger, Schachter, & Back, 1950), it quickly migrated into the laboratory. In fact, researchers in this school played a major role in creating a powerful *experimental technology* for studying groups in laboratory experimental settings. In large part because this technology became the dominant paradigm for studying groups, small group research was a central topic within a developing experimental social psychology in the 1950s and 1960s. The very success of this experimental technology, however, helped separate many researchers from the study of natural groups with which they had begun.

Small group researchers continue to be interested in influence processes in groups, although the emphasis on majority influence in this early work has broadened to include minority influence processes (e.g., Moscovici, Mugny, & Van Avermaet, 1985; Nemeth, 1986; for a recent review, see Wood, Lundgren, Ouellette, Buscerne, & Blackstone, 1994). The theory of social impact (Latané, 1981) and its successor, dynamic social impact theory (Latané & L'Herrou, 1996; Nowak, Szamrej, & Latané, 1990), integrate majority and minority influence into a single framework and also take dynamics seriously.

The features of this work that have informed our approach to groups are its substantive emphasis on how groups fulfill member needs, its conceptual emphasis on the importance of member-member and member-group relations, and of course the methodological approach of studying groups experimentally.

Groups as Vehicles for Patterning Interaction

Another large portion of early research on groups regarded groups as *vehicles for patterning human interaction* (e.g., patterned sequences of problem-solving phases). Bales's (1950a, 1950b) interaction process analysis (IPA) theory and coding system and its applications to analysis of group processes (Bales, 1953, 1955; Borgatta, 1962), leadership and group structure (Bales & Slater, 1955; Borgatta, Couch, & Bales, 1954; Talland, 1955), and problem-solving phase analysis (Bales & Strodtbeck, 1951; Psathas, 1960), as well as his later SYMLOG theory (Bales & Cohen, 1979), provided the benchmark work on group interaction process for decades.

In the same era, Bion, Thelen, and colleagues (Bion, 1961; Stock & Thelen, 1958; Thelen, 1956; Thelen, Stock, & Associates, 1954) developed an alternative theory of work and emotionality in groups and an alternative system for coding interaction. That work had and continues to have an enormous influence on research and theory in group psychotherapy (e.g., Ettin, Fidler, & Cohen, 1995; Verdi & Wheelan, 1992; Wheelan & McKeage, 1993). Both the Bales IPA system and the Bion system for observing interaction (a) are highly labor intensive and demanding, (b) focus on interaction process but not on its content, and (c) are tightly tied to particular theories and hence less useful for researchers working out of other theoretical frameworks.

This work is important to our theory because of its emphasis on the key role of group process and because of its early concern with the patterning of interaction process over time. The focus on dynamic processes continues in recent work based in this school, such as Polley's (1988, 1989) development of group field dynamics. See Bales (1999) for a recent summary and integration of this body of work.

Groups as Vehicles for Performing Tasks

Another large body of early research on groups viewed groups as *vehicles for task performance.* That work, much more diffuse, dates back to the 19th-century work of Triplett (1898), to Allport's (1920) early research on social facilitation, and to the work of other scholars in the early 20th century (e.g., Dashiell, 1930). Much of this work studied military units and sports teams (e.g., Altman & Haythorn, 1967; Carter, Haythorn, & Howell, 1950; Goodacre, 1953; Havron, Fay, & Goodacre, 1951; Havron & McGrath, 1961; Roby & Lanzetta, 1956; for reviews, see Dyer, 1985; McGrath & Altman, 1966). The majority of work, however, used ad hoc laboratory groups to study topics such as leadership styles (e.g., Fiedler, 1964; Glanzer & Glaser, 1959, 1961), communication patterns (e.g., Guetzkow & Simon, 1955; Shaw, 1954, 1958), and various

aspects of group problem solving, decision making, and task performance (e.g., Davis & Restle, 1963; Hackman & Morris, 1975, 1978;
Laughlin & Ellis, 1986; Lorge & Solomon, 1955; Shaw, 1932; Steiner,
1972; Taylor & Faust, 1952; for reviews, see Davis, Laughlin, &
Komorita, 1976; Levine & Moreland, 1990; McGrath & Kravitz, 1982).

Because task performance was central to this school, a portion of the
work from this perspective dealt with the effects of different types of
tasks (e.g., Carter, 1950; Kent & McGrath, 1969; Laughlin & Shippy,
1983; Laughlin, VanderStoep, & Hollingshead, 1991; McGrath, 1984;
Roby & Lanzetta, 1957, 1958; Steiner, 1972). This school's emphasis on
task performance as an outcome and its concern with differential effects of different tasks have both been important to our own thinking.

Groups as Vehicles for Improving
Member Self-Understanding

Simultaneous with these three schools of basic research on groups,
work at the National Training Laboratory at Bethel, Maine, was exploring small groups from a more applied standpoint, investigating how
groups could be used to help individuals learn, grow, and gain greater
understanding of themselves. This work, which also originated with
the insights and teachings of Kurt Lewin (see Moreland, 1996, for an account of how this tradition got started), led to a host of alternative approaches by many research and practice groups, all of them exploring
how groups can contribute in a quasi-therapeutic way to individual
growth and development. Each research or practice team tended to develop its own protocol for establishing and directing groups and established its own criteria for assessing the progress of members on their
self-insight and self-development tasks.

One long-standing contribution of this body of work was the insights
it contributed to how small groups developed over time (see, e.g.,
Bennis & Shepard, 1956; Hill & Gruner, 1973; LaCoursiere, 1980; and
integrative reviews by McGrath, 1984; Tuckman, 1965; Tuckman &
Jensen, 1977). For examples of more recent work on group development
that draws on this tradition, see McCollom (1995b) and Worchel
(1994). This work is important for our thinking because of its focus on
developmental issues and also because of the importance it placed on
the personal and interpersonal consequences of group activities.

Groups as Intact, Holistic,
Sociotechnical Systems

The work of researchers at the Tavistock Institute in London, using what came to be known as the "sociotechnical" approach, related both to the basic issues of the first three schools and to the applied focus of the fourth. That work viewed groups as intact systems, consisting not only of a collection of members but also of the tools, resources, and technology available to (or imposed on) them. It studied groups in the field (see, e.g., Trist & Bamforth, 1951) and revealed how changes in technology could not be viewed separately from the group structure that had grown up around a particular technology and set of tasks. The sociotechnical tradition of studying naturally occurring work groups in context has been continued by contemporary researchers inspired by this tradition (e.g., Goodman, 1986; Kolodny & Kiggundu, 1980).

This work has been important to our thinking because of its focus on technology and the interconnection between members, tasks, and tools. More fundamentally, this body of work was one of the earliest to study groups as intact, complex systems, embedded within larger contexts that set constraints on these systems.

Informal Groups in Work Settings

Much early applied research on groups was conducted in work organizations. Unlike the sociotechnical school (and a later tradition to be discussed below), most of this research was not concerned with analyzing how formally organized work groups did their tasks; indeed, this work stumbled on the importance of groups in the workplace serendipitously. Perhaps the most notable part of this body of work were the well-known "Hawthorne studies" (Homans, 1950; Roethlisberger & Dickson, 1939), conducted at the Western Electric Company's plant in Hawthorne, Illinois. The researchers conducting these studies were not, initially, studying groups. Instead, they were interested in the impact of workplace conditions and incentives on individual productivity. To facilitate their studies, however, they separated out small groups of workers and placed them in separate rooms for easier observation. They found—to their surprise—that these informal groups of workers developed and enforced strongly entrenched "group norms," which sometimes worked against the higher productivity goals of management, counteracting the expected impact of production incentives, and sometimes promoted enhanced production.

Other group researchers (e.g., Coch & French, 1948; Kahn & Katz, 1953) began investigating informal groups in work settings more deliberately. They were interested in how emergent informal groups—the unplanned patterns of interpersonal relations that developed among coworkers—affected task performance and worker satisfaction in those settings. They found that informal groups had a strong impact on what formal work groups could accomplish and on how they carried out their work. This body of work is important to our thinking because of its emphasis on the importance of emergent groups and because of its early investigation of how the group as a distinct entity mediates the impact of a larger embedding context (typically work organizations) on individuals.

The Interplay of Intergroup Relations
and Within-Group Processes

Some early group research also tackled the question of intergroup relations and how those intergroup processes are intertwined with intragroup activities. A classic early study that epitomizes work on this topic was the Robbers Cave study by Sherif, Harvey, White, Hood, and Sherif (1961), which showed that rivalry between groups typically worsened under close contact but could be transformed into cooperation through the manipulation of a common fate affecting both groups.

This study and other early work exploring intergroup relations (e.g., Blake & Mouton, 1961; Rabbie & Horwitz, 1969) continue to inform studies of conflict between groups ranging in size from a few people to whole nations or societies. A primary emphasis has been understanding the roots of intergroup hostility and violence, demonstrating the ineffectiveness of mere contact between members of different groups in counteracting hostility, and searching for more effective ways to prevent or defuse intergroup conflict in schools (e.g., Johnson, Johnson, & Maruyama, 1984; Schofield, 1978), in the workplace (e.g., Brown, Condor, Matthews, Wade, & Williams, 1986), and between large racial and ethnic groups (e.g., Staub, 1989; White, 1969). This body of work has been important to our thinking because of its focus on the dynamic ten-

sion between cooperation and competition, on the importance of contextual factors in understanding intragroup relations, and on the two-
way interchange between a group and its embedding contexts, which
also contain other groups.

More Recent Bodies of Group Research

As noted above, work on the core topics of many of the "early"
schools has continued to the present. Small group researchers have not
lost interest in influence processes, the patterning of interaction, group
performance, and so on, and contemporary work on these themes can
be viewed as contributing to a continuous line of research established
by this early work. So the work of many of these schools is ongoing.

In this section, we identify recent bodies of work that are less easily
identified as continuations of one of these prior streams. Others survey-
ing the field might come to different conclusions about which bodies of
work constitute "continuations" or "new themes," and we have no
doubt left out some bodies of work that others would include. The bodies of work that we have decided to call new "schools" or "streams" of
research strike us as different from continuations of the early schools
for one or more reasons. Some are pursued primarily by researchers in
disciplines other than experimental social psychology. Some integrate
multiple themes from different early schools; others coalesce around
new metaphors for thinking about groups. The first one we describe ex-
emplifies the emergence of a new metaphor.

Groups as Information-Processing Systems

The metaphor of the computer, which inspired the development of
modern cognitive psychology and contributed to a new interest in cognition by social psychologists, has also been applied in the past few decades to small groups. This growing body of research treats groups as
systems for *organizing and processing information*—that is, acquiring,
encoding, processing, storing, exchanging, and using "information,"
broadly construed. It is exemplified by the theory and research of
Wegner and colleagues, and others, on transactive memory in groups

(Hollingshead, 1998; Wegner, 1986; Wegner, Erber, & Raymond, 1991); the work of Davis and colleagues, and others, on group decision-making processes, information exchange, and group memory (Clark & Stephenson, 1989; Davis, Kameda, Parks, Stasson, & Zimmerman, 1989; Hartwick, Sheppard, & Davis, 1982; Hinsz, 1990; Hinsz, Tindale, & Vollrath, 1997; Laughlin & Adamopoulos, 1982; Stasser, Taylor, & Hanna, 1989; Stasser & Titus, 1985, 1987; Tindale, 1989); and the work of Levine, Moreland, and others on sociocognition (Gruenfeld & Hollingshead, 1993; Levine & Moreland, 1985, 1991). This work emphasizes what we see as one of the crucial "instrumental functions" of a wide variety of kinds of groups: the acquisition, storage, processing, generation, and use of information.

Groups as Conflict-Managing
and Consensus-Seeking Systems

Another body of more recent work treats groups as systems for *managing conflict and generating consensus*. Scholars who take this perspective focus on the political work that groups do. It contrasts with the earlier stream of research on conflict because it emphasizes what happens when group members work together to try to resolve conflict and thus tends to focus on intragroup, rather than intergroup, conflict. It is exemplified by theory and research on negotiations and mediation and on the experience and effects of intragroup conflict (e.g., Bazerman, Mannix, & Thompson, 1988; Deutsch, 1949a, 1949b; Deutsch & Krauss, 1962; Jehn, 1995, 1997; Komorita, 1973, 1974, 1979; Pruitt & Kimmel, 1977; Vidmar & McGrath, 1970).

In this body of work, groups are viewed not so much as problem-solving systems but, rather, as interest- or perspective-blending systems. They are looking not for a correct answer but for consensus. This work is important to our thinking because it makes clear that rational information processing and problem solving is not the only thing groups do, because it recognizes the importance of dynamic political tensions in groups, and because it focuses on consensus as an emergent group-level product of interactions among members. It complements the cognitive focus of the information-processing school with an emphasis on affective processes.

Groups as Systems for Motivating,
Regulating, and Coordinating Member Activities

A third body of recent work treats groups as systems for *motivating, regulating, and coordinating member behavior.* Work along these lines includes research and theory on socialization of members by Moreland, Levine, and others (e.g., Goodman & Leyden, 1991; Goodman, Devadas, & Hughson, 1988; Moreland & Levine, 1982, 1984; Salas, Blaiwes, Reynolds, Glickman, & Morgan, 1985); work on habitual routines by Gersick and Hackman (1990) and others (e.g., Weiss & Ilgen, 1985); and the work of Poole and colleagues on adaptive structuration (e.g., Poole, 1981, 1983; Poole & DeSanctis, 1989, 1990; Poole & Roth, 1989a, 1989b; Watson, DeSanctis, & Poole, 1988). Much work in sports psychology (e.g., Ball & Carron, 1976; Carron, 1988) also takes this perspective.

This body of work views groups as the medium within which much human development and activity takes place and in which interaction and resulting interpersonal relations are motivating forces, normative-regulatory forces, and behavior-coordinating forces. This body of work has been important to our thinking because of its emphasis on ongoing group processes and because more than any of the other current "schools" it stresses the dynamics of group operation.

The Development and Use of Teams
in Work Organizations

In the last decade or so, there has been a resurgence of interest in groups in the workplace, coincident with the growing use of "teams" as a basic unit of organizations (e.g., Beyerlein, Johnson, & Beyerlein, 1997; Guzzo & Salas, 1995; Hackman, 1990; Salas, Dickinson, Converse, & Tannenbaum, 1992; Sundstrom, De Meuse, & Futrell, 1990; see Guzzo & Dickson, 1996, for a recent review). This body of work shows both that teams can be very effective units of the work organization and that teams can fail to provide high performance effectiveness, depending on the features that they incorporate and the contextual conditions under which they operate. That work also shows that organizations often create units they call teams and expect the benefits that are purported to flow from them but create those teams in a way that undercuts

their effectiveness as autonomous performing units—by failing to provide needed resources, including training; by placing responsibility on
the team but rewarding individuals; and by failing to provide an appropriately supportive embedding context for the team to do its work. We
draw on this body of research not only because it emphasizes teams or
groups as intact systems but also because it stresses the importance of
both initial conditions and interrelations with embedding contexts.

Groups as Vehicles for Improving the Learning and Adjustment of Members

The early work on "t-groups" and other forms of groups designed to
benefit members' psychosocial adjustment has its parallel in current
bodies of work within group psychotherapy, social work, and educational and clinical psychology (e.g., Corey & Corey, 1992; Kaplan &
Sadock, 1993; Yalom, 1995). Some of that work, done in classroom settings, explores the benefits of group activities both for individual learning and for the development of positive patterns of interpersonal relations (e.g., Christensen, 1983; Michaelsen, Watson, & Schrader, 1985;
Watson, Kumar, & Michaelsen, 1993). Application of these ideas,
within a wide range of types of groups, explores how group settings can
be beneficial to individual psychosocial adjustment, whether those individuals are children and adolescents (e.g., Duncan & Gumaer, 1980;
Scheidlinger, 1984), adults suffering from the after-effects of childhood
trauma such as incest (e.g., Herman & Schatzow, 1984), people with behavioral problems such as eating disorders (e.g., Brisman, & Siegal,
1985; Hendren, Atkins, Sumner, & Barber, 1987), battered women (e.g.,
Sadock, 1983), or the men who batter them (e.g., Grusznski & Bankovics, 1990). This work emphasizes the two-way interchanges between the group and its members and highlights a wide range of group
types and a wide range of group-related phenomena.

Identity in Groups

One body of work currently receiving considerable emphasis is the
study of social identity, group identity, in-group/out-group perceptions, members' attributions about self and others, and other concepts

involving groups and identity. Unlike the earlier work of Sherif and others on intergroup relations, current work is much more focused on basic research issues, and rather than studying more natural groups longitudinally, it primarily studies either short-lived, ad hoc laboratory groups or "minimal groups" whose members are informed of their membership but do not interact.

This body of work, which draws on social identity theory (Tajfel, 1974, 1978; Tajfel & Turner, 1979) and social categorization theory (Turner, 1985; Turner, Hogg, Oakes, Reicher, & Wetherall, 1987), focuses on the cognitive process of perceiving groups and group boundaries and identifying oneself as a member and on the consequences of this process, such as in-group favoritism and discrimination against out-group members. The emphasis has been largely on intergroup relations (e.g., Brown, 1978; Tajfel, Billig, Bundy, & Flament, 1971; Taylor & McKirnan, 1984; van Knippenberg & Ellemers, 1993) rather than on intragroup process (for some exceptions, see Brewer & Gardner, 1996; Hogg, 1987, 1996; Hogg & Hardie, 1991; Rabbie & Lodewijkx, 1996). This work is important to our thinking because of its emphasis on individual cognition and perception about groups, on the group boundary, and on the ways in which the context of intergroup relations may affect group members' cognition, emotion, and behavior.

∞ SOME STRENGTHS
AND LIMITATIONS
OF PAST THEORY AND RESEARCH

The research from these 13 streams of work on small groups, plus other work that does not fit neatly within any of these categories, encompasses an enormous number of published studies (see McGrath & Altman, 1966; Moreland et al., 1994; and Sanna & Parks, 1997, for overviews). Research in all of these approaches has been done well for the most part—as well as can be done by working with the methodological tools that have dominated our field during this era. These multiple research streams have provided key ideas for our theory of groups. The ideas that we will draw from these bodies of work, and some crucial limitations of that work that make a new formulation useful at this time, are considered in this section.

Key Ideas From Past Research

As noted above, we have learned from all of those research programs. We think existing research and theory about groups justifies the following set of characterizations. First, groups serve more than one purpose or function. All of the themes underlying both the early schools and the more recent work are valid ideas about what groups are and do. Groups do influence members' attitudes, values, and behaviors. They do pattern member interactions. They can aid individual learning and self-fulfillment. Groups process information, manage conflict, attain consensus, and motivate, regulate, and coordinate member activities. Groups and their members have intentions and goals, some assigned to them and some group generated, and they carry out activities to attain those goals.

Second, although a group contains individuals who are its members, a group is more than just a collection of individuals. What the group is doing—its purposes and therefore its tasks—has important consequences for how it behaves and what the group and its members gain from group activities. The group's technology and resources affect what the group decides to do, how it proceeds, and how effective the results are. Members, tasks, and tools are interconnected in complex patterns.

Groups are intact systems with boundaries but are never completely isolated or closed; the boundaries are permeable. Spanning these boundaries, groups engage in continual two-way interchanges with a number of contexts in which they are embedded—organizations, communities, and physical and cultural environments. They also carry on continual two-way exchanges with their own individual members.

Third, groups develop and change over time. Not only do groups carry out their tasks and purposes via patterned sequences of activity; they also learn from that experience and hence modify those activity sequences. They also change as they interact with and adapt to changing conditions in their various embedding contexts.

Some Limitations on
Our Extant Body of Knowledge

Despite its strengths in contributing to our understanding, much work done within these early and more recent streams of research shares conceptual and methodological features that also limit what we can learn from that work about groups. Certain limitations that beset work from many of these perspectives, we believe, are unintended but inevitable consequences of the dominant methodological paradigm within which almost all of that work has been done and of the underlying conceptual paradigm to which that methodology is tied. Much of North American and European social psychology and the related disciplines within which small group research has recently flourished have been heavily committed to a positivist-reductionist-analytic perspective or paradigm. Within that perspective, the laboratory experiment is the idealized methodological strategy, but the interpretative epistemology of that paradigm extends even to studies carried out by other data collection strategies, such as field studies, field experiments, and sample surveys.

The positivist paradigm carries a strong preference for empirical research that permits very precise measurement and effective manipulation and control of variables. Those features, which are maximized in laboratory experiments, allow researchers to make strong directional causal inferences, an essential for gaining definitive knowledge. At the same time, that paradigm purchases those advantages at a serious cost in some other essentials. Specifically, it gives up considerable amounts of contextual realism, and its pays a heavy price in generalizability, both of which are also important for advancing our knowledge of a domain (Runkel & McGrath, 1972).

For both methodological and practical reasons, work done within the positivist-reductionist-analytic paradigm tends to gain its precision and control from several design compromise strategies that generate other problems. First, work in the positivist paradigm examines groups from an analytic and reductionist perspective, stripping them as much as possible from their contexts. Second, work in that paradigm studies only a limited range of variables, ignoring, holding constant, or putatively randomizing all other aspects of the group and its context.

Finally, work in that paradigm typically entails relatively static (one-shot or short-term) designs, testing key hypotheses either about differences (at a given point in time) between groups that were created experimentally and randomly assigned to different experimental conditions or about covariations (at a given point in time) of two or more properties of a number of "cases," all presumably comparable in all respects except for the properties under investigation.

The huge volume of empirical research on small groups done from the positivist paradigm has been well done, by and large, and it has yielded bountiful results, often with high precision and a strong basis for directional causal inferences. But at the same time, those results, inevitably, give us only a limited conceptual picture of groups. In particular, commitment to the positivist paradigm by small group researchers of all schools virtually ensured that groups would be studied and construed in ways that prevent us from fully appreciating three of their major features, namely that groups are *complex, adaptive,* and *dynamic* systems. Those features are addressed more extensively below.

Groups as Complex Systems

With the exception of the sociotechnical school and scattered studies in other traditions, small group research typically treats groups piecemeal, rather than holistically. For the most part, both early and more recent group research has examined only a narrow band of variables potentially relevant to its own perspective. This is an almost inevitable consequence of the preferred positivist-analytic-reductionist research methodology and of the analytic forms of theory that are its natural accompaniment. Both treat phenomena in analytic-reductionist fashion, rather than as holistic-emergent systems.

The analytic-experimental strategy limits what we can learn in two related ways. First, it permits us to gain information about only a limited range of variables. In any experimental study, a small increase in the number of independent variables and in the number of levels of each included in a study yields a huge increase in terms of numbers of cells (i.e., number of combination of levels of conditions), hence in terms of number of cases required to obtain adequate experimental power. Second, this approach usually deals inadequately with (or ignores) higher-order interactions within that paradigm. This strategy can be very effective if most of the important features of groups function unidirectionally, linearly, and additively. This "building block" approach, however, will not help us achieve a full understanding of groups if, as we strongly believe, many of the important phenomena regarding groups function as *nonlinear, recursive, systemic* relations—hallmarks of complex systems. If, as we believe, groups are most appropriately construed as complex systems, then our past ways of conceptualizing and studying groups not only will never lead us to that conclusion but will systematically mislead us.

Groups as Adaptive Systems

A second major limitation of past and current work also arises from a heavy commitment to the positivist-analytic-reductionist strategy. With the exception of work from the sociotechnical tradition (e.g., Emery & Trist, 1965, 1973; Katz & Kahn, 1976; McCollom, 1995a, 1995b; Trist & Bamforth, 1951) and research on how work groups in organizations deal with their organizational environments (e.g., Ancona & Caldwell, 1988, 1990), most research and theory pay little attention to the interaction of groups with their embedding contexts. Most empirical work on groups treats them as if they were isolated systems whose only important relation to their embedding contexts involved the experimenter-imposed stimuli or tasks. Moreover, that work seems to assume that these stimuli and tasks impinge on the group with unidirectional effects. That work does not construe groups as acting systems continually engaged in intricate two-way interchanges with many facets of their embedding contexts—with other work groups and individuals within the same organization; with customers and suppliers; and with families, friends, and communities, as well as with a physical environment *from and to which* information, stimulation, and resources may flow. Although experimental laboratory groups do have a context—the academic environment, the "subject pool," and more immediately, the experimenter who structures the experimental experience and serves as the external director of the group—the impact of these contexts is not explicitly considered in most experimental work.

Small group research studies done in the typical experimental setting not only fail to study the interactions between group and embedding context but take great pains to strip away "irrelevant" contextual factors. Similarly, group research studies done in field settings make serious efforts, often statistically, to unconfound the group as a unit of study from those troublesome interactions with contextual features. But we strongly believe that groups are *adaptive* systems that *actively engage with their embedding contexts* in two-way interchanges. Therefore, both group and embedding contexts adapt to one another.

We believe that attempts to strip context from groups are both limiting and doomed to fail. What is most successfully stripped away is the researcher's attention to context. Although a group without a context can be imagined as a theoretical entity, all real groups have multiple embedding contexts. We need to study groups *in context*. This may be inconvenient from a methodological point of view. But pretending that groups can exist without a context is, we believe, counterproductive.

Groups as Dynamic Systems

Partly as a consequence of the laboratory-experimental methodology and partly as a consequence of the underlying analytic-reductionist conceptual paradigm, most group research has studied group activities for only a very limited span of time—often for a single 50-minute research session. For groups that are created in the laboratory for research purposes, that 50 minutes usually encompasses the entire life span of the group. Such groups have no history; their formation is not very interesting because it is entirely experimenter determined; their members have neither expectations for nor a commitment to the group in even a short-run future; and the group plays no meaningful role in their lives.

For both practical and methodological reasons, short-span experimental studies have been far more popular than longitudinal ones within the small group domain. Longitudinal studies are extremely costly in time and resources; age, generational, and historical effects are often difficult to untangle; and imperfect member attendance makes for differential "mortality" (Cook & Campbell, 1979) and change-in-membership problems.

But even though longitudinal studies pose these problems, a body of research made up almost entirely of very short-term studies of groups leaves something missing from our knowledge base. Most groups to which we might want our findings to generalize exist far longer than the typical single-session life span of laboratory groups. As such groups develop, they generate a history that may be quite different from the histories of other comparable groups, and aspects of that history may affect current group actions at any given point in their life span. Moreover, the processes by which groups carry out their activities, develop as systems, and react adaptively to their embedding contexts, as well as the outcomes of those processes, are fruitful matters for study in themselves if our aim is to arrive at a full understanding of groups as ongoing systems.

If those temporal matters are worthy of study, then we need to somehow extend our study designs to permit their exploration. That poses several methodological problems. First, to learn about the processes by which groups carry out their activities, develop over time, and adapt to external contexts, we must obtain repeated measurements of important processes and their consequences at appropriate time intervals, over appropriate periods of time. Second, if we wish to interpret results of longitudinal studies in the form of between-cases comparisons, within the nomothetic logic of inferential statistics, we face huge resource requirements (numbers of cases over extended periods of time), even if we are studying only one or a few experimental conditions.

Longitudinal studies face two other problems. They must deal with the naturally occurring absences and attrition of group members over a group's lifetime. Moreover, in longitudinal studies, later events are inevitably confounded with the effects of earlier events within a given group. Note that both of these latter problems are matters of confounding in terms of experimental design but are simply features of "life as we know it" from the point of view of the group and its members. That is, group activity at any given time really *is* in part a function of that group's own past history, including its history of changing membership, even if that "confounds" research information about it.

Not only is a group's activity in part a function of its own past history; it is also, in part, a function of its future, as carried in the expectations of its members (and, perhaps, as carried in the expectations of agents in its embedding contexts). Group activity is dynamic in many other senses too. The group-member interchange, like the group-context interchange, involves continuing, dynamic, bidirectional transactions. The ongoing interactions of group members with one another and with their technology and tasks are continuing, adaptive processes. Data based only on one-shot measures, or on before-and-after measures testing unidirectional effects of specific experimenter-manipulated variables (e.g., of the effect of group pressure on members' attitudes), do not give us very much leverage for understanding those continuing, two-way processes. Here, again, choices driven by the limitations of our dominant methodological paradigm get in the way of our substantive understanding. When we study groups by creating ad hoc laboratory groups that have no past and no anticipated future beyond the single session, we are thereby imposing not just methodological limitations but substantive ones as well.

∞ NEEDS FOR THE FUTURE

In our view, group research seems to be approaching the limits of what can be learned about groups using the currently dominant methodological paradigm, the data-gathering and analysis methods that are its main tools, and the theoretical conceptions that arise from it. If we want to achieve major progress in our understanding of groups and their activities, we need a major paradigm transition. We need to borrow and invent new ways of thinking about groups and new tools for doing research on them that allow us to conceptualize and study groups as complex, adaptive, dynamic systems.

At least three other fields of study have been concerned with such systems, and some of their concepts may be useful in our field as well: (a) general systems theory, whose key concepts are already partly integrated within psychology and social psychology (e.g., Katz & Kahn, 1976); (b) dynamical systems theory, a branch of mathematics with useful concepts regarding dynamic systems as well as crucial analytic tools; and (c) complex systems theory, which is beginning to be prominent within the physical and biological sciences, though not yet in the behavioral sciences. All have had some behavioral science uses (see, e.g., Baron, Amazeen, & Beek, 1994; Katz & Kahn, 1976; Latané & Nowak, 1994; Nowak & Lewenstein, 1994; and other studies presented in Vallacher & Nowak, 1994), but their implications have not yet fully penetrated the thinking of our field. Furthermore, the exploration of their applications to groups has been very limited.

We believe that concepts and tools from all three of those areas have great promise as the underpinnings of a theoretical conception of groups as complex, adaptive, and dynamic systems. To use such concepts in our theory of groups requires, at the same time, that we shift both the logic of our study designs and the tools we use for collecting and analyzing data. In the next chapter, we introduce the core of our theory, which applies concepts from general systems theory, dynamical systems theory, and complexity theory to small groups. We also discuss how shifting our way of thinking about groups leads to a new logic of inquiry.

∞ *3* ∞

Groups as Complex Systems

Overview of the Theory

*I*n Chapter 2, we reviewed the history of small group research and proposed that the field needs a broader, more integrative, and more dynamic approach. The goal of our theory is to build on findings and insights from past research while transcending some of the conceptual limitations that have hampered progress in the field. This chapter presents the core of our small group theory, packaged as five propositions that establish its main concepts. The chapter also develops some of the implications of taking dynamics and complexity seriously in thinking about groups. The five chapters of Part II then unfold our theory in detail.

The five propositions include statements of several kinds. Some are definitional assumptions. Some are, in effect, the axioms and postulates of our theory. Some are potentially testable hypotheses. The propositions address (a) the nature of groups, (b) causal dynamics in groups, (c) group purposes or functions, (d) the elements and the network of relations among them that constitute group composition and structure, and (e) modes of group life over time.

We draw on a broad interdisciplinary foundation, incorporating ideas and perspectives from general systems theory, social network theory, dynamical systems theory, and complexity theory. The connections between our ideas about small groups, on the one hand, and concepts borrowed from other disciplines and fields, on the other, are noted in the discussion. The focus of this chapter, however, is not on explicating the many conceptual insights that have nurtured our ideas but on presenting an integrated theory of small groups in which the insights we have gleaned are embedded. We present and discuss each of the five propositions in turn.

Proposition 1:
The Nature of Groups

Groups are open and complex systems that interact with the smaller systems (i.e., the members) embedded within them and the larger systems (e.g., organizations) within which they are embedded. Groups have fuzzy boundaries that both distinguish them from and connect them to their members and their embedding contexts.

This proposition incorporates several concepts central to a systems view of groups. These include the ideas that systems are open, complex, adaptive, and dynamic; that systems entail recurrent patterns of interaction among elements at multiple levels; and that systems have permeable boundaries that regulate the exchange of resources among levels. We unpack these ideas in the following sections.

Definition of a Group

A group is a complex, adaptive, dynamic, coordinated, and bounded set of patterned relations among members, tasks, and tools. Just as the boundaries between the different levels of systems are fuzzy, however, no sharp line distinguishes interacting small groups from uncoordinated collections of elements. We use the following criteria to determine how "groupy" a given system of relations is: (a) whether the people involved consider themselves to be members of the group; (b) whether they recognize one another as members and distinguish members from nonmembers; (c) whether members feel connected to the other members and to the projects of the group; (d) whether members coordinate their behavior in pursuing collective projects; (e) whether members coordinate their use of a shared set of tools, knowledge, and other resources; and (f) whether members share collective outcomes (both rewards and costs) based on their interdependent activity in the group. The sharing of collective outcomes based on group membership is sometimes referred to as *common fate* (Brewer & Kramer, 1986).

A given set of relations may fit some criteria more than others or may fit all of them very weakly. Although we believe that these criteria capture the essential qualities that define a small group system, they should not be considered an exhaustive set. They also should be viewed as continua rather than dichotomies, so that any given set of relations among a number of individuals (any given "putative group") will fit to some degree. Thus, the term *group* spans a broad conceptual range, from ephemeral groups that meet for an hour to engage in activities that are relatively unimportant to the members (e.g., the typical laboratory group) to long-lived, multiproject, strongly interconnected groups such as multigenerational family households.

Another definitional issue involves the minimal set of elements and connections required to form a group. Clearly, a single individual cannot constitute a group, no matter how many links that person has to different tools and tasks. Group researchers differ, however, on whether two people constitute a group. A dyad has only one member-member link. Some group researchers feel that dyads are sufficiently different from larger groups that they fall into a separate domain (e.g., Levine & Moreland, 1990). Many group researchers, however, have defined dyads as the minimal case of groups (e.g., Hare, Blumberg, Davies, & Kent, 1996). In this book, we treat links among people as a basic building block for groups but focus our attention mainly on groups that have more than one dyadic link.

At the other end of the spectrum is the distinction between a small group and a larger collective (e.g., an organization) that is composed of multiple interconnected small groups. At what point the former becomes the latter can be addressed with the same criteria used to identify a group, namely: Do members see themselves as belonging to a group that is a "proper part" of a larger collective? Do they agree, more or less, on that smaller group's membership? Do the group members' activities show more tightly coupled interdependence within the group than with others in the larger collective? Do members of the group share a common fate not totally shared by the larger collective? Again, the boundary is fuzzy.

Groups as Open Systems

Much of the work from several of the bodies of early group research (see Chapter 2) treated groups as closed systems. Work done from the groups-influencing-members perspective emphasized a unidirectional process by which characteristics of groups as inputs (e.g., cohesion) affected characteristics of members as output (e.g., attitudes). Even when members' connections to a broader environment were considered, members were nonetheless tacitly viewed as wholly contained within a group, rather than as being partially embedded in a group and simultaneously embedded in and influenced by a wider social environment. There were exceptions. For example, Newcomb's (1943) Bennington College study treated members' connections to and identifications with their families as key factors affecting the degree to which students' attitudes were influenced by their fellow students.

Work from the task performance perspective focused on inputs from the embedding environment, such as task demands and member preferences, and outputs to the environment, such as task products and group decisions. But the experimental paradigm typically used in those studies precludes the study of how groups go about acquiring their task goals and resources (they are provided by the experimenter) and how their relationship to the embedding environment and its response to their outputs shape group dynamics. Even in studies of natural groups such as military crews, groups were generally not conceptualized as actively procuring and processing resources from the environment or as actively affecting that environment. Early work dealing with patterns of interaction was similarly constrained, mainly studying small discussion groups as isolated entities. That research seldom paid attention to attributes or resources brought to the group by particular members or to active interchanges with embedding contexts.

Conceiving small groups as closed systems precludes studying the active two-way exchanges between group, members, and embedding contexts. We believe that this ignores some of the most fundamental features of small groups. For that reason, our theory emphasizes multiple levels and the permeable boundaries that regulate exchange among those levels. We conceive of small groups as *open systems* involved in *active two-way exchanges* with individuals, groups, and other entities within an array of embedding contexts, as well as the individuals who are the group's own members. The sources we draw on for our interpretation of the systems approach include general systems theory (von Bertalanffy, 1968) and systems theories of organizations (Kast & Rosenzweig, 1972; Katz & Kahn, 1978), of small groups (Homans, 1950; McGrath, 1991), and of groups in organizational contexts (Arrow & McGrath, 1995; Emery & Trist, 1965; Gillette & McCollom, 1995; Trist & Bamforth, 1951).

We view groups as intact social systems embedded within physical, temporal, sociocultural, and organizational contexts. Embedded within groups are the group's members, who are also complex, adaptive systems embedded in multiple contexts—including multiple groups. Effective study of groups requires attention to at least three system levels: individual members, the group as a system, and various layers of embedding contexts—both for the group as an entity and for its members. We also need to attend to the interchanges that connect the different levels, the group's interchanges with its various embedding contexts, and the group's interchanges with its members.

Groups acquire members, projects, and tools from their embedding contexts. Depending on the type of group and the nature of its relation to its embedding contexts, those contexts may or may not actively supply elements (e.g., assign members, specify projects, allocate equipment and space), make demands (such as a change in tasks or rules), and set constraints on group activity (such as deadlines).

Similarly, groups negotiate exchanges with their members. Group members are never fully embedded in a single group but, rather, belong simultaneously to other groups and operate as intact systems within a wider environment. Groups receive contributions from and make contributions to their members and their embedding contexts. A family, for example, draws on the physical energy of its members and the money they earn in the outside economy to support the feeding, housing, development, and education of its members. An airline crew uses the energy and knowledge of its members and depends on the flow of information into and out of the crew to fly planes from one place to another for the airline. Its members are paid a salary and get other benefits from the airline in exchange for their contributions to the group's activities, hence to the airline's goals.

Groups as Complex Systems

From complexity theory (e.g., Casti, 1994; Cowan, Pines, & Meltzer, 1994; Gell-Mann, 1994; Kauffman, 1993; Kelso, 1995; Prigogine & Stengers, 1984; Waldrop, 1992) we borrow some definitions of system complexity and adopt the idea that groups are self-organizing systems in which global patterns emerge from local action and structure subsequent local action. (This idea is developed in more detail under Proposition 2.)

Complex systems are systems that are neither rigidly ordered nor highly disordered. A snowflake is not a complex system—it is too orderly. Turbulent flow in a fluid is not a complex system—it is too chaotic and not adaptive. Complexity theorists are interested in systems whose behavior falls in the region between fixed order and deterministic chaos and whose behavior is influenced by and takes advantage of random noise.

Complexity theorists have developed multiple definitions and measures of system complexity (see Gell-Mann, 1994, Chapters 3-5, for a readable overview). All capture aspects of the commonsense meaning of complexity—as referring to something with many interconnected parts and a complicated structure. We define *system complexity* as the number and variety of identifiable regularities in the structure and behavior of the group, given a description of that group at a fixed level of detail. This definition incorporates two of the definitions from the complexity theory literature that seem particularly useful for our purposes: *effective complexity* (the length of a description of system regularities; Gell-Mann, 1994, p. 56) and *crude complexity* (the length of the shortest possible description of a system; Gell-Mann, 1994, p. 34).

Random events and random behavior do not count toward complexity because they exhibit, by definition, no regularities. Loose aggregates of people whose collective behavior shows little coordination and lots of random activity would have low complexity as systems. Highly ordered patterns that adhere to a single rule also contribute very little to complexity. Groups in which every member performs basically the same task in the same way (an impromptu group on one end of a tug of war, for example) would have low complexity. Systems with high complexity have many kinds of regularities generated by multiple rules, including contingencies and exceptions. Groups in which members are both connected to and distinguished from one another in a highly articulated structure of roles, relationships, and activities, for example, would have high complexity.

Given that definition, we suggest that groups tend to increase in complexity over time. This means that the number and variety of patterned regularities in the structure and behavior of the group increase over time. A description of the regularities and patterns in groups tends to get longer (controlling for level of detail) as the group accumulates experience and changes throughout its history (Casti, 1994; Gell-Mann, 1994; Horgan, 1995).

Groups with fewer distinguishable kinds of members, fewer different projects, fewer distinguishable kinds of tools and rule systems, and fewer distinguishable types of connections (relations) among the elements are less complex than those with more of any of those features. Groups that take on a broad array of projects that require different procedures and tools for completion will have higher complexity than groups that take on a single project.

Implications of Proposition 1:
Multiple Levels and Change Over Time

Applying insights from complexity theory to groups yields the following implications about the nature of groups:

1. The structure and behavior of groups includes both regularities—which contribute to complexity—and random elements.
2. Group behavior involves interactions across at least three levels: constituent elements of groups, the group as an entity, and the contexts in which a group is embedded.
3. The structure and behavior of groups changes over time, yielding temporal patterns of development.
4. As groups change over time, they tend to become more complex—which means the number and variety of regularities in structure and behavior proliferate.

As will be elaborated in later propositions, change is driven in part by the effects of experience and history and in part by the group's adaptive response to the impact of events.

The assertion that groups change over time and that this change typically involves the emergence of new regularities or patterns across time suggests that "snapshot" observations of groups as a single point should not be taken as evidence of what that group was or will be like at an earlier or later period in its history. It also calls into question the practice of generalizing about the behavior of groups in general (which includes groups that have extended histories) on the basis of the observation of ephemeral groups that form, complete a simple task, and disband. The next proposition elaborates on the cross-level dynamics inherent to complex systems.

Proposition 2:
Causal Dynamics in Groups

Throughout a group's life, three levels of causal dynamics continually shape the group. *Local dynamics* refers to the activity of a group's constituent elements: members using tools to do tasks. Local dynamics give rise to group-level or global dynamics and are shaped and constrained by them. *Global dynamics* refers to the evolution of system-level variables that emerge from and shape local dynamics. *Contextual dynamics* refers to the impact of features in the group's embedding contexts that shape and constrain the local and global dynamics of a group.

Our analysis of causal dynamics in groups draws on *dynamical systems theory,* a branch of mathematics that models systems that change over time. Dynamical systems theory takes evolving relationships among variables as the object of inquiry (Abraham, Abraham, & Shaw, 1990). The focus is not on differences in *values* of variables between distinct social entities at a given time but rather on qualitative *patterns* of dynamical variables exhibited by social entities or systems over time.

The concepts we adopt from dynamical systems theory include the following ideas. First, dynamical systems model the behavior of different levels of dynamical rules and variables—features of system operation that change, interdependently, over time. Dynamical rules and variables can be classified into three categories that are demarcated by fuzzy boundaries. *Local dynamics* refers to rules of activity for parts of the system, *global dynamics* refers to rules of activity for system-level properties that emerge out of local dynamics, and *contextual dynamics* refers to the impact of system-level parameters that affect the overall trajectory of global group dynamics over time and whose values are determined in part by the group's embedding context. In many dynamic systems, global variables tend to settle into certain values or sets of values called *attractors*. Which attractors are available to the system—for example, whether a system settles into a single state (a "point" attractor) or a recurring cycle (a "periodic" attractor)—depends in part on the values of contextual parameters.

To give an example from the physical sciences, distance from the equator (a contextual parameter) determines whether a region will experience a single year-round climate or a cycle of seasons. To give a small group example, the individualism or collectivism of the national culture (a contextual parameter) in which a family is embedded should affect the level and pattern of change in family members' commitment to the needs of the family over time. In strongly individualist cultures, children are expected to become increasingly independent of the family as they mature and build their lives according to individual preferences; in strongly collectivist cultures, commitment to the needs of the family should remain more constant over time. Local variables for these two systems might be daily temperature and humidity in a particular location and the commitment of a particular group member to a particular family project, respectively.

The logic of dynamical systems theory holds that although detailed predictions about the values of micro-level variables of a nonlinear dynamic system will break down very quickly, we often can make predictions about evolving patterns of key global variables if we know the initial values of local variables, the settings of key contextual parameters, and the rules that govern system dynamics. Just as weather forecasts are only reasonably accurate in the short term, and at a limited level of resolution, the details of group behavior (as opposed to the general patterns of group behavior) are inherently unpredictable over time.

Local Dynamics

Local group dynamics involve the activity of system parts, or local variables, and the rules that govern that activity. These rules might be implicit norms or procedures, as when group members use cognitive schemas such as stereotypes to infer other group members' abilities and intentions, or these rules might be more explicit norms or procedures that specify, for example, how members should interact on the basis of relative seniority in the group or who should do which tasks in what order for a particular type of project on the basis of established member roles.

The central concept we draw on to describe local dynamics is *coordination*. The idea of coordination within a group has been given at least three different meanings. In its most common usage, *coordination* means the spatial and temporal synchronization of overt behaviors of two or more people so that those actions fit together into an intended spatial and temporal pattern. This defines *coordination* as *spatial, temporal, and interactional synchrony,* or the *coordination of action.*

In a second meaning, one becoming more frequent with the recent surge of interest in cognitive processes, *coordination* means achieving either explicit or tacit agreement among group members regarding the meanings of information and events. This includes shared understanding of the nature of embedding conditions and the threat or opportunity they pose; agreement on procedures for pursuing goals; agreement on criteria by which to assess progress toward goals; and agreement on division of labor, status, and reward structures. This defines *coordination* as *agreement on shared meanings* and on *norms* about who should do what and how. This is the *coordination of understanding.*

A third meaning of *coordination* has been studied by researchers interested in goals, mixed motives, and social dilemmas. Whereas *coordination of action* refers to interactional synchrony, and *coordination of understanding* to shared meanings and norms, the mutual adjustment of individual purposes, interests, and intentions among group members yields the *coordination of goals.*

To coordinate goals, understanding, and action, members must adjust to one another interpersonally; they must also order and sequence a host of logical and temporal links among tasks, tools, and members. Coordination is always relative, not perfect. There are many paths to most group goals, and member interests often cannot be fully harmonized.

More members may be more able (and motivated) to carry out given tasks with available tools than an efficient division of labor can accommodate, as when several members of a basketball team want to take the potentially winning final shot in the closing seconds of the game. Some tools have many uses but cannot be used simultaneously for more than one task or by more than one person. Thus, members may compete for desirable task assignments and for access to particular tools (e.g., a specially equipped computer, a large office, or the role of leader in a hierarchical group). The meshing of member-task-tool components into a coordination network thus entails setting priorities, allocating desirable resources, planning alternating uses of tools and alternative task assignments, and other coordination strategies. These matters are discussed in considerable detail in Chapter 5.

Global Dynamics

Complex, adaptive, dynamic systems exhibit system-level structure and behavior that cannot be fully specified from a detailed understanding of isolated system components. The global structure or pattern generated by the interaction of local variables in turn constrains the future behavior of these local variables. This is what we mean by *global dynamics.*

Global variables index coherent relations among the interacting parts of a system (Kelso, 1995), not details of the individual parts. The most promising candidates for global variables will be emergent aspects of the system rather than simple aggregates of local variables.

The status structure of a group is a good example. We can think of it as a set of asymmetric influence relations between members in which one person tends to be influenced by words or actions of another. By adulthood, every person has plenty of experience enacting and observing high- and low-status roles. Yet even with detailed information about those past experiences, it is difficult to predict which members of a group will achieve high-and low-status positions in different aspects of group activity if roles are not specified and imposed in advance (e.g., by job descriptions). But when a group actually forms, the role system that emerges from group interaction produces a patterned set of influence links among members. A simple status structure would be a highly centralized system in which one person always leads (influences) and the others always follow (are influenced). Status in a more complex role system might involve different leaders for task and social activities (Bales & Slater, 1955) or might specify contingencies (Fiedler, 1964) and complexities such as deputies or substitution rules.

Once such an emergent status structure is in place, however, it patterns the subsequent activities of members, which are likely to reproduce those same or very similar influence patterns. So the interplay between micro- and macro-system levels is a two-way influence. Global variables emerge from, and subsequently guide and constrain, local action of the system. These issues are discussed in more detail in Chapter 6.

Contextual Dynamics

Contextual parameters are features of a system that affect the dynamic operation of local variables and hence constrain the pattern over time of global variables. In a physical system such as the flow of water in a river, for example, the rate of flow determines whether the water will flow smoothly (laminar flow) or break up into rapids (turbulent flow). In this example, rate of flow is the contextual parameter, which varies on the basis of conditions in the physical context for the river— rainfall, snowpack, and human release of water from dams, for example. The smooth or turbulent flow of the river is the global variable that indexes the qualitative pattern of global behavior.

The recruitment and socialization of group members (Moreland & Levine, 1982) offers a small group example. Average member commitment to groups and the turnover in group membership (two related global variables) should follow different dynamic patterns depending on the supply of potential members in the group's embedding context and the number of alternative attractive groups that members can choose among. The supply/demand balance for potential new members is the contextual parameter. If there are only a few alternative groups in the embedding context and there is an ample supply of desirable potential members for a given group, overall member commitment to groups should increase rapidly after recruitment and remain high. Turnover should be low and stable. When attractive groups are numerous and potential new members scarce, however (a different setting of the supply/demand contextual parameter), member commitment is likely to rise and fall rapidly on the basis of small changes in the perceived relative attractiveness of different groups. Turnover should be higher, with stronger fluctuations, and members should switch groups in a more chaotic fashion. The impact of contextual parameters on groups and the efforts of groups both to adapt to fixed features of the environment and to change features of their immediate embedding contexts are discussed in more detail in Chapter 7.

Implications of Proposition 2: Qualitative Versus Quantitative Prediction

This conception of causal dynamics entails a logic of study that differs markedly from the logic of positivist-reductionist-analytic approaches to studying small groups that have dominated research in the past century. In the traditional paradigm, we measure and compare average levels of specific dependent variables, at a given point in time, for sets of cases that are exposed to experimental conditions with differing (experimentally manipulated) levels of (one or more) independent variables. When we use the correlational variant of that paradigm, we measure the levels of two or more features of the cases (i.e., the groups) that we are studying and then assess the degree to which those features covary over cases at a given point in time.

In contrast, a dynamical systems approach to studying a complex system of interacting elements is to *track the trajectory of system-level variables over time*, examine their qualitative patterns, and relate these qualitative patterns (a) to the rules of interaction among system components and (b) to aspects of the group's context. The focus is on how the system-level properties of interest (global variables, also called *state variables* in the dynamical systems literature) emerge from and subsequently shape the dynamic interactions of micro-level variables (local dynamics) and how these local and global dynamics are in turn affected by the levels of one or more contextual parameters (called *control parameters* in the dynamical systems literature). In some cases, mapping the relation between the evolution of global variables and the settings of control parameters is the main focus, and the details of local dynamics are ignored (although control parameters are understood to shape the hidden local dynamics from which global variables emerge).

There are three crucial differences in the logic by which we interpret data in the two paradigms. First, in the complexity paradigm, we look at the operation of the entire system, as evidenced by emergent variables, not at the directional causal effects of specific individual features of the system on other specific features (i.e., the effects of one local variable on another). Because all local-level elements are understood to interact with one another in a recursive, nonlinear fashion, dynamic attributes of these elements and their interaction in the system are interdependent variables, which cannot be usefully decomposed into "independent" and "dependent" variables.

Second, the complexity approach presumes that the state of the system as reflected in the global variables emerges from the dynamic interaction of myriad local dynamical variables that make up the system. Rather than trying to predict the exact values of particular local variables in the future, however, researchers focus on discovering the rules of interaction among variables at the local level.

Third, in the complexity paradigm, the matter of most interest to the researcher is the *evolution over time* of the group as a system, as evidenced in the *trajectory over time* of a given set of global variables for a given group as a system. The complexity researcher also has far less interest in the average levels of these global features of systems over a given period of time than one would using the conventional paradigm. Nor are those researchers interested in average levels of local variables that have been aggregated over a set of groups that are regarded as equivalent because they were in the same experimental condition. In the complexity paradigm, researchers understand that the detailed evolution of each system in the "same" condition may vary on the basis of even small differences in initial conditions, so that differences in levels of variables between groups are *not* viewed as random (and normally distributed) deviations from a canonical path of development. Studies of nonlinear dynamic systems in which the rules of operation are completely deterministic reveal that tiny differences in initial conditions can lead to rapid divergence in the quantitative levels of local and global variables, a phenomenon known as *sensitive dependence on initial conditions.* What is expected across groups in the "same" condition is qualitative similarity in dynamic patterns rather than quantitative convergence on a particular sequence of values.

These profound differences in the logic of interpretation will, in turn, require us to rethink the data collection strategies and tools and the data-analytic techniques that we use in our empirical inquiries. These issues are discussed at length in Part III of the book. The functions of small groups themselves (as opposed to the function of research on groups) are the focus of the next proposition.

Proposition 3:
Group Functions

All groups have two generic functions: (a) to complete group projects and (b) to fulfill member needs. A group's success in fulfilling these two functions, or purposes, affects the viability and integrity of the group as a system. Thus, a third generic group function—(c) to maintain system integrity—emerges from pursuit of the other two and in turn affects the group's ability to complete group projects and fulfill member needs.

This triad of primary group functions is based on prior theorizing (e.g., Hackman, 1990; McGrath, 1991) about purposes, goals, and criteria for assessing group functioning. The third function of maintaining system integrity is somewhat different in nature from the other two. Whereas groups are formed to complete projects and to fulfill member needs, system integrity emerges as an issue only after a group is formed. Maintaining the group as an intact system is also less likely than the other two functions to be considered an explicit group purpose by members.

The extent to which a group succeeds in completing group projects and fulfilling member needs affects the group's well-being as an intact system. Members of groups with high system integrity are both willing and able to invest energy into carrying out group projects and addressing member needs. Members of groups with low system integrity are less committed to future activity in service of the group's intrinsic purposes. Attaining and maintaining system integrity are thus dependent on and instrumental to the other two functions. The three functions are interconnected in a circular chain of interdependent causation.

Groups differ in the relative priorities they place on fulfilling member needs, accomplishing group projects, and maintaining the group as a viable ongoing system. Furthermore, those priorities do not (and probably cannot) remain static over time. In the longer run, they must all be fulfilled to some minimal extent for the group to continue as a viable system. Bales's (1953, 1955) early theoretical work on equilibrium within the group's interaction process held that groups had a continual, and somewhat dialectic, interplay between task and socioemotional needs. Bales proposed an oscillation or alternation between them. As groups pursue their tasks, they neglect socioemotional concerns. These needs build up as a consequence of that neglect, and eventually the group must turn to its fulfillment via socioemotional behaviors. This produces a neglect of task needs and a consequent buildup in tensions with regard to those needs. This forces a return of the group's attention to its task activities, and the cycle begins again. Bion's (1961) theory of work and emotionality contained premises postulating a similar, and perhaps even more elaborately patterned, picture of dynamic interplay between similar competing functions.

Although a cyclical pattern of alternation among competing group functions is no doubt a global pattern in some groups, we do not believe it is the only pattern. We believe that all groups exercise some degree of self-regulation over how they pursue their multiple functions over time but that the balance among them, and changes in this balance over time, will also be affected by constraints in the embedding contexts that group members have.

Self-regulation implies several features of groups as systems: group goals or desired states, ideas about how to stay on or move toward a path that will attain the desired state, a monitoring process to determine whether group activity is having the intended effect, and a procedure for changing course if the gap between the group's current state and its desired future state is widening rather than closing. This set of requirements suggests the idea of negative and positive feedback loops as they are used in cybernetics (Weiner, 1948) and control theories (Campion & Lord, 1982; Powers, 1998).

Some past group research has paid attention to negative (dampening) and positive (amplifying) feedback loops. An example is Janis's (1972, 1982) work on groupthink, a state of pathological unity in groups in which all information or member tendencies that might cause a group to deviate from its current position are actively eliminated from the group. The dynamics of this state involve strong negative feedback loops that are triggered by small departures from the status quo. Resocialization in Moreland and Levine's (1982) model of group socialization is a healthier example of a negative feedback loop, in which a group attempts to draw a marginal member back to full membership status.

The self-correcting activity of group members has three prerequisites: (a) a sense of what the preferred state or path is for the group, (b) attention to information indicating that the group as a whole or some of its members are drifting (or have been pushed) off track, and (c) procedures for taking corrective action. Groups can drift from their preferred path as a consequence of internal group dynamics, or they can be pushed (or lured) off course by outside forces.

Unlike mechanical systems, groups can change their own settings or invent new ways to respond to information. A physical cybernetic system, such as a house's heating system, has fixed "goals" set by forces outside the system, and it cannot acquire new strategies (such as "open a window") to alter the prevailing conditions. The boundaries of "too hot" and "too cold" for a heating/cooling system are set by entities *outside* the system. Group goals may also be set by people outside a group. Group members, however, have the ability to reset their reference points by adopting new goals.

A social system such as a group can adapt to a new situation by generating novel responses. Furthermore, even if the goals and the external situation remain the same, a group can alter its plan of action in pursuing its goals. Thus, groups are self-regulating as to both ends and means. They can modify their ends, and they can attain their ends via multiple alternative means. Of course, the implications of changing group goals or paths, and the likelihood that this will happen, will depend somewhat on the type of group and its relation to its immediate embedding context. Processes by which groups organize themselves (and are organized by others) to fulfill group functions are discussed in Chapters 4 and 5. Learning and adaptation are discussed in Chapters 6 and 7.

Implications of Proposition 3: Nonlinear Effects

Feedback loops, whether negative or positive, create nonlinear effects. A small change in a local variable that triggers a positive (amplifying) feedback loop can ultimately result in a big change at the global level, as interactions among coupled elements at the local level ratchet up to effects that are noticeable at the group system level. Self-regulation that depends on negative (dampening) feedback loops means that influences originating outside group boundaries do not necessarily have the impact one would expect if one conceptualized the group as a static, passive object acted on by outside forces. In the bank-wiring experiments at the Hawthorne Western Electric plant (Homans, 1950), for example, management attempted to boost production by changing the incentive system for workers. The bank-wiring group, however, maintained its preferred level of production by sanctioning members who strayed too far from the target level by either underproducing (free riding) or overproducing (rate busting).

The self-regulating activity of open systems such as groups does *not* imply a centralized control mechanism like those used in engineered systems—for example, heating systems regulated by a thermostat. The global state of the system can be noted by members who take action without any need for collective consultation. In the Western Electric study, all members were aware of the group's preferred level of production (a global norm), and any member might detect deviations from that norm (change in a global variable) and impose sanctions (a local-level action). The next proposition addresses the structure of relations among group elements that enables a group to fulfill its multiple functions.

Proposition 4:
Group Composition and Structure

In groups, three types of elements—people who become a group's members, intentions that are embodied in group projects, and resources that become the group's technologies—are linked in a functional network of member-task-tool relations that we call the *coordination network*. This dynamic structure, which enables groups to complete projects and fulfill member needs, is made up of six sets of relations: (a) the *member network* of member-member relations, (b) the *task network* of task-task relations, (c) the *tool network* of tool-tool relations, (d) the *labor network* of member-task relations, (e) the *role network* of member-tool relations, and (f) the *job network* of task-tool relations.

The Elements

The three types of elements included in the group structure—members, tasks, and tools or resources—are not equivalent. The people who are the group's members have a special relation to the group that is quite different from the relations of projects and technology to the group. Individuals have intentions, and those intentions shape a member's role and choice of actions in a given group. This, of course, is not true of projects or tools. Projects are expressions of intentions, and some tools are designed with intended uses in mind, but projects, tools, and resources do not "have" intentions.

The resources and tools that we group under the general rubric of "technology" comprise a broad range of elements that includes hardware such as hammers, computers, and washing machines; software such as the knowledge of how to use hammers, computer programs and programming knowledge, and procedures for washing clothes without turning white shirts pink; and resources such as money, meeting spaces, and languages that group members share. Thus, the "software" knowledge of how to do things has a dual status as something that members have (a member attribute) and an element in the "tool kit" of resources available to the group. Tools and resources differ in the actions they afford to members. A given tool may support or constrain interpersonal interaction, be used for a variety of task activities, or facilitate planning and other coordination activities.

Members will differ in what "software" resources they bring to the group, as well as in a host of other attributes. Members differ in interpersonal, task, and process skills; values, beliefs, and attitudes; and personality, cognitive, and behavioral styles. They also differ in demographic attributes, such as sex, race, and age, and in the needs they seek to fulfill via group membership. The mix of needs for affiliation, achievement, power, and material resources that members seek to satisfy via their activities in any given group will often change over time in groups that have an extended lifetime.

Group projects vary in the balance and types of interpersonal activity, task activity, and procedural activity they require. They also differ in their requirements for instrumental functions such as processing information, managing conflict and consensus, and coordinating member behavior. Groups vary in how many different projects they need to coordinate at the same time.

Relations Among
the Elements

For a group to engage successfully in coordinated activity to carry out its project(s) and fulfill member needs, it must (a) contain members who have, among them, the attributes necessary to accomplish their projects and fulfill member needs; (b) break down each project into a set of concrete tasks and match the members with these tasks in a division of labor that suffices to get the activities done and fulfill member needs; and (c) import, develop, or acquire the resources of needed tools, equipment, and knowledge and develop a role system that specifies member access to concrete tools and resources (hardware) both for completing tasks and for fulfilling member needs. This "matching" allows for the coordination of action.

A group may have all the resources it needs and include members capable of completing their tasks yet still fail to function effectively if members fail to develop coordinated understandings about how all of these components will fit together. Groups may also settle on a match of people and tools to tasks that is dysfunctional for completing a project. They may match people to tasks and tools entirely on the basis of project requirements while ignoring member needs. In this case, members with the ability, the tools, and the shared understandings necessary for coordination of action may lack the motivation to carry out their tasks successfully. Such a group has failed to achieve an adequate coordination of goals. Thus, a full consideration of the forces that drive groups must attend to the needs as well as the attributes of group members, along with the attributes of tasks and tools.

The links (called *ties* in social networks theory) that connect the elements (also called *nodes*) in a network differ in nature depending on what type of elements they connect. Links among members may represent symmetrical relations such as friendship or asymmetric, directional relations such as influence or advice. Links among tasks may involve temporal ordering, specifying which tasks follow one another in a particular order (e.g., alternatives must be generated before the group can meet to choose among them) or which tasks must be completed simultaneously (the furnace must be installed while the house is still being framed).

Carrying through with this network conception of group structure, we call the division of labor that links each member to a subset of tasks the *labor network*. The labor network specifies who does what. Each member does his or her tasks using some tools and other resources. As noted above, some resources arrive in the group as part of members' "software" repertoire, so these resources cannot be "allocated" to members. The allocation of intangible resources such as status determines the distribution of power in the group and also should be correlated with access to tangible resources. We refer to the set of links between members and resources as the *role network*. The role network specifies who gets what and who decides, as well as how members do what they do. Each tool or procedure is useful in carrying out some tasks but not others, and tasks vary in requirements for other tangible and intangible resources. The allocation of tools and resources to tasks establishes the group's *job network*. The job network constitutes a set of operating procedures.

Implications of Proposition 4: Limited Role of Reductionism

A network conception of groups highlights the reasons why reductionist approaches are of limited use when the object of study is a complex system. Studying a system by decomposing it into its basic elements and varying these elements one at a time is a problematic strategy when the elements are strongly interconnected. In such systems, the links between elements are as important as the elements themselves and are far more numerous. So, for example, a membership change that involves removing one person from a group does not simply change one element; it removes all of the ties that the member had with the other members, with the group tasks, and with the tools and knowledge by which the group could accomplish its tasks. This set of ties is what made the person a member of the group.

Proposition 5:
Modes of Group Life

The life course of a group can be characterized by three logically ordered modes that are conceptually distinct but have fuzzy temporal boundaries: formation, operation, and metamorphosis. As a group forms, people, intentions, and resources become organized into an initial network of relations that demarcates that group as a bounded social entity. As a group operates in the service of group projects and member needs, its members elaborate, enact, monitor, and modify the coordination network established during formation. Groups both learn from their own experience and adapt to events occurring in their embedding contexts. A group undergoes metamorphosis when it dissolves or is transformed into a different social entity.

The formation mode, by definition, is the process by which a group emerges, and the metamorphosis mode, if it occurs at all for a group in any given time frame, is by definition the process that ends the existence of that group. The operations mode encompasses most or all of the group's existence and may occur concurrently with formation and metamorphosis. The three levels of causal dynamics discussed in Proposition 4 take place in all three modes, continuously and simultaneously.

Formation

Groups differ in the degree to which formation is shaped by forces external to and internal to the group and in the degree to which formation results from deliberate attempts to create the group or as an unintended consequence of events. The relative influence of different forces active during formation affects the kind of structure that a group will develop. The relative importance of different types of ties in the group network is reflected in the temporal sequence in which the different networks among members, tasks, and tools form. This in turn affects that group's initial pattern and its subsequent pattern of development and adaptation. It also affects the group's strengths and vulnerabilities. Those issues are discussed in Chapter 4.

Operation

As the group works on group projects and tends to its members' needs, its members elaborate, enact, maintain, and modify the coordination network established during formation. Recurrent patterns of local and global dynamics emerge during operation. The operation mode is discussed in Chapters 5, 6, and 7, which focus in turn on the three levels of causal dynamics identified in Proposition 2. *Coordination* is used as an overall label to refer to local dynamics—the ongoing patterning of interaction among the group's constituent elements as the group pursues its functions. *Development* is used as an overall label to refer to global dynamics—the continual changes that occur (via learning and experience) in the global patterns by which the group carries out its activities. Development encompasses the continual mutual adjustments between the group as a system and its constituent parts—its members, technology, and projects. *Adaptation* is used as an overall label to refer to contextual dynamics—the group's adjustment to and alteration of features of its embedding context(s). This encompasses the continual mutual adaptation between the group as a system and its physical, cultural, organizational, and temporal embedding contexts.

Metamorphosis

During metamorphosis, the group dissolves or is transformed into a different social entity that is not reasonably regarded as the "same" group. *Metamorphosis* refers to the processes by which *some* groups end. Metamorphosis may occur due to a breakdown or change in local, global, or contextual dynamics. This is the topic of Chapter 8.

∞ **CONCLUDING COMMENTS**

Implications of the Theory:
A Different Logic of Inquiry for Studying Groups

The logic of inquiry implied by our theory of small groups can be summarized as follows. Groups are complex systems. In small groups, local action consists of recursive, nonlinear interaction among many elements. Local group process creates, activates, replicates, and adjusts dynamic links in a coordination network. Our conceptualization treats this as an interaction among many local variables. From local action, global-level patterns emerge—behavioral and cognitive patterns such as group norms, cohesion, division of labor, a role system and influence structure, and temporal patterns such as cycles of conflict and consensus, regularities in changing group performance, and the ebb and flow of communication. These global-level patterns are conceptualized as global variables that emerge from local interaction and then structure subsequent local action.

Local action for any given group shows regularities, which can be modeled as a set of "rules" that the system follows. Although the interaction among local-level elements may be highly complicated, the rules governing the action and interaction of group elements are often relatively simple. Which rules guide local action, however, and which global patterns emerge from the operation of these rules, depends on initial conditions and on subsequent situational factors and external conditions, conceptualized here as contextual parameters. This is not the kind of relationship traditionally modeled by independent and dependent variables. Rather, we are talking about contextual factors that constrain the operation of local-level rules without determining the outcome. The whole pattern of global dynamics that emerges from this local action may shift when a contextual parameter shifts to a different value. Or it may remain unchanged. This depends on where in the range of possible values the shift occurs.

Given the range of potential interactions among local variables, it is not possible to predict the individual and joint values of these variables accurately, even if their values are known with high accuracy at a particular point in time. Complex systems whose behavior depends largely on interactions among local elements—the weather, for example—are predictable only in the short run, and these predictions are for global variables (arrival of cold fronts, conditions favorable to tornadoes), not local variables (the precise pattern of a tornado through a neighborhood). Patterns of key global variables, however, do show substantial regularities over time. The qualitative pattern of these regularities may differ for groups under different operating conditions, or for the same group if the value of a contextual parameter changes beyond some critical threshold. The pattern over time of a given global variable such as the division of labor, for example, may be qualitatively different (e.g., centralized or decentralized), depending on the "setting" of a contextual parameter such as the level of external threats to the group.

In the language of dynamical systems, global variables settle over time into relatively small regions in state space (the space of possibilities for that variable). These regions, called attractors, vary in type. One aim for research is to identify the attractors—single or multiple; stable or unstable; fixed point, periodic, or quasi-periodic—into which a given global variable will settle over time and to discern variations in the landscape of attractors at different levels and combinations of key contextual parameters.

The aim of this approach, therefore, is not to predict average levels of specific local variables, either at a given time or aggregated over time. Rather, the aim is to track the characteristic evolution of the system through different system states, as reflected in the pattern of global variables over time, and to investigate which contextual parameters affect this pattern of evolution and how.

Looking Ahead

These five propositions form the core of our group theory. The definitions, relations, and claims they make develop a theoretical picture of groups as complex systems. The discussion of the propositions thus far has explicated some of the corollary claims and implications of our conception of groups. Additional ideas and implications embedded in these propositions are elaborated in Part II of the book.

PART II

THE THEORY IN DETAIL

∾ *4* ∾

Group Formation

Assembly and Emergence

The cross-functional task force we described in Chapter 1 was assembled by two managers—we'll call them Ali and Barbara—to complete a single project: develop a plan for a new notepad product. Ali and Barbara decided together on the membership for this task force. The cross-functional approach dictated that people from different departments should be included, and the number of departments to be represented dictated the size of the group. The cross-functional composition presumably will ensure that various tasks implicit in the project, such as researching the market for notepad computers, selecting designs that are feasible given the company's manufacturing capacity, forecasting costs of production, and developing a sales strategy, can be handled by appropriate group members. Members need to have the interpersonal skills to work collaboratively with others, and someone will need to serve as group leader. Some, if not all, of the members need to be creative thinkers. Ali and Barbara are committed to the success of this group and will see to it that the group has access to whatever resources—space, research support, release time from their primary departments, and so on—they decide they need.

Ali and Barbara realize, of course, that skill levels, creative abilities, and department affiliations of potential group members are not all they need to know. Motivation matters. They consider whether various potential members would be excited to be assigned to this task force, or resentful, or indifferent, and they make preliminary inquiries to see which candidates express strong interest. They consider the leadership styles of different potential members and the possible pitfalls of assigning different members as task force leader. Barbara, who is familiar with research on creativity in groups, wants the group to be demographically diverse, with a mix of men and women and representation from some different ethnic groups. After weighing these various requisites and constraints, Ali and Barbara assemble the group, designate a leader, and arrange an initial group meeting at which they clarify the objectives of the group, the resources available, the deadline for completion, and the frequency with which they would like to hear progress reports from Richard, the group leader. Then they hope for the best.

Contrast this with the formation of a three-person flight crew, such as the one described by Ginnett (1990). Tom, Bill, and Greg were assigned by the airline to be the captain, first officer, and flight engineer in this group on the basis of their availability in time and space and their certification to perform one of these three roles. Tom and Greg had flown together before, as it happened, but past experience with the other crew members was, according to Ginnett, the exception rather than the norm for such crews (p. 428). This crew was expected to fulfill its mission of flying planeloads of people back and forth along the Eastern seaboard, in challenging weather conditions, with many lives and staggeringly expensive organizational resources at stake. Airline managers presumably had high confidence that any given crew assembled in this fashion would complete group formation and be ready to perform this challenging task successfully within minutes of meeting for the first time. In stark contrast to the lengthy decision process that Ali and Barbara went through to assemble their task force, the airline might well have used an automated scheduling program to assign pilots and flight engineers to crews.

Finally, consider a group of nine students who form a new a capella singing group. No one assigns these students to the group; instead, one or more of them come up with the idea of creating a group, and somehow they find one another. No one assembles this group by assigning members to it. Instead, people transform themselves into members as the group assembles itself. The group includes men and women; sopranos, altos, tenors, and basses; and members with a range of singing backgrounds and skills. No one has a predetermined conception of how many people will be in the group or what attributes they will have, apart from a shared interest in membership. A leader emerges. A group identity and boundaries develop. The group invents projects, figures out what tasks the projects entail, and acquires or develops tools and resources for completing the tasks. In contrast to the planning task force and the flight crew, the singers are a completely self-organized group.

As these examples illustrate, group formation is not a single process with minor variations. Instead, distinctly different sequences of events can result in the formation of new groups. In this chapter, we view group formation as resulting from the planned assembly of elements plus emergent dynamics. These processes are driven both by the individuals who become group members and by external forces that either initiate or facilitate group formation. On the basis of the relative importance of internal and external forces, and of planning and emergence, we define four categories of groups. A section on the "prehistory" of groups covers the context in which groups form, social integration, and planning that occurs in advance of group formation. We then discuss the impact of initial conditions and initial events that set the group on a path of development, and we define six prototypical project-focused and member-focused groups.

∞ FOUR FORCES OF FORMATION

The creation of a new interacting group requires the assembly of components into a new whole; the transformation of people, resources, and intentions in the context of the whole; and the emergence of group-level features as the members of the new group come together. The formation of new groups is driven in part by the motivated action of their members. The structure of new groups is also determined in part by constraints, opportunities, and demands in the group's embedding contexts. People who are not group members are often instrumental in forming new groups. In the early history of the group, potential group members interact both with one another and with aspects of the embedding context to create a new collective entity. The new group then mediates and moderates the interaction between members and environment and creates a new boundary that defines what is internal and what is external for the group. External and internal forces contribute to both assembly and emergence.

Assembly is the deliberate combination of parts to form an envisioned whole, according to an implicit or explicit plan or plans. The primary challenge of assembly, as illustrated by Ali and Barbara's experience in putting together the notepad task force, is to select and combine people and resources in a group that is likely to complete its projects successfully, keeping in mind how different combinations of elements with different arrays of attributes are likely to fit together. The task force and the flight crew examples illustrate very different solutions to this assembly problem.

Structure and order can also emerge from initially uncoordinated local interaction among individuals who transform themselves into members of a group without any overall orchestrated plan. The formation of the singing group illustrates this process. In this case, the logic of the structure is determined not by a blueprint and careful engineering but by characteristic dynamics that entrain and order interacting parts, replacing independence with complex patterns of interdependence. Even the most carefully assembled groups have features—such as group boundaries, group identity, norms, and collective memory systems—that emerge as the group begins to operate.

The most important "elements" in a group are people, whose identity and behavior will change to some degree in the process of psychological group formation. Ali and Barbara "hope for the best" because they realize that the success of the group will depend very much on emergent processes. Some aspects of group structure, such as leadership, may be either predetermined or emergent. When elements of the group are transformed in the context of the whole, generating new dynamic patterns, we view this as a process of emergence.

∞ THE GROUP FORMATION SPACE

External and internal forces, planned assembly, and emergent processes play a part in the formation of all groups. However, the balance of forces that shape their formation differs markedly across groups. Together, the four forces define a group formation "space" in which new groups can be arrayed. By dividing this space into quadrants we identify four categories of groups (see Figure 4.1):

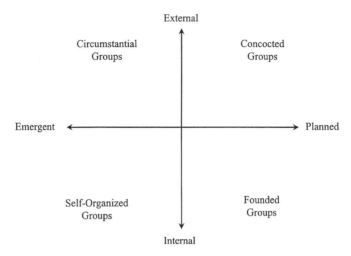

Figure 4.1. Forces in the Group Formation Space

1. *Concocted* groups (external, planned forces predominate)
2. *Founded* groups (internal, planned forces predominate)
3. *Self-organized* groups (internal, emergent forces predominate)
4. *Circumstantial* groups (external, emergent forces predominate)

When external agents deliberately form new groups according to some plan, we call these *concocted groups*. Many work groups in organizations, for example, are established by a manager who "creates" them by fiat, assigning members, tasks, and/or tools to them. These correspond to what Walton and Hackman (1986) called work teams. The notepad task force and the flight crew are both concocted groups.

Alternatively, one or more persons who will be charter member(s) of a group may deliberately assemble a new group by linking up with other people. We call these *founded groups*. A small business start-up would fall into this quadrant. Both concocted and founded groups are formed because some person or persons—outsiders in one case, future members in the other—set out deliberately to connect people and resources into a coordinated whole that will complete collective projects.

Other groups, such as the singing group described at the beginning of the chapter, come into being without much planning. These groups arise more or less spontaneously from self-organized activity that flows within existing patterns of relations among members, tasks, and tools. We call groups that emerge from local interactions among persons pursuing their individual agendas *self-organized groups*. Many friendship groups form this way. Walton and Hackman's (1986) category of self-enacted groups at work includes many groups of this type.

Groups thrown together by unexpected environmental circumstances that dictate both the project and the membership of the group fit the fourth quadrant of *circumstantial groups*. A group of people stranded together on a broken-down bus, for example, may form a circumstantial group. In self-organized groups, the primary impetus for group formation comes from group members; in circumstantial groups, the primary impetus emerges unexpectedly from the environment or embedding context. Neither is planned in advance.

Our designation of these four categories emphasizes the relative balance of forces in a group's formation, but all groups are formed by a combination of forces. The people in a stranded bus, for example, become aware of themselves as a bounded set of people who share a common predicament because of an unexpected external event, but no group will form if the people fail to make contact and simply continue reading or staring out the window. By the same token, dyadic contacts among people who are linked in a social network will not generate a bounded, functionally coordinated group if the context provides no opportunities or rewards for doing so. Instead, interpersonal contact will simply lead to more interpersonal contact.

∞ WHAT THE CATEGORIES ILLUMINATE

The distinction between planned assembly and emergence is, in part, a distinction between groups that are to some degree "built" by designers (whether members of the group-to-be or not) who deliberately connect the elements and groups that "grow" out of an embedding context as ties among certain elements become denser and more closely coordinated with one another.

We believe that this typology is useful because the primary issues involved in group formation differ depending on where in this space a new group falls. When external forces predominate, a primary issue for the new members of the group is how to conform to external demands. When internal forces predominate, a primary issue is how new members will coordinate and integrate their own goals, intentions, and expectations. The distinction between internal and external forces is, in part, a distinction between groups for which the member-group interchange develops first and plays a prominent role in a group's early development and groups for which the group-context interchange develops first and thus takes precedence over member-group relations in shaping a group's early development.

When a group is planned and deliberately created, the problems of assembly come to the fore—how to choose among, gain access to, recruit, and combine possible components. What to plan and what to leave to "chance" or emergent dynamics are also an issue. The external and internal creators of concocted and founded groups, respectively, are attempting to optimize (or possibly satisfice) the group composition, given their intentions for the group. The process of planning that precedes group formation determines some but not all aspects of the group composition. In groups that emerge more spontaneously, the composition is also emergent. Understanding the formation of such groups requires that we look at the forces that tend to bring people together into new collectives and consider the impact these forces have on the likely composition of emergent groups. In the next section, we discuss the "prehistory" relevant to groups in all quadrants of the group formation space.

∞ THE PREHISTORY OF GROUPS

Although it is often not possible to identify the starting point of a new group with precision, we propose that a group "begins" when people who think of themselves as belonging to a new group interact withother new members and begin coordinating their actions for some collective purpose. Thus, group formation is both a cognitive and a behavioral process. All groups form in some context, in which people and resources are available, to serve one or more purposes via collective action. In the next section, we identify features of the embedding context that should affect the prevalence of forces during group formation.

The Context in Which Groups Form

The embedding contexts from which new groups emerge offer both opportunities and constraints. Some contextual factors that should affect the rate of group formation are the proximity and ease of interaction among potential group members; the level of unsatisfied needs among potential group members; the current "saturation" of groups within the embedding context and hence the availability of unexploited "niches" for new groups; the capacity of existing groups to handle the array of projects that powerful individuals in the embedding context want to see addressed; and the level of threat and uncertainty that people perceive in the environment generally.

The coexistence of individuals in a common physical, temporal, and sociocultural environment provides opportunities for ties to form between them and for existing sets of ties to become elaborated into a group. People are more likely to form connections with people they encounter frequently (e.g., Festinger et al., 1950; Newcomb, 1961). They may be connected in a labor network by working together at the same workplace, for example, at jobs that facilitate but do not require interaction. They may work physically close to each other.

People are also connected through numerous social networks based on kinship, professional identity, religious affiliation, and a host of social collectives that may be widely distributed across space. Closeness of two people within a social network (i.e., having a short path of indirect ties between them, such as being the friend of a friend) is also predictive of future direct ties among people (Milardo, 1986). The recent development of technologies for long-distance communication, such as telephone, fax, and especially the Internet, also allows people to inhabit a common virtual environment even when they are geographically distant. Moreland (1987) called the tendency of people who live in the same physical or social environment to form groups *environmental integration*.

Potential group members have many competing demands on their time. People who already have many friends and acquaintances may not be motivated to seek out new contacts, and people already overloaded with projects should be less motivated to take on new ones. In general, people who feel their needs are being met by their membership in existing groups should not be motivated to form or join new groups.

The higher the "saturation" of groups in a particular sociocultural ecology, the less the likelihood of new groups' forming in that space. Saturation should be highest when the embedding context is stable or changing quite slowly. In such conditions, the transaction costs for starting a new group are likely to exceed the effort needed for existing groups to take on new projects or make other adjustments.

In an environment that is changing more rapidly, potential group members may become available when existing group ties are severed or when the demand of existing groups for members, projects, or resources declines. When lots of people are moving in and out of a particular embedding context, this creates opportunities. Once formed, groups, like institutions and organizations, often persist even when returns to their members diminish. When the environment is "shaken up," people may shake loose from these groups and look to form new ones.

The combined operation of environmental integration and environmental constraints suggests that groups are most likely to form when new projects, resources, and potential group members emerge in the environment or existing elements become available, when conditions promote lots of contact among people, and when existing groups have little flexibility in tackling new projects. Chaotic "mixing" of people who are interested in new relationships, things to do, or resources to do things with should facilitate the emergence of new groups by creating a high volume of new contacts, some of which will bring people with compatible goals and interests together for the first time.

In such a context, powerful individuals often provide the impetus for new group formation. The architects of concocted and founded groups can take advantage of changes in the environment that create new opportunities. A big influx of new people, for example, creates an opportunity to recruit new members who do not yet have extensive ties in their new setting. In organizations, rapid growth, restructuring, and downsizing all disrupt established groups. A concocted group's "architect" may be someone in a formal organization who has the power to reallocate other people within the organization—by reassigning them, relocating them, or redirecting their time and energy—and who also has the power to allocate resources and assign projects.

When threat and uncertainty are high in the environment, people's attachment to existing groups will increase, and the boundaries of groups should become more rigid. At the same time, enhanced needs for social support and protection will increase the tendency of people to seek out others. If existing groups provide inadequate response to threat and uncertainty by failing to protect members or failing to provide a satisfactory interpretation of events, their members should be open to recruitment into new groups that appear to hold more promise. When threat is high and changes in the environment break up existing groups, the proliferation of new groups should be especially high.

Disruption creates the context for circumstantial groups, which form among people who are "thrown together" by outside forces, especially if the situation includes strong incentives for collective action. Neighbors on a hill who find themselves cut off from the rest of the town by rising flood waters are faced with a new physical boundary that defines a set of people with interdependent problems. The emergence of a functioning group is not guaranteed, but the environmental conditions make group formation likely. The challenge posed by shared circumstances motivates people toward collective action to address the challenge through what we may call a search for appropriate technology.

High levels of external stress on existing groups can also lead to new groups formed when existing groups either merge or split. Stress on families, for example, increases the prevalence of marital breakups. When the children are split between parents, two new households are formed. The unmet needs of divorced or separated parents also go up. One result, if the search for a new partner is successful, may be yet another new household: a blended family of two adults and their children from previous partners.

Mergers can resolve the somewhat contradictory effects of high stress—increased attachment to existing groups and unmet needs for protection and support. When groups merge together and pool their resources, member needs can be met without relinquishing existing social ties.

Social Integration

Within an environment that provides opportunities and incentives for people to connect with one another, a given person is more likely to interact with some potential contacts than with others. People may be drawn together on the basis of emotion and shared identity. Following Moreland (1987), we call these *affective* and *cognitive integration.* The operation of social processes that tend to pull people together is part of the prehistory of self-organized groups and affects the composition of such groups.

Affective integration refers to emotional forces that draw people together. Dyads formed on the basis of interpersonal attraction may become the building blocks for emergent groups through the chaining together of overlapping dyads, for friends of friends are more likely to interact than are people who are totally unconnected. The empirical evidence for chaining (see Moreland, 1987, for a review) is consistent with balance theory (Heider, 1946; Newcomb, 1981) and other theoretical explorations of how friendship groups form (Hallinan, 1979; Zeggelink, 1993, 1995). Affective integration suggests that self-organized groups are most likely to form among people who already know and like one another. Founders of new groups—even if the purpose of the group is not primarily social—will typically favor potential members they already know.

According to social comparison theory (Festinger, 1954), people also seek out others who share their opinions to reinforce their own interpretation of important but ambiguous issues and events. Within a discipline, for example, people will tend to interact more with others who share their paradigms for viewing their area of interest. Founders establishing a new group will find it relatively easier to attract those who agree with their beliefs and values. People who interact frequently with one another tend to develop shared understandings, as their store of shared information increases and their conversations lead to common interpretations of this information (Carley, 1991). Thus, cognitive integration both is driven by and generates increased similarity.

As demonstrated by Latané and colleagues (Latané & Bourgeois, 1996), the opinions of a collection of randomly assembled people who share their views with neighbors quickly begin to cluster into coherent subgroups, following the predictions of dynamic social impact theory. When people share their views on a range of apparently unrelated topics, initially uncorrelated views begin to show correlation, illustrating that over time, people begin to agree (or disagree) consistently with people they talk to about a wide range of topics. Minority viewpoints tend to lose ground (a process called consolidation), but pockets of disagreement remain, ensuring continuing diversity. The process of simultaneous mutual influence generates patterned structure in a pool of interacting people.

Another cognitive dynamic that draws people together and pushes them apart is the categorization of self and other. Individuals within a larger social context who classify one another as belonging to the same category are biased (i.e., have positive attitudes) in favor of one another (Turner et al., 1987) and tend to prefer one another as group members (Hamilton & Bishop, 1976; Turner, Sachdev, & Hogg, 1983). This dynamic influences self-selection into relatively homogeneous self-organized groups.

Of course, any given person fits into many social categories based on attributes such as sex, race, religion, and age and has varied interests, talents, and preferences. So which individuals "gravitate" toward one another depends on which of the many attributes that make up their social identity are salient at a given time. Social identity is a flexible, dynamic construction of self. Salience is in turn influenced by situational factors such as the relative proportions of people who fit various categories within a person's immediate embedding context. Skewed proportions on any attribute heighten attention to distinctions based on that attribute (Kanter, 1977a, 1977b).

Planned Assembly:
The Prehistory of Concocted Groups

When groups are "built" to fulfill the purposes of their creators, rather than emerging spontaneously among interacting individuals, the problem of choosing and assembling the component parts comes to the fore. The coordination network of an operating group connects members, tasks, and tools—both the tangible resources of hardware and money and the intangible resources of knowledge and procedures—into a functional whole.

Concocted groups (Moreland, 1987, called them "artificial" groups) differ in the level of detail specified by the designer. In a group with minimal preassembly planning, people may be assigned to a group that has a defined project but no articulated set of tasks, no designated resources beyond those indigenous to the members, and no designated leader. In a highly planned group, both the elements and specific ties among elements are specified in detail.

The amount of planning that precedes group formation is not always evident to the casual observer, however. In the examples of the notepad task force and the flight crew, a great deal of effort was expended to select members of the former group, but hardly any was evident for the latter. We consider the flight crew, however, to be a maximally planned group, whereas the task force formed with only moderate advance planning. The real difference between the two, however, is in the strategy for assembly.

In the crew, the tasks to be completed were well defined and articulated, and equipment and procedures carefully designed for those tasks were assigned and designated. The job network linking tools and tasks was thus extensively developed in advance. The people who would complete the tasks were trained to use the equipment and procedures in a standard way, based on well-defined roles. In effect, the whole coordination network was designed in great detail before the members came together and interacted for the first time. When this type of group design is used, the particular person who fills the role of captain or first officer is in theory not important, as long as the person who fills the role is adequately trained—just as it should not matter which particular Boeing 727 from the airline's fleet the crew flies. As described in the actual case involving this flight crew (Ginnett, 1990), two captains were accidentally scheduled for the same flight, but they quickly sorted out who would take the job. It shouldn't matter. The technology is engineered and the people are trained with the aim of making them functionally interchangeable parts that can snap together and go to work immediately.

In planning the notepad task force, the desired end result was clear, and the architects of the group had a general idea of the tasks involved. The deadline for completion was also defined in advance. Members were chosen primarily on the basis of their functional specialty, but the architects did not expect all people from the same department to be interchangeable. People were not specifically trained to be a member of this group. Instead, the architects relied on careful selection to pick people who would be a good fit because of their array of task-relevant skills and interest in the task. Apart from designation of a leader, the roles each member would play in the group remained undefined. How the group would accomplish its mission, and with what resources, was left for the group to determine.

Two general issues of composition that designers of group need to consider when planning a group are size and diversity. Moreland, Levine, and Wingert (1996) provided an excellent review of the abundant advice and somewhat sparser research evidence about the pros and cons of larger and smaller groups and of diversity and homogeneity. The two issues are to some degree related, for groups with more members have a wider range of potential diversity than small groups. Because much of the research on size and diversity discusses implications for the later development of the group, we cover these topics in the next major section, which focuses on the initial conditions of a newly formed group.

∞ TIME ZERO: INITIAL CONDITIONS

The initial composition of people, tasks, and resources; the clarity and permeability of group boundaries; and the prevailing external conditions at formation can together be considered the *initial conditions* for group formation.

The initial conditions of a group affect its early development and can have long-lasting effects, even when the conditions that prevailed at formation change a great deal. A perfect knowledge of initial conditions will not necessarily tell which path a group will take. The same set of initial conditions may define multiple *attractors*—consistent patterns in time and space toward which a dynamic system moves. However, knowledge of initial conditions allows us to narrow down the likely future development of a group to a subset of outcomes that are more or less likely.

Group Size

If we compare groups with different numbers of members, the number of possible ties among members grows much more quickly than the number of members. Restricting our attention to dyadic ties, dyads have 1 tie, triads have 3 potential ties, quartets have 6, quintets have 10, and so on. If more than two members need to act in concert, the coordination difficulties multiply much faster than the number of people. If the project is a complex one that involves many tasks and a wide array of tools and procedures, the difficulties multiply. The coordination problems of large groups can interfere with their performance (Diehl & Stroebe, 1987; Steiner, 1972).

Motivation losses also tend to increase as group size increases (Steiner, 1972). This may manifest in a range of problems, from social loafing (Latané, Williams, & Harkins, 1979) to interpersonal conflict to absenteeism and active exploitation of the group (Moreland et al., 1996). Possible reasons for these problems include fewer opportunities to participate productively, a sense that one's contributions are not critical or identifiable, and greater depersonalization. The proper size for a group depends, of course, in part on the group's goals and projects. Because of the many problems created by larger group size, however, the risks of overstaffing exceed the risks of understaffing. One study found that understaffing can actually have positive effects on member motivation, satisfaction, and participation (Wicker, Kirmeyer, Hanson, & Alexander, 1976).

In voluntary groups where membership is based on individual decisions, rather than controlled by outsiders, starting out with too many people is less important because members who feel redundant can quickly prune themselves out of the group. Thus, the impact of size as an initial condition determining the future outcomes of a group is liable to be stronger in groups that have less control over their membership.

When groups need to be large, formal structures are useful to deal with coordination demands. Spontaneous conversation is typically constrained to no more than four people (Dunbar, Duncan, & Nettle, 1995), and this constraint limits informal coordination. In general, the smaller the group, the more effective informal coordination processes will be. As group size increases, the role of a leader (or some pattern of influence) in coordinating members becomes increasingly important. If no leader is designated, the emergence of an informal leader (or influence pattern) will be of pressing importance.

Groups in the upper range of the "small group" size—the size of petit juries (12), for example, up to Simmel's (1902) limit of 20 or so—are apt to handle the coordination problem initially by treating subsets of members as subgroups of people who are more or less equivalent, with ties linking members according to their subgroup membership and with a simple role division differentiating a few members of each subgroup. For example, members of a jury beginning deliberations may organize themselves according to their preferences for a guilty or not-guilty verdict, and each subgroup may tacitly agree on a spokesperson for its position. In juries, the relative size of the guilty and not-guilty factions, combined with the size of the overall jury (6 or 12), affects the probability of different verdicts—the most important outcome for such groups (Davis, 1982). This illustrates one type of interdependence between size and the distribution of attributes among members.

Diversity

Members of groups can be relatively homogeneous or diverse on a broad array of attributes, including knowledge, skills, and abilities (KSAs); values, beliefs, and attitudes (VBAs); personality, cognitive, and behavioral styles (PCBs); and demographic attributes such as sex, age, race, religion, and ethnicity, plus attributes that indicate a person's standing or role in a particular social context, such as socioeconomic status, immigrant versus native born, or reputation in a professional community (McGrath et al., 1995).

At the point of group formation, salient attributes that members hold in common are likely to be incorporated into the identity of the group as part of psychological group formation. In some cases, these attributes are important to the purpose and projects of the group, and members have been selected—or have chosen one another—on the basis of this shared attribute. However, similarity on attributes that are logically irrelevant to the group's purposes can also be incorporated into members' image of the group, either explicitly or implicitly. This can make it difficult for the group to integrate new members who are different on that attribute because they will not seem to "fit" the group.

As noted above in the discussion of social integration, people with similar values and beliefs form bonds more readily than those who perceive one another as different (e.g., Newcomb, 1961). Groups whose members have similar values are also likely to come to agreement more easily regarding group objectives and goals. Demographic similarity or dissimilarity also affects interpersonal attraction. Homogeneity in values and demographic background, however, may limit the perspectives and alternatives considered by groups, thus limiting creativity and variety in group products and solutions. For some attributes, complementarity rather than similarity is best. Two people, one high and one low in dominance, for example, will work together more smoothly than two people who are either both high or both low in dominance (e.g., Schutz, 1958).

For juries, the most important compositional feature is the initial distribution of beliefs concerning the proper verdict in a trial. The social decision scheme approach (Davis, 1973, 1982) predicts the group verdict in a criminal trial on the basis of this initial condition plus the decision rule that specifies how individual preferences should be transformed into a group decision. The behavior of the whole is thus predicted from a knowledge of members and a particular tool (the decision rule). Many distributions lead with high probability to a single verdict, which we would view as a single fixed attractor.

Demographic attributes that mark a person's position in a group's sociocultural embedding context become important if members differ. When demographic attributes are used as diffuse status cues (Ridgeway & Berger, 1986), they influence status within the group, and hence access to resources and primacy in choosing more desirable roles, unless these roles are determined by the preexisting design of the group.

Diversity in skills, abilities, values, and demographic backgrounds among members will prolong the formation process unless the fit between members, tools, and tasks has been carefully engineered in advance. In the long run, diversity increases the flexibility and path multiplicity of groups whose projects require diverse skills and allows for greater complexity, but in the short run the cost is a longer start-up period (McGrath et al., 1995).

A common error in studying composition effects is to reify diversity as something a group has in a fixed quantity based on the distribution of attributes among members. People tend not to express all aspects of self in a given group or to be aware of all dimensions of other members. They also acquire a new dimension of identity as the group forms (Turner et al., 1987), and the transformation of identity will be stronger the more important the group is to the person. This is one reason why an exhaustive listing of attributes of people within a group does not fully define the membership composition. The composition and distribution of attributes perceived by group members will instead include some subset of this array, and *which* subset depends on what the group requires, what other members attend to, and what members' personal agendas are for their involvement.

Boundaries

By definition, a newly formed group has members who consider themselves members interacting with other members. The distinction between member and nonmember creates the psychological boundary of the group. The physical and temporal boundaries of groups are also important initial conditions. Group boundaries serve as both barriers and conduits for exchanges among members, groups, and their multiple embedding contexts (Arrow & McGrath, 1995).

Temporal boundaries include the beginning and end point of groups that define their duration or life course. Some groups have an end point that is known in advance, keyed to task completion, calendar time, or temporal patterns in the group's embedding context. Other groups— the U.S. Supreme Court, for example—have open-ended temporal boundaries: They are expected to continue indefinitely. Temporal boundaries also mark the times and days that groups meet—the slice of time for each member that is committed to the group.

Physical boundaries delimit the physical space and equipment that are used by a group. Some groups have spatial boundaries that are also temporal, as when a group has rights to a particular space during a particular time slot but has no claim to this space at other times. When a group is assembled or actually uses its equipment, the spatial boundary is manifest, but nonmembers may also recognize that certain spaces or other physical resources belong to a group even when that group is not in session. Spatial boundaries may also be abstract and metaphorical. Groups that meet online, for example, may have their own mail groups or bulletin boards to which only members have access.

Clear boundaries and the ability to regulate movement across boundaries promote effective internal coordination and external relations.

Confusion about who is and is not a member of the group makes it difficult to coordinate action, and unclear temporal boundaries make it difficult for groups to schedule, pace, and synchronize their activities. Clear boundaries also promote effective exchanges between the group and its members and between the group and its embedding context.

The *permeability of boundaries* refers to the ease with which people and resources move into and out of the group. McCollom (1995a) proposed that the vitality of the group system depends on whether its boundaries are sufficiently permeable that it can access the resources it needs but not so permeable that either outside input overwhelms the system or group resources are drained from the group by its members or by outsiders.

The primacy of the group's boundary at the interchange with the embedding context, versus the boundary at the interchange between members and group, differs between groups that are formed primarily to complete collective projects, which we call *work groups,* and groups that are formed primarily to meet member needs, which we call *clubs.* We elaborate on this distinction later in the chapter. First, however, we move the clock ahead from time zero to consider the impact of initial events on a newly formed group.

∞ INITIAL EVENTS: SETTING OR ADJUSTING THE PATTERN

Initial conditions are important because they predispose a group to develop in qualitatively different ways. However, any new group may fall into more than one possible pattern. Which of the many possible patterns will characterize the group's unfolding global dynamics also depends on *initial events* that occur in the sensitive early period of group life. Small differences in these initial events can set a group on a very different path of development. This sensitive dependence on initial events should be especially marked when new members have no previous experience with one another, when the purpose of the group is vague or the project is ill defined, and when members feel anxious and uncertain—in other words, when the situation has little structure and either the goal or the path to the goal is unclear. Almost anything can happen, theoretically. Whatever *does* happen in new groups operating under these conditions makes a deep imprint on the future of the group.

Groups can usually complete their projects by more than one path. The intentions underlying a project usually do not dictate either a single "correct" set of tasks (subintentions) into which the project must be divided or a single correct "mix" of interpersonal, task, and process activities to complete the project. Rather, the paths groups take to achieve their goals are characterized by equifinality. Groups can complete a given project by dividing it into different subprojects (i.e., tasks, subintentions), by assigning those tasks to different combinations of members, or by using different sets of tools to carry out the tasks, and thus by carrying out those tasks with different patterns or mixtures of kinds of activities. If one path does not seem to be leading toward the goal, groups can and often do switch to other routes to accomplish their goals. However, groups rarely switch routes immediately, and the path they set out on will lead them in directions that will alter the relative costs of switching. As soon as a group starts acting as a collective, it acquires direction and momentum.

That momentum can be surprisingly strong, even when the group heads off in an ill-advised direction. This type of instant and persistent pattern was evident in Gersick's (1988) study of eight task forces whose life spans were defined by the time it took them to complete their assigned project. In every case, the first part of the first meeting of each group established a pattern of interaction and an approach to the task and outside context that persisted for half the life of the group. This was not because the groups engaged in careful deliberation and planning. Instead, they seemed to step collectively into the marsh of possibilities and simply keep going in whatever direction was set by that first step. Dynamically, what seems to be happening is that a very small movement acquires astonishing inertia. Order emerges from a chaotic swirl of possibilities, and the group does not stop to evaluate the usefulness or appropriateness of that order—until much later, long past the formation stage.

Another example of an instantly established norm appears in Bettenhausen and Murnighan's (1985) study of decision-making groups who completed a series of bargaining tasks. Norms for allocating payoffs formed immediately (typically during the first of 48 trials) and persisted, despite changes in the incentive structure of the bargaining game.

In groups in which a high degree of order is present at group formation, such as the carefully preengineered flight crew, initial events should have a much less dramatic effect. The project is already elaborated into a carefully sequenced set of tasks, with little room for adjustment. However, because some of the "parts" in this assembly are human, variance between theoretically interchangeable members is inevitable. Thus, a first task is to discover the ways in which the particular crew members are different from the prototype and to adjust.

The relevant model for understanding what happens in the initial interaction may be the carpenter principle. Boulding (1953) applied the analogy of building a house out of two-by-fours, windows, doors, and other parts that will always need some adjustment as the carpenter fits them together. In this analogy, planned groups are built according to a blueprint, but even in this careful blueprint, human behavior will vary, and some important behaviors—such as demonstrating effective leadership—are hard to define and inculcate. If the crew members are strangers, some brief socializing will allow them to get a feel for how they will interact and sense how well the leader fits his or her role. As Ginnett (1990, p. 444) reported, interviews with airline pilots indicated that they could tell within a few members of meeting a new captain whether he or she would be a good leader, even though they couldn't say what exactly an effective captain did.

In both concocted and founded groups, the vision of what the group will be is an important guide to adjusting and tuning ties in the group network as the group begins to operate.

In groups created by multiple founders, however, different visions of the group can complicate the formation process. Just as too many cooks can spoil the broth, multiple founders can wreak havoc by setting off confidently in different directions. Lower-status members find that fitting in and establishing a valued role is especially difficult when multiple blueprints are in use (Arrow, 1996).

In self-organized groups, such as a collection of like-minded senators who meet every Wednesday at breakfast to talk strategy, the winnowing process of self-selection is likely to ensure that seriously mismatched members are not included in the group. The operation of affective and cognitive integration will tend to pull together people who already feel the same way about matters pertinent to the group and tend to identify with one another.

∞ WORK GROUPS AND CLUBS:
SIX PROTOTYPICAL GROUPS

The two primary functions of groups, as defined in the previous chapter, are completing group projects and fulfilling member needs. The charter purpose of a group, an important initial condition that shapes member expectations and actions, will typically emphasize one and neglect the other. Work groups, whose primary function is to complete group projects, can be further distinguished by the strategy of group design, which depends in part on how the temporal boundaries are defined. Clubs, whose primary function is to fulfill members' needs, can be distinguished by the kind of need they are designed to address.

Work Groups

The functional importance of elements in new work groups is strongly influenced by members' expectations about how long the group will continue, how long they will continue as members, and the nature and range of projects that the group will undertake. The time a group is expected to stay together, the expected stability of its membership, and the expected stability and multiplicity of its projects will affect the time and effort likely to be devoted to developing different types of ties. This in turn affects the relative strength of these ties and the constraints they place on other components of the group network. The three work group exemplars are task forces, crews, and teams. The formation of a task force and a crew were described in the examples at the beginning of this chapter.

Task Forces

Members of task forces expect to work together until they complete their assigned project and then to disband. They often have a deadline, which they use to organize and pace their work. The expected lifetime of task forces is thus defined by the projects to which members have been assigned, and the most important order of business for new task forces is to decide what tasks the project involves and get busy addressing them. A group assigned to write a report on television violence, a

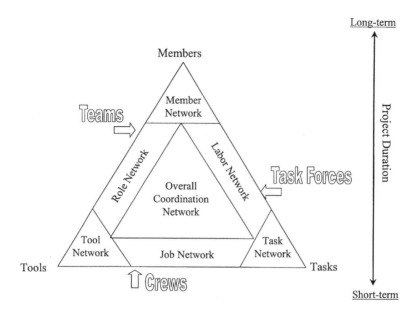

Figure 4.2. Work Groups Motivated by Projects

group that coordinates the move to a new office building, and a search committee to select a new employee or faculty member all fit this prototype. In task forces, the project, the task network that specifies how the project will be completed, and the member-task ties that link members to the project are primary (see Figure 4.2).

In task forces, interpersonal relations receive little attention and are important only for their instrumental role in either facilitating or impeding progress on the project. Members typically identify only weakly with task forces. In the notepad example, members were all "on loan" to the task force from their primary departments, which served as more permanent anchors for group identification.

Crews

Crews, as typified by the three-person flight crew of captain, first officer, and flight engineer, are short-term groups assembled in a modular fashion, usually to perform specialized tasks with specialized equipment. Members fill slots within this job network until their time is up—

their shift, tour of duty, or other defined period. They do not necessarily see a whole project from start to finish. The tasks that the crew will work on may be determined in advance, or crews may simply be assigned to the project-technology system for a certain time period and deal with tasks as they arise. The airline maintenance crew described in Denison (1990), for example, fits this description.

In crews, the integrated project-technology system, which is typically designed for a certain class of projects, is the most important component. The job network of task-tool ties may be extensively engineered in advance to ensure fit and facilitate system performance, and members are also often trained in advance to carry out designated jobs—that is, a specific set of tasks with a specific set of tools. Thus, the role and labor networks are clearly defined, but the fit between people, tasks, and tools is typically accomplished by modifying people via training, not by modifying the technology or the projects.

Along with flight crews (Ginnett, 1990), the surgical team that performs an operation or set of operations (Denison & Sutton, 1990) and a utility line repair crew also fit this prototype. Crew members are typically drawn from a larger pool of people with the necessary training who can be put together in a modular fashion. In crews, psychological boundaries are weak. Crews are often acting groups that have no long-term identity, unlike teams or task forces, whose members view themselves as belonging to these standing groups even when they are not actively working together. The primary identity of crew members often lies with a pool of other potential crew members who share the same training rather than with their concurrent crew mates. Surgeons, for example, will see themselves as more similar to and connected to other surgeons than to the nurses who assist them as part of the crew that staffs a surgical operation.

Teams

Some authors use *team* as a generic term for work groups. However, we reserve it for work groups whose group lifetime is expected to span many projects. The duration of a team is typically open-ended. Because members will be working together indefinitely and need to become cohesive and resourceful in tackling a range of projects, interpersonal relations in the member network are highly important, as are the soft tools of decision rules, communication protocols, and conflict resolution methods. Sports teams, collaborative research groups, top management teams, and string quartets fit this prototype. The care with which members are selected for these groups illustrates the instrumental primacy of the members, the interpersonal network that connects them, and the role network.

The "team-building" exercises that organizations sometimes use to help members of concocted teams develop stronger bonds also illustrate the importance of the member network in these groups. Because of the individualized character of the member-member ties, team formation is a relatively lengthy process. Sports teams and musical groups typically go through a long process of training together to "tune" the ways in which members coordinate their ideas, emotions, and actions. The projects and tasks that make up the third component of a team are more ephemeral, and the member-task mapping may be quite flexible. Self-governing teams choose or develop their own projects (Hackman, 1986).

Clubs: Groups Motivated
by Member Needs

In contrast to work groups, clubs are formed primarily by members to fulfill member needs. Projects are chosen and completed on the basis of whether members find them satisfying and useful. We distinguish clubs on the basis of which member needs are emphasized and the relative importance of different elements and networks. Economic clubs are formed to address member needs for resources, so members' ties to resources are primary. Social clubs are formed to address member needs for affiliation and social power, so relationships among members are primary. In activity clubs, formed to allow members to participate with others in valued activities, member-task ties are primary (see Figure 4.3).

When a club is formed, the life of the group is defined by the collective need of the members for the benefits (economic, social, or activity) that club membership provides. Members form and contribute to clubs primarily because they provide access to opportunities available through coordinated action. The expected lifetime of a club depends on how long resources continue to meet member needs and whether suffi-

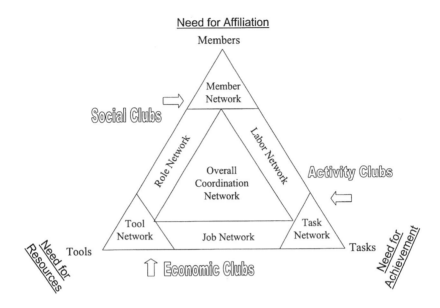

Figure 4.3. Clubs: Groups Motivated by Member Needs

cient new contributing members are available to replace departing members.

Club theory presumes that members form groups to gain access to valued resources, social contacts, or activities. In exchange for access to club resources, members contribute time, money, or other assets necessary to make these goods available and accessible to the membership. To survive, the club must retain enough members so that member contributions are sufficient to generate the club goods, while avoiding overcrowding that depletes the resources that members value.

Economic Clubs

The original notion of a club in the economic literature (Buchanan, 1965) stressed member pursuit of individual economic self-interest. Coalitions of people who trade off support (e.g., rotating credit groups that pool money and risk to fund one another's projects); sets of professional associates (attorneys, architects, etc.) who share office space, facilities, and support staff; members of a car pool; and groups of room-mates who live together and share household expenses but are not close friends all fit the prototype of economic clubs.

According to club theory, economic clubs are typically formed through the self-organizing efforts of members who see a way to improve their own economic position by pooling resources and efforts with others. However, outsiders may arrange conditions to promote the formation of economic clubs in pursuit of some larger goal. In the service of economic development and reducing poverty, for example, the Grameen Bank of Bangladesh promotes the formation of collective credit groups among poor people, who pool their resources to obtain small loans and rely on one another's commitment to paying back the loans as a form of group-based collateral.

Social Clubs

In social clubs, the primary "resource" that attracts members is the social interaction with other members and connection to the club itself. Interpersonal ties are primary. Members of social clubs may do things together that they could do alone, such as watching movies, completing writing exercises, or going out to eat, because they enjoy doing them with others. They may also engage in fundamentally social activities, such as playing bridge or throwing parties, that cannot be done alone. In social clubs, however, the primary purpose of a group gathering is affiliation with others, and the particular project or activity is usually a means to that end rather than an end in itself. If one activity proves implausible, they find something else to do.

In social clubs, a poor match among members leads to serious problems. In this, social clubs resemble teams. The particular projects a club undertakes may vary a great deal over time and are subordinate to maintaining the social network. A group of writers who meet for lunch to do writing exercises, for example, may switch to a new task—reading and commenting on stories that one of the writers is using to teach literature, or watching movies together, depending on the varying needs and preferences of members. Social clubs are especially likely to form via the chaining together of dyadic links among people who know and like one another and already do things together socially.

Activity Clubs

When the primary attraction of a group is the opportunity to engage in a desired project or activity that requires other people, this fits the prototype of an activity club. A book discussion group and a game that requires multiple players are some examples. Activity clubs resemble crews in that members usually need to have advance knowledge of rules and procedures and are relatively interchangeable. Instead of being assigned to a shift of duty, however, members show up because they enjoy the activity. Anyone can join a college club sport such as soccer, football, softball, or ultimate frisbee if he or she has some rudimentary knowledge of and skill for the sport. Any particular member may participate in only one weekend pickup game or may participate all semester or all year.

Most long-standing clubs, of course, serve a combination of member needs and may serve different needs for different members. We expect newly formed clubs, however, to have a narrower focus at first.

∞ THE FORMATION "STAGE"

Some groups have an extended period during which they develop the structure of the group, and these groups have what might be called a "stage" of group formation. However, many other groups begin their work immediately and thus are both operating and forming at the same time. It is for this reason that we prefer to focus on modes and processes rather than positing discrete stages of group development. Many of the dynamic principles introduced in this chapter continue to shape the behavior of groups that have already begun operations. The carpenter principle, for example, influences both how a group changes as a result of experience and how it responds to external events while preserving the network that enables it to function as an integrated whole. In the next chapter, we turn to the coordination processes that elaborate, stabilize, and maintain the pattern of activity established during formation.

∾ 5 ∾

Local Dynamics

Coordinating Members, Tasks, and Tools

*A*s a group assembles a network of connections that allows it to operate—the focus of formation—it also begins to operate as a collective entity. Some groups have a distinct beginning stage during which the focus is formation. Other groups set to work immediately, even as they are assembling a network or activating a detailed blueprint for the group. Similarly, groups may complete their projects and then unravel, or they may continue to work on group projects and attend to member needs even as the network that holds them together dissolves. Operations, the mode covered in Chapters 5 through 7, is conceptually distinct from the processes of beginning and ending, even though the modes of formation, operations, and metamorphosis overlap in many groups. In the operations mode that spans most of group life, three levels of dynamics take place continuously as group members act and interact over time. Although these three levels operate simultaneously and interdependently, we discuss their functioning in three separate chapters, sandwiched between Chapter 4, which discussed formation, and Chapter 8, which covers metamorphosis.

This chapter explores the local-level processes (i.e., local dynamics) that are involved in the coordination of members, tasks, and tools. The elaboration, enactment, and modification of the coordination network are driven by efforts to serve member purposes and needs, to serve group purposes (Moreland & Levine, 1982), and to maintain the group as a viable system that makes the pursuit of member and group goals possible. The evolution of global-level variables that emerge from these local-level processes is the topic of Chapter 6. Chapter 7 examines the impact of contextual dynamics: how features of the group's external contexts affect a group's operations and how groups both adapt to and create changes in these contexts.

∞ LOCAL DYNAMICS

Local dynamics in the operations mode include all the everyday activities of group members as they carry out their work. Coordination requires a shared set of expectations about how each member will act, a way to determine whether members are fulfilling expectations and whether their actions are fitting together effectively, and processes to detect and resolve problems that hamper progress on achieving group and member goals. This chapter examines coordinated activity on a relatively micro level. In dynamical systems terms, this chapter describes the local activity of the group, out of which global patterns emerge.

In considering any complex system, one can always include multiple system levels both larger and smaller in scope than the reference system. The choice of what is global and what is local is always in part arbitrary. We treat the elements of groups (members, tasks, and tools), their attributes, and the individual ties that connect them as the micro level. We treat group-level variables such as the division of labor, the level of conflict in the group, and overall group productivity as global variables.

We divide our discussion of local dynamics into several parts:

- *Elaborating the coordination network.* Although the creation of a coordination network is the focus of the formation mode, this network is further articulated during group operations.
- *Enacting and maintaining the coordination network.* As the group produces and reproduces coordinated patterns of activity, this stabilizes the core structure of the coordination network and maintains continuity.
- *Modifying the network: feedback and learning.* As groups receive feedback about group performance and member satisfaction, members may modify ties in the coordination network. The feedback process occurs continuously and con-

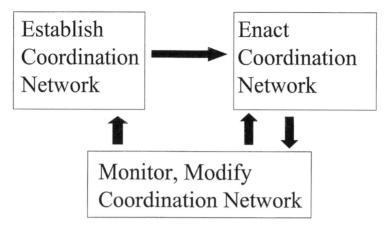

Figure 5.1. The Coordination Cycle

currently with both elaboration and enactment. Members may adjust ties and elements on a more or less continuous basis or sporadically.

Figure 5.1 shows these aspects of local dynamics: elaboration of a coordination network, enactment of that network in pursuit of both project goals and member needs, and learning from experience. They unfold together as highly interdependent processes that constitute not a single series but a continuous recurrent cycle. We discuss these aspects in turn, recognizing that the first (elaboration) overlaps in part with formation and that the latter (modification) overlaps in part with group development, the focus of Chapter 6. We treat micro-level feedback and learning as part of local dynamics. The outcome of this process on a more global scale is discussed in Chapters 6 and 7.

Dynamics of Elaboration

Complex systems tend to increase in complexity over time, and the proliferation of ties in the coordination network is part of this process. In group formation, what we are calling the elements of a group—its membership, the tasks that make up its projects, and the tools of its technology—are linked together to form a functional unit called a group. Elements of all three sets must be linked to make coordinated action possible. Some ties are established as the group forms, some predate the formation of the group, and others are implicitly or explicitly developed as the group goes about its everyday business. Ties established before or during formation form the skeleton that is fleshed out as the group elaborates the network with a rich set of connections.

The basic dynamic of elaboration is the proliferation of elements and ties. Elements may be added to the group, and these elements connected via new ties to existing elements. That is one form of elaboration. Much of the proliferation of elements, however, involves unpacking and unfolding aspects of the group that were not evident at first to the members. The identification of tasks needed to complete a project, for example, is not a matter of "importing" new tasks but a matter of discovering necessary tasks by analyzing the project into components. Similarly, the proliferation of tools available to the group may result from a census of member resources and expertise. In this way, elaboration involves unearthing, generating, and sharing information about aspects of the group. Ties may also proliferate via the creation of new ties, the discovery of existing ties, or both. Two group members who find that they went to the same university are discovering a tie; the ensuing sense of camaraderie may also be the basis for a new tie of friendship between the two.

As existing ties are revealed and new ties developed, similarities and differences among elements and ties also become evident, and the elaboration of ties is affected by the perception of these relations. Ties are more likely to be formed among some elements than others, with the result that certain elements are clustered together by dense ties, whereas others are not. Elements and ties can also be organized on the basis of perceived differences. When previously undifferentiated elements are ordered either in importance or in temporal sequence, this breaks the sameness among them and provides the basis for further clustering. Symmetry breaking creates new levels of order in an organized network, increasing its complexity. Clustering and ordering ensure that the proliferation of ties is not indiscriminate. New patterns emerge as tasks are differentiated and ordered by temporal priority and sequencing requirements, tools are differentiated and ordered by priority of use and attractiveness, and members are differentiated into jobs and roles and ordered in one or more hierarchies of relationships. The elaboration of ties thus reveals and creates new microlevel structure.

Dynamics of Enacting
and Maintaining

As this structure is activated, the ties specified by members' (and, for groups, outsiders') plans and mental models are put to the test and are tuned and selectively reinforced. Those connections that are activated early and often will tend to stabilize into habitual routines while other connections wither away, pruning the coordination network down and sharpening the differentiation between members who have different patterns of connections with other members, tasks, and tools. At the same time, information is generated about the group and its patterns that serves to bring members' models of the group system into greater alignment as their expectations about what others might do are compared with what other members are actually doing and as the outcomes of this action are assessed. Whatever actions group members hit upon and then repeat as they work together will tend to be adopted as normative, especially if there is no immediately obvious problem with these actions or their results. As this happens, members' ability to predict the actions of other members should improve. Information about overall group effectiveness and potential problems is also generated as the group operates, alerting members about friction, redundancy, incompatibility, conflict, and problematic holes in the existing network of ties.

Just as external and internal forces, planning and emergence, shape the structure of the initial coordination network, these forces guide the dynamics of group activity. Some of this activity follows explicit or implicit plans about what needs to be done and who should do what in what manner. Some of these plans exist at the group level, having been either established by the creators of the group or negotiated among the group members. Other plans exist at the individual level and constitute members' own scripts and beliefs about how things should be done, which are not necessarily held in common with other members. When a plan is specified by outsiders, the goal of action may or may not be clear to group members. Members' perception of the intended goal of a particular plan may also differ from the goals that inspired the plan, particularly when it was created by someone outside the group.

Group activity can also be driven by emergent, unplanned responses to evolving situations as members generate partial solutions to problems that were not identified in advance or for which the initial plan proves unworkable. These responses include actions by individual members who act without consulting with others, joint actions by a subset of members, or collective actions by the whole group that are coordinated "on the fly." The logic of such self-organized activity involves identification of a desired goal or state, the perception that the member or group is not in that desired state, and execution of actions intended to bring the member, subset of members, or group closer to that desired state. Because members sometimes differ in both their goals and their perceptions, the actions of group members will not always move the group in a single coherent direction.

An important difference between plan-driven activity and goal-driven activity is the criteria for determining whether a member or the group collectively is on track. Self-organized action in pursuit of goals is guided by and evaluated on whether it seems to be bringing the person or the group closer to the desired state. Preplanned actions, in contrast, may be evaluated by how closely they adhere to the plan, whether or not the execution of the plan is having desirable effects. This is especially true when the goals and the timetable for achieving those goals are not entirely clear to group members. As group members accumulate a history together, a third model emerges as a guide for activity: the set of actions the group took in the past, which is incorporated into the group culture of expected patterns.

Extant group theory tends to emphasize group activity as the execution of plans in a static environment. Unplanned, goal-directed activity is more like feeling one's way in a dynamic environment, which includes many false steps and course corrections along the way. The emergence and reproduction of habitual routines is a form of automatic, culturally conditioned action. We believe that day-to-day operations in most groups includes all three types of activity.

Dynamics of Modification

The small adjustments that bring member actions into coordination and keep them either aligned to plans or on an envisioned path to goals are an aspect of group maintenance that stabilizes the core pattern of group activity. However, the information generated by collective action also provides a basis for altering the network by changing elements, links, tactics, strategies, or goals. The distinction is like the difference between the constant small corrections needed to keep a car between the painted lines on the road and a change in course that involves either a different route or a different destination. In line with the focus of this chapter on local dynamics, we focus on micro-level changes that occur at the member level rather than large-scale changes that are adopted by (or imposed on) the group as a whole.

Group members obtain performance feedback in a number of ways, depending on how performance is being judged and the nature of the group project. Evaluations of actions differ in (a) how obvious and objective the criteria for evaluation are, (b) how quickly the effects of an action can be assessed, and (c) the degree to which outcomes depend on multiple intertwined actions or a single action. The success or failure of some types of actions is immediately obvious—for example, whether a violinist hits the correct note, whether all of the musicians are following the same tempo, or whether another person praises, rejects, or ignores a suggestion. The success or failure of other types of actions and group products, however, is more ambiguous. The beauty of a glass sculpture, the musical worth of a particular interpretation of a Beethoven sonata, or the relative value of a policy suggestion is harder to assess. For these more ambiguous performance products, group members must rely on some system of judgment, which may involve acquiring information from their surrounding environment (e.g., clients, management, or an audience) and from other group members.

Some actions can be evaluated relatively quickly, such as the number of units produced in a given time period or the technical accuracy of a violin solo. Products created by other actions, such as the structural integrity of a bridge or the effectiveness of a governmental program designed to reduce poverty, take much longer to evaluate. The source of success or failure may also be much more difficult to trace back to particular actions when the product involves many interdependent actions taken over an extended period of time.

Finally, actions and outcomes differ in whether they can be improved by one member acting alone or whether a meaningful change requires a coordinated modification of actions by two or more members. If the cello player habitually messes up a particular passage, for example, or a basketball player misses a free throw, these problems usually can be corrected by individual effort even though their causes may involve extraindividual factors. If the piece lacks a unified interpretation, however, or if an offensive strategy doesn't work because players fall out of coordination, collective, explicit adjustments are needed. Because of the greater complexity of links involved, the path to improving collective coordination problems tends to be more ambiguous than the steps needed for correcting independent action.

To use the information generated by experience to make changes, group members need to evaluate what they did right, what they did wrong, and what external forces may have influenced the group's performance. Preliminary research results on group performance attribution (Rantilla, 1996) suggest that groups tend to show the same kind of self-serving biases found in individuals: That is, members attribute success to the group (e.g., ability and effort) and attribute failure to external circumstances (e.g., luck and project difficulty).

With regard to both making attributions about group performance, and making ameliorating modifications, a group faces a more complex set of conditions than individuals do. Whereas individuals may change their own behavior to improve performance (e.g., work harder, practice more), groups have the complicating factor of how individual performances fit together. The actions and network ties that group members believe to be effective will be reaffirmed and will be less likely to be modified in future rounds of project activity. The elements and ties that group members believe to be responsible for poor performance are more likely to be altered or eliminated.

Members may attribute poor performance to one member, a subset of members, or all members, depending on the project type, on how project contributions get combined, and on the task responsibilities of the members. They may blame poor performance on one or more tools and decide to follow different procedures for future tasks. Members may also conclude that the task network is inadequate (e.g., tasks are not being completed in the right order, or people are doing the wrong tasks). Poor project performance may also be attributed to some combination or intersection of members, tools, and tasks—in other words, to the division of labor, to member roles, or to the organization of jobs. Group members may also reach different conclusions about the source of problems. The self-serving bias will guide members to find fault not in themselves or the tasks they complete but in other members or tasks.

While they assess the value of outcomes for the group, members are also assessing the value of their own personal outcomes. This can lead to modifications that appear to an outsider to make no sense, as when a member whose actions appear highly effective stops doing the work or seeks to switch tasks or tools with other members. Such modifications may be driven by an individual member's belief that the benefits received from his or her actions do not justify the effort or by a judgment that the current coordination network is not meeting important personal needs. Members may also change their personal goals and preferences as they gain experience with the group, raising or lowering their expectations about how much power or resources they deserve—for example, changing their minds about how much they like working with other group members and hence becoming more or less satisfied with aspects of their position in the labor, role, or member network.

∞ COOPERATION AND CONFLICT AT THE GROUP-MEMBER INTERCHANGE

In this section, we discuss in turn how local dynamics are (a) driven by individual efforts to achieve member goals and (b) driven by efforts (individual and joint) to achieve collective group goals. Elaboration, action, and modification in the service of member needs and group projects coordinates member interests, understandings, and action in a pattern that combines elements of cooperation and competition, convergence and conflict.

Member Needs and Goals as an Engine of Local Dynamics

Individual member goals and needs can be pursued both via independent action and through negotiations between the group and the member regarding what the group will supply to the member in return for the member's contributions to the group. An account of the latter process is found in Moreland and Levine's (1982) model of group socialization. We draw heavily on concepts from that model, which delineates the ongoing processes of the member-group exchange as members join a group, change position within a group, and eventually leave that group. The model fits our theory especially well because it is based on a dynamic rather than static concept of groups (Baron et al., 1994).

According to the group socialization model, the degree to which a member has valuable contributions to offer a group (as perceived by the rest of the group) determines the level of the group's commitment to the member, and the degree to which a group has valuable contributions to offer a member (as the member perceives it) determines the level of the member's commitment to the group. Member and group commitment levels mutually determine the member's status within the group at any given time, as well as the relative power that each party has in negotiating the exchange. Because commitment levels reflect the dynamic exchange between the member and the group, membership status changes over time.

Members have varying needs for affiliation, achievement, power, and resources and also have different expectations about which of those needs will be met by their participation in a group. Assuming that all group members have all of these needs to some degree, we can anticipate what kind of negotiations will be necessary to establish, enact, maintain, and modify selective ties in the coordination network to fulfill member needs. We discuss the coordination requirements separately for each need.

Need for Affiliation

For group activity to address group members' needs for affiliation, coordination requires shared expectations for social interchange and the elaboration and activation of interpersonal ties. Members need to reach an adequate level of agreement, explicit or implicit, on norms regarding the following:

1. How much group time can legitimately be spent on interpersonal activities such as social outings, celebrations, and discussions of personal matters
2. How group members should respond to other members' affiliative needs (e.g., whether to attend outside social events to which they may be invited, how to respond when someone divulges personal information, and whether to send cards or visit a member who is in the hospital)
3. Interpersonal relationships within the group (e.g., whether close friendships or romantic intimate relationships between members are encouraged, permitted, discouraged, or proscribed)

These norms vary widely across groups. They may be adopted independently by group members as a constraint on the social network or may be imposed by the embedding system. Work groups in some organizations are expected to conform to organizational norms proscribing close interpersonal relations, especially romantic relations, on the premise that they would interfere with effective project performance. Such norms prevail in many graduate study programs with respect to faculty-student relations, and "fraternization" is explicitly prohibited between different "classes" of members in military groups. In other groups (e.g., family businesses), close interpersonal relations among members are pervasive.

Beside group norms, interpersonal relations are also affected by the group's communication technology. Research (e.g., Hollingshead & McGrath, 1995; Lebie, Rhoades, & McGrath, 1996) suggests that interpersonal activity is greatly diminished in groups that can communicate only via computer conference systems, compared to groups meeting face to face. This difference may interact with differences in types of projects. Performance on some kinds of projects, such as those requiring extensive negotiations and high levels of interpersonal trust, can benefit from richer interpersonal communication. For other types of projects, such as solving intellective problems with demonstrably correct answers, interpersonal communications may be a distraction. Thus, the extent to which a given group provides affiliation opportunities that fit a given member's needs is in part constrained by the nature of the group's tasks and tools, in part determined by its embedding environment, and in part determined by ongoing member-group negotiations.

Need for Achievement

For group activity to address members' needs for achievement, members need to develop shared expectations about task responsibilities and about how credit is assigned to member accomplishments. This involves agreement, explicit or implicit, on procedures by which

1. Member preferences for certain tasks and tools are considered when allocating tasks and tools to members
2. Members are promoted to new levels of responsibility and assigned high-status, high-profile tasks

3. Members receive explicit recognition for their contributions to group projects

These "soft" tools of procedures may be imposed by the embedding environment, negotiated among members, or both. Task and role assignments determined by outsiders, for example, may be either reinforced or subverted by informal strategies for allocating tasks and acknowledging member contributions (Homans, 1950). The formal and informal systems may be based on different criteria (e.g., seniority vs. skill and differential need for achievement), so that members end up doing tasks that are supposedly some other member's responsibility. This can be a satisfactory arrangement, for example, if the senior person is more concerned with achieving power goals and the more competent member cares mainly about the intrinsic rewards of a skilled performance.

Need for Power

Negotiations among members about power needs and goals typically involve both dyadic struggles to clarify relative power and collective norms about the status and influence structure. Group members need to attain a functional level of agreement, explicit or implicit, regarding the following:

1. How membership status is established within the group (e.g., determined by a leader, based on the value of contributions to group projects, based on seniority)
2. The degree of power disparity between members allowed by the group
3. The acceptable uses of power to influence others in the group and how to sanction violations of these norms

Of course, members' power goals may also be fulfilled by belonging to a relatively powerful or prestigious group, regardless of their status in the group hierarchy.

Work by Raven and colleagues (French, 1956; French & Raven, 1959; Raven, 1993) distinguishes among six bases of power: reward, coercion, legitimate, expert, referent, and informational. The type of power available to group members will vary both among groups and within groups depending on role assignments and member attributes. Group constraints on power disparities and the use of power may also vary depending on the type of power. Disagreements among members on these issues that have not been resolved by the adoption of an explicit norm are liable to surface as members pursue their own quests for power within the group.

Also relevant to the pursuit of power is research on leadership (e.g., Fiedler, 1964), although not much of that research deals explicitly with issues of power in groups. Interpersonal influence has also been studied extensively, in terms of both the influence of majorities on dissenting members (e.g., Asch, 1951; Myers & Lamm, 1976) and the influence of minorities on majority decisions (e.g., Moscovici, 1985; Nemeth, 1986). Very little of this work, however, illuminates how membership and activity in groups fulfill (or fail to fulfill) member needs for power. It is also unclear whether different types of power are sought differentially by members or whether the desire for power, and the satisfaction of that desire, is more generic. If the former is true, then power conflicts among members might be resolved by acknowledging greater expert power for one person, for example, but greater legitimate power for another.

Need for Resources

Negotiations among members and groups about the tangible rewards of group membership in general, and the differential allocation of resources among members, require agreements, explicit or implicit, regarding the following:

1. Which benefits of group membership are automatically conferred on all members, such as use of shared tools or other perquisites
2. How divisible goods produced directly by the group, or obtained by the group in exchange for group products and services, will be divided among members
3. How conflicts among members over divisible goods will be resolved

Club theory (Buchanan, 1965) focuses on the production of nondivisible "club goods" that are conferred on all members by virtue of belonging to the group. This relation would be represented in the coordination network by ties connecting all members to a particular tool or other resource. Club theory has focused primarily on predicting the optimal size of clubs from an economic perspective. The optimal size is large enough to generate the resources desired by members but not so large that the resources diminish in value due to crowding effects. In groups that are not at this optimal size, conflicts over modifying the group structure by either admitting new members or expelling existing members are likely.

Theory and research regarding equity, equality, and other bases of resource allocation within social units are relevant to the disposition of divisible goods owned by, produced by, or procured by the group. A growing body of research (e.g., Fiske, 1991, 1992; Triandis, 1994) documents cultural (and subcultural) differences in the assumptions made about allocation norms in different types of relationships. Even within the same culture, however, allocation norms can and do differ among groups of the same type. Such differences may stem from a different mix of needs and goals of the individual members of groups. If access to tangible resources is not an important motive for group members, a default norm of equality may be automatically applied, for example, because it is the simplest to administer. However, if one member is highly motivated by access to resources whereas other members care more about affiliation, power, or achievement, the negotiation between this member and the rest of the group may result in a very unequal distribution of resources that is nonetheless satisfactory to all.

Coordinating Interests, Understanding, and Action in the Service of Group Projects

If the process of working on group projects and the outcomes from completing those projects do not advance the individual objectives of members and fulfill needs that members expect to be satisfied by the group, the group is unlikely to function effectively for long. Thus, the purposes that underlie group projects must be integrated in some way with the intentions and objectives of the members. In this section, we discuss the coordination of interests, understanding, and action that make coordinated pursuit of collective goals possible.

The process by which groups coordinate the completion of single— let alone multiple—projects has received relatively little attention in the social psychology literature. This neglect is not surprising, as most research in this tradition has studied laboratory groups tackling simple projects that consist of one or more obvious tasks specified by the experimenter. The relation of tasks to one another within larger instrumental frameworks such as projects has been considered by von Cranach, Tschan, and colleagues (Tschan, 1995; Tschan & von Cranach, 1996) and others (e.g., Frese & Zapf, 1994; Hacker, 1985) who draw on theories of action regulation.

Tschan and von Cranach's (1996) framework is very compatible with our theory of groups. They proposed that groups work toward relatively molar purposes that require many kinds of tasks or activities. This corresponds to our conception of projects. Activities toward group goals are organized hierarchically, at three levels: a high level characterized by purposeful thought, an intermediate level characterized by scripts, and a more micro level characterized by more or less automatic behaviors. These three levels are knowledge based, rule based, and skill based, respectively. The authors proposed that the parts of the project (which corresponds to our notion of task) are organized sequentially. Action at each hierarchical level, and within each segment of the temporal sequence, is carried out by recurrent cyclical regulatory processes.

Tschan and von Cranach decomposed this recurrent cycle into three processes: (a) orientation, goal choice, and planning; (b) execution; and (c) evaluation (feedback). These resemble the phases used in early studies by Bales and colleagues (e.g., Bales & Strodtbeck, 1951), but the application differs. Bales and colleagues saw orientation, evaluation, and control as time-ordered phases and expected that acts of orientation would occur mostly in early parts of task performance, that evaluation would peak in a middle period, and that control would predominate near the end. In contrast, Tschan and von Cranach argued that each task or subtask requires all three phases of the cycle, although often parts of the cycle are done tacitly or with minimum attention. Action regulation theory has been applied both to groups doing primarily cognitive tasks and to groups doing tasks primarily involving motor behavior.

These concepts fit well with our theoretical formulation. Elaboration corresponds roughly to Tschan and von Cranach's (1996) orientation and planning aspect of the task performance cycle, although we focus more broadly on all component networks, not just those involving tasks. Enacting corresponds to their concept of execution, and evaluation is an important process for both the maintenance of ties and their modification.

Adaptive structuration theory, a body of research that views group activity as the production and reproduction of patterned interaction (Poole & DeSanctis, 1990), offers insight into the micro-level process of elaboration and adjustment. Coordination is the structured patterning of within-group activities by which groups strive to achieve their goals. A precondition for coordination is that group members have or develop reasonably "predictive" expectations about the who, what, when, and how of others' actions and also understand what others expect of them. Norms about handling conflict, coordinating action, and processing information help establish shared expectations and coherent group behavior.

In Chapter 4, we proposed that group projects can be classified according to the degree to which they require activities geared toward attaining consensus and managing conflict, regulating behavior, or processing information and solving problems. Although much past theory and research on groups has focused on one of these activities, we presume that most groups engage in projects that draw on all three activities, which require the coordination of interests, of actions, and of understandings, respectively. Where projects differ is in their relative emphasis on each of these kinds of activities. We also presume that projects in most real groups require members to carry out a variety of activities, including directly task-related activities (e.g., proposing answers to the problem posed by the project or kicking a field goal), interpersonal activities (e.g., praising a teammate), group process activities (e.g., suggesting the next play in football), and activities that combine two or all three of these.

Conflict and Consensus

All groups must find a way to coordinate the interests and goals of individual members, which will rarely be in complete harmony from the outset. The group socialization model presumes, in fact, that there will always be some friction based on competing interests, with all members hoping to maximize the benefits they receive compared to the contributions they make to the group. Incompatible interests can generate what Jehn (1995) called relationship conflicts, which are often the most destructive and disruptive type of conflict in a group. Establishing norms for adjudicating and resolving competing claims is thus a key issue for groups that have autonomy in such matters.

Depending on the type of project that the group is engaged in, the process of discovering and resolving conflicts may also be important to the task itself. In some groups—a debate team would be one example—what Jehn (1995, 1997) called task conflict is central to the group's work. In others, such as juries, the core project is for members to reach consensus on a controversial matter. To engage in productive conflict, manage potentially destructive conflicts, and reach consensus on issues important to the group, members need to settle, explicitly or implicitly, on norms that establish the following:

1. How members will present their claims or views to the group (e.g., in a structured or unstructured group discussion, through informal conversations with other members, by speaking with the group leader privately, or by appealing to outsiders who have the power to influence group actions)
2. How each member's claims or point of view will be evaluated and how much they will be weighted compared to the claims or opinions of others
3. How disparate interests or viewpoints will be reconciled (or discounted), and by whom
4. How (and by whom) a group decision will be established when a group consensus is required and members' views diverge

According to Bettenhausen and Murnighan's (1985) analysis, when group members define a situation similarly and retrieve similar scripts (the intermediate level of rule-based action, according to Tschan & von Cranach, 1996), their interactions will be relatively unproblematic. When members agree on the norms specified above, we anticipate that this will be largely true even when members' interests and opinions are in conflict because they have a common framework for expressing and resolving conflict. If group members lack collective norms that settle these matters, interaction can lead to procedural conflict (Jehn, 1997).

Groups often develop their conflict-handling and consensus-attaining procedures "on the fly," settling on norms by trial and error, and often with considerable turbulence. Much of this process is played out in groups at the level of local dynamics and involves friction between individual members rather than group-level conflict and consensus procedures. As Jehn (1995) noted, conflicts of one type can also change into conflicts of another type, with unresolved conflicts on task or procedural matters, for example, spawning relationship conflicts between members who disagree.

Considerable research bears on these issues. Research on bargaining and negotiation investigates how groups manage explicitly conflicting interests. There also is a growing body of research on the occurrence, expression, and management of conflict within groups that are considered to be cooperative rather than mixed-motive groups (Jehn, 1995; Rhoades & O'Connor, 1996). For the consensus process, research on how group members combine their opinions into a single group decision is relevant (e.g., Davis, 1982; Laughlin et al., 1991). Research on the impact of opinion minorities and opinion majorities within groups seeking consensus is also relevant (e.g., Nemeth, 1986). This work investigates not only the relative amount of influence exerted by majority and minority factions but also the quality of the products generated by minorities and majorities. For example, Gruenfeld (1995) discovered the highest level of integrative complexity in products generated by members of nonunanimous opinion majorities and the next highest in products generated by members of opinion minorities. Members of unanimous groups generated products with the lowest integrative complexity (see also Gruenfeld & Fan, 1996).

Synchronization of Member Activity

For projects that depend on synchronized physical activity, coordination requires that members develop shared expectations about the intensity, content, and timing of their actions and execute those actions as expected. Much of this coordination, especially at the micro level of individual actions, is implicit and is developed through the process of working together. Effective coordination of action requires:

1. Agreement on who will do what, where and when (either in clock or calendar time or relative to other group members' actions)
2. Well-rehearsed performance habits for individual actions and well-practiced performance habits for each pair or larger subset of members whose actions need to be closely coordinated in time and space
3. Mechanisms for monitoring deviations from the intended "who-what-where-when" of actions
4. Procedures to correct these deviations

The latter two requirements may be addressed by a leadership or control hierarchy or handled in a self-organized fashion, with all members monitoring their own actions and comparing them against an ideal of how collective action should be choreographed.

Most research on the coordination of physical actions has been carried out in the context of team training (Ilgen, Major, Hollenbeck, & Sego, 1995; Salas et al., 1985) and has been geared to specific projects or types of activities—(e.g., a military unit executing a reconnaissance patrol or an attack on a specific objective (Goodacre, 1953; Greer, Galanter, & Nordlie, 1954; Havron et al., 1951; Havron & McGrath, 1961). Both limitations arise for good reason. For one thing, action coordination has an emergent and iterative quality; smooth coordination between members is attained only after much experience and practice. Hence, training and rehearsal are prerequisites for high-level performance. At the same time, the synchronization of actions with tight time tolerances is typically very specific to the particular activity of the group. For example, both an orchestra playing a particular passage of a symphony and a basketball team executing a fast break require close coordination and split-second timing by teammates, but they are dramatically different in content, so one would expect virtually no generalization of skills from one activity to the other.

As people work together closely, especially when similar actions are repeated over time, their actions become entrained (McGrath & Kelly, 1986), so that the temporal patterning of different people's actions is aligned with respect to phase and periodicity. In some types of activity, long-standing experience in social interaction suffices to ensure quick entrainment on the automatic, skill-based level. An example is the patterning of conversational flow in groups, which can also extend to gestures and even breathing patterns (Warner, 1988).

Information Processing and Problem Solving

All groups obtain, interpret, and use information in their interactions, and the process of group interaction itself constantly generates information about its members and about the workings of the coordination network that links members, tasks, and tools. Projects differ, however, in the kind and intensity of information-processing and problem-solving activity required. Coordination of understanding entails sharing information and establishing the meaning of that information for the group. Effective coordination of understanding requires that group members:

1. Determine what information the group needs
2. Identify potential sources of information and evaluate their credibility
3. Determine the relevant meaning of information for the group's project goals
4. Decide who will monitor which sources of information and how this information will be shared with others
5. Agree on how, and by whom, information will be interpreted and integrated with other information before it is shared

Relevant work on collective information processing by Wegner and colleagues (Wegner, 1987; Wegner et al., 1991) and on transactive memory by other researchers (e.g., Hinsz et al., 1997) investigates how group members divide up information access, processing, and storage tasks. Stasser and colleagues (e.g., Stasser & Titus, 1985, 1987; Stasser, Stewart, & Wittenbaum, 1995) have examined how group members share—and fail to share—information that would improve the quality of group decision making.

Groups often gather and process information working from a very incomplete conception of the possible sources of information and the importance of various pieces of information. Moreover, the information that is objectively accessible in the group's environment depends not only on their information-gathering technology but also on the procedures by which members come to agree on the meaning of information. Information processing involves not only a reduction of uncertainty, which is caused by incomplete information, but also a reduction of equivocality, the ambiguity caused by multiple possible interpretations of the same information (Daft & Lengel, 1984).

∞ LOCAL DYNAMICS IN DIFFERENT TYPES OF GROUPS

In this section, we discuss some ways in which local dynamics differ in different types of groups. Depending on the type of group, ties between group elements may be (a) largely predetermined by an outside "architect" (e.g., a manager who created the group); (b) determined by one group member or a subset of group members (e.g., the group's founders or appointed leaders); (c) collectively created by members of a self-organized group; or (d) implicitly assumed by, and enacted by, all or a subset of group members, perhaps on the basis of their prior experience in similar kinds of groups.

In groups formed according to the plan of either outsiders or group members (concocted and founded groups), many ties may be specified in advance. The ties most likely to be specified are those that are most important for completing group projects. Ties that are important primarily for satisfying member needs are less likely to be specified and will instead develop as group members interact. In groups formed in a bottom-up fashion (self-organized and circumstantial groups), ties and component networks are developed primarily through elaboration and modification as the group feels its way toward an effective system of connections.

Actual groups do not generally attain an ideal set of relations among their elements, except in the minds of their creators, designers, or leaders. Often, they satisfice, with respect to both group projects and member needs, with less than optimal coordination patterns. A system of ties that seemed ideal to a founder or architect may prove less workable in practice as actual members prove less competent than envisioned, tools do not work as expected, and members compete over the more desirable tasks and depart from specified operating procedures.

Formation driven by the dynamics of emergence (which predominates in self-organized and circumstantial groups) also creates initial coordination networks that need to be elaborated, tuned, and adjusted. Groups may form to complete projects that prove unworkable given the tools and resources that members have on hand. Members drawn together on the basis of a perceived commonality of interests and intentions may discover that their goals are not entirely compatible after all, that completing group tasks is not as rewarding as they had anticipated, or that their initial conception of the group's project overlooked key tasks. For such groups to persist and succeed, elaboration and modification of the network will be critical.

If the initial network is highly structured and the group's duration short, then elaboration may be minimal. In short-lived groups, the brief time horizon may dissuade members from any serious effort at modifying the network unless it is so dysfunctional that the group cannot proceed with its work. Instead, members may satisfice, putting in their time and looking ahead to their next assignment rather than investing energy into making changes. In circumstantial groups in which the overwhelming objective is to solve a pressing crisis and disband, members may show a great deal of tolerance for suboptimal structures as long as they are minimally functional.

In groups that closely approximate the crew exemplar, members often have a detailed understanding of what they are supposed to do, in what order and in what way. Similarly, they can make very accurate predictions about what others will do based on knowledge of the structured roles that other crew members inhabit. When crew members not only are well trained but have substantial experience working on similar crews, little elaboration is necessary, especially if the project remains routine. A surgical crew performing a routine coronary bypass, for example, has little need to elaborate or adjust the coordination network, especially if all members of the crew work at the same hospital and are familiar with the norms that govern not only the actions specified by their designated role (surgeon, anesthesiologist, scrub nurse, or circulating nurse) but also those that are particular to the embedding system of the hospital. (See Denison & Sutton, 1990, for a case study of surgical crews on which this description was modeled.) Elaboration in prototypical crews occurs primarily when the group encounters nonroutine conditions or tackles novel projects. The assignment of members and tools to emerging tasks should follow the logic of the established structure.

Surface changes in behavior patterns in crews typically indicate that the group is activating a different set of ties in the network, rather than modifying the coordination network itself. The local coordination of action among members may require minor tuning as the crew sets to work. When members have substantial experience doing highly similar tasks with people who have been trained using the same scripts and routines, entrainment should be quick and should operate on the automatic, skill-based level. Adjustments that change existing ties, especially when new ties violate standard role or job definitions, are most likely when the situation is not only nonroutine but radically novel. According to Zaccaro and Burke (1998), an important responsibility of crew leaders is to determine when contingencies warrant a modification that violates familiar roles and routines.

In groups that are closer to the task force prototype, however, elaboration of ties during operations is the rule rather than the exception. The initial network is generally too sparse to allow reliable predictions and thus must be further articulated to reduce uncertainty. Norms need to be established and tested and conflicting expectations resolved. As the initial network is activated to do the group's work, discrepancies between expectations and reality become apparent. Because of the intensity of interaction, elaboration and modification of ties in the member network of interpersonal relations are particularly important for teams. In task forces, the elaboration of the task network is a more prominent concern. The global evolution of group-level patterns studied in research on group development results from myriad changes and adjustments at the more local level of individual elements and ties in task forces and teams.

The patterning of elaboration, maintenance, and modification is hardest to predict in clubs. Depending on what members expect to receive from a club and how much interaction is required to satisfy these needs, a sparse network that is quickly assembled may function quite well, especially for a short-lived group. The components of the coordination network most likely to be elaborated and modified should depend on the type of club. A transient activity club of people playing pickup basketball together is likely to show change and development in the coordination of action as people notice and adjust to one another's styles of play. In contrast, the interpersonal ties that form the member network should be the densest and most active in a friendship club formed primarily for social purposes.

In groups created by a merger of two smaller groups, elaboration is least likely among the elements of each preexisting subgroup; instead, new ties should proliferate between members, tasks, and tools of the two previously separate groups as members learn the rules and procedures followed by others and redistribute tasks. In groups created by partition, the severing of ties with the elements in the former, larger group context creates opportunities for new ties to develop within the new group.

∞ COORDINATION IN THE SIX COMPONENT NETWORKS

In the next four sections, we focus on tasks, then on tools, then on members in relation to tasks and tools, and then on members in relation to one another. We apply the local dynamics of elaboration, enactment, maintenance, and modification to the six component networks in the process. For each network, elaboration involves identifying elements and their attributes, clustering elements by creating or strengthening ties, and ordering elements and ties based on temporal priority, logical sequence, member preferences, or importance to the group. Enactment and maintenance involve activating these ties through group interaction, strengthening and reaffirming ties through repetitive use, or letting ties wither away if they prove ineffective. Modification involves deliberate alteration of elements and links in the coordination network in response to information about its functioning.

In the first section, we examine the task network. In the next section, we focus on tools, discussing both the tool network and the job network that coordinates tools and tasks. The elaboration, enactment, and modification of these three networks are driven primarily by the requirements of group projects. In the next two sections, we focus on networks involving members: the labor network that connects members to tasks, the role network that allocates tools and resources to members, and the member network of interpersonal relations. Along with project requirements, local dynamics in the latter three networks are influenced by member needs, goals, and intentions.

Creating and Executing Project Plans:
Local Dynamics in the Task Network

To carry out their projects, groups must implicitly or explicitly elaborate a set of tasks into a "game plan." Unless the tasks involved are already prescribed or the project involves a simple unitary task that members do in parallel, such as bagging trash along a highway or loading a moving van with boxes, group members need to break a project down into tasks. This corresponds to identification. Members then need to specify how the tasks are related, including which tasks go together (clustering) and what temporal sequencing of tasks makes sense (ordering). Groups may also order tasks by importance, especially when some tasks are not absolutely necessary for completing the project.

The result of dividing a project into tasks, grouping the tasks into functional sets, and sequencing them is a network of task relations. The elaboration of tasks may occur before, during, or after other parts of the coordination network are developed. It can happen before the group begins work, intermittently throughout the life of a group as it takes up new projects, or via a process of continual discovery as the group's work unfolds.

In crews performing routine projects, members may simply check with one another that they have identified the project in the same way and have the same conception of which tasks will be completed in what order. If no discrepancies are discovered, no elaboration is required, and the group sets to work. If the script for a particular project involves some alternate choices—a question mark in the task network—crew members will need to agree on which alternative set of tasks they will complete.

Depending on the structure of the crew, the task network may be specified by the leader, who communicates the plan to the other crew members as they commence operations. The crew leader may also add some tasks or specify details about sequencing that are not required by the general script. In a case study of an airline cockpit crew, for example (Ginnett, 1990), the captain tells the flight attendants that he will put the no smoking sign on 10 minutes before landing to ensure that they can do a very thorough safety check and be in their seats well before landing. Although safety checks and getting seated always take place before landing, they do not always happen as promptly as this captain prefers. This counts as an elaboration of the general script for landing.

In a broader study of cockpit crews, Ginnett (1987) found that some captains creatively elaborated the core expectations that all crew members had about their own and others' behavior, others simply affirmed standard expectations, some went through the motions during briefing without providing any information about the task network, and others actively undermined preexisting organizational expectations. He found that these different approaches led to significantly different patterns of interaction among crew members. This indicates that even the relatively minor elaboration that occurs in highly structured crews can have important effects.

In task forces, the elaboration of a project into tasks is generally the responsibility of the members, even in task forces commissioned by outsiders who specify what the final product should be. For a task force of bankers formed to create a new money market account, Gersick (1990) found that the broad outlines of the account and when it could be implemented were specified by an act of Congress that approved this new product for banks. Because the product was new, group members were unclear about just what would be involved in creating it. Some details of the account were still being worked out by a banking regulatory committee. Thus, the group began its work by identifying some of the tasks that would be involved and by noting the areas of the task network that could not be specified yet because of missing information.

The details of the bankers' conversation illustrate that this group started with identification. A brainstorming session about "the things we have to decide" resulted in a list that was, as the banker notes, "not necessarily in order of importance" (p. 115). This was followed by a discussion that took up these tasks in no particular order—the group did not bother to cluster or sequence them. They did, however, pay attention to clustering and sequencing the tasks involved in implementing the new account, which the members accomplished primarily by working individually or in pairs (p. 121). Modification and further elaboration of the plan occurred at several points, triggered by new information created as the regulatory committee completed its work. This on-line, periodic task modification may be characteristic of task forces, just as preplanned blueprints are characteristic of crews. Gersick's (1988, 1989) research suggests that members of task forces identify an incomplete list of tasks in their first meeting and then set right to work, with little attention to the logic of clustering or ordering.

Teams, which take up many projects over time, may develop a process that has elements of both. Although a team's projects are likely to differ, over time members may create a general blueprint for what tasks are typically involved in their projects and may use this blueprint as a starting point for each new project. Unlike groups that have the preprogrammed nature of crews or the single-project orientation of task forces, teams may also select their own projects.

Clubs of the economic or social variety may have few "projects" that have a beginning, middle, and end. Instead, the activities of the group are driven more by the goals and preferences of individual members, so that the distinction between pursuing group projects and satisfying member needs is blurred. Activity clubs are more likely to have defined projects, such as a sports tournament or a camping trip, that need to be broken into relevant tasks. Members of such groups may also get together to execute enjoyable tasks—such as playing bridge or singing together—without any overall "project" or overarching goal.

Developing Norms and Procedures:
Local Dynamics in the Tool
and Job Networks

To perform tasks successfully, a group must implicitly or explicitly have at its disposal an array of tools that will suffice to perform them. Tools include both tangible objects and resources and the "softer" tools of procedures and rules. Identifying the former is more straightforward, typically, than identifying the latter. In some groups, the tools may comprise a standard technology of hardware and procedures issued to the group by people in the embedding context. In crews, the members will typically know how these tools map to the tasks. In work groups embedded in organizations, the organizational infrastructure, including information systems, rules and policies, and physical equipment, provides a preexisting technology and set of resources that are already elaborated into a working system.

Members of groups embedded in environments that are less familiar may receive explicit guidance about their choice of procedures and their access to resources. Juries, for example, are instructed by the judge about the decision rule they should follow in rendering a judgment. Juries depend on the larger system to provide a space in which to conduct their deliberations and other tools to help them integrate the information provided during the trial.

If members are unfamiliar with the range of resources that are potentially available, or with the possible uses of the tools they have at their disposal, they may appeal to outsiders for assistance or may discuss the problems among themselves. This corresponds to the knowledge-based level of purposeful thought. Work groups in organizations may need clarification, for example, about which organizational resources and tools they may legitimately either claim as their own or share with others. Members may also simply tackle tasks with whatever tools are at hand, generating information about what works via trial and error and modifying the job network as they go. For a circumstantial group of people in a lifeboat, for example, the projects may be quite clear: Tend to the wounded, attract the attention of rescuers, and keep everyone alive in the meantime. The tasks that are feasible in pursuing these projects will depend in part on what tools are available, in the form of supplies stashed in the boat and techniques and procedures either explained in instructions or known to one or more of the survivors. In this case, the tool network and job network develop in tandem. Trial-and-error matchings help the group learn what tools are useful for which tasks and how they should be used. Collective recall and preliminary efforts may help members recover little-used tools, such as procedures learned in first aid classes but never before applied.

The soft tools of rules and procedures potentially available to a group may be specified in written instructions, but most are carried in the forms of scripts—Tschan and von Cranach's (1996) rule-based level—in the heads of the group's members. This is the presumption of Bettenhausen and Murnighan's (1985) model of norm emergence. They proposed that individuals first define the situation they are in (drawing on what Gell-Mann, 1994, called a schema, a model of the environment) and then retrieve possible scripts that apply. When group members' definitions and scripts are similar, interactions confirm the validity of their choices. Thus groups may "fall into" a pattern of majority-rule decision making or consensus without ever discussing the appropriateness of alternative models. The associative links that exist in the members' scripts become ties in the job network of the group as they set to work. Many procedures, such as turn taking in face-to-face discussions, are enacted by group members without conscious attention rather than identified from a range of alternatives and specifically chosen. This would correspond to the automatic, skill-based level of the action regulation model. This type of elaboration occurs throughout the life of a group as new tasks are tackled in a habitual, routine manner.

When members define the situation similarly but have different scripts, initial interaction should be unproblematic, but disagreements are likely to surface later. At this point, the group will need to develop a group-based understanding (the highest level of purposeful thought), using whatever norms the group has developed for discussing and resolving differences in opinions. In this case, initial elaboration is minimal, but interaction creates conflicts and a poor match between expected actions and actual behavior. When group members realize that the poor fit is based on different expectations among members, the path to adjustment should be relatively clear. However, if members interpret the friction interpersonally and blame others rather than recognizing that different scripts are a structural problem in the job network, the ensuing local dynamics are likely to play out more in the member network than in the job network. If groups spend more time in planning and elaboration, members may discover up front that they hold incompatible scripts that specify, for example, a majority-rule voting system versus a consensus model. In this case, they will need to choose among the procedures or assign different ones to different tasks.

When members have similar scripts but different definitions of the situation, interaction should make the problem clear very quickly. Other members' actions will not fit expectations, but the logic of their actions should be relatively clear. In a task force, for example, one member may begin to execute a part of the job plan prematurely but according to the rules that the group has agreed on. It should be quickly evident to others that this person has a different conception of what stage the group is at, rather than seeing the behavior as strange or illogical. The actions of a group member who begins executing emergency procedures when there is, in fact, no emergency are similarly easy to interpret and correct.

The more often a rule is used in a particular group, the more likely it is that this particular rule will be seen as generally appropriate. Group members may elaborate the task-tool network by applying an agreed-on rule indiscriminately to all tasks that seem vaguely similar. A group of teachers and parents who had explicitly agreed to use the consensus model for making important decisions about the curriculum, for example, found themselves applying this decision rule to relatively trivial decisions such as whether to put a water cooler in the classroom. After the meeting, members agreed it was somewhat ridiculous to spend 45 minutes on this issue, an outcome that was a direct result of their unthinking application of a familiar script for decision making to an emergent task. On the basis of the information generated by the experience and the discussion, the group agreed that issues that were relatively trivial could be decided using a different procedure, an alteration of the task-tool mapping.

Groups may cluster tools together on the basis of function (e.g., the group's computers and a printer; an information-gathering procedure and a procedure for integrating that information); clustering also involves matching hardware with the procedures for using that hardware. Another form of clustering is based on the links among members and tools. In groups with well-defined and highly differentiated role systems, for example, how a task is accomplished, and with which tools, may depend heavily on who is doing that task.

Finally, depending on the task network and the relations of tools to one another, it may make sense to order the use of tools to mesh with the task sequence or to handle possible competing needs for the tool. An example of the former would be using a computer database to find out about consequences of past policies before taking a vote about policies. An example of the latter would be setting priorities that establish the primary use of a tool, with secondary uses allowed only when the tool is not needed for the primary task it is matched with. Of course, this issue can also be resolved by tying primary and secondary claims on a tool to privileged *users* rather than privileged *uses*.

Mantovani (1996) discussed the relation of tools to one another, as well as to tasks and users, for task performance at three levels. Level 1, called the *construction of context*, involves the interplay of structure and action to generate the group's history. Level 2, called *interpretation of situations*, involves the interplay of opportunities and intentions to generate goals. Level 3, called *local interaction with environment*, involves users interacting with tools to accomplish tasks. The concepts in this formulation and in ours are quite intertwined, as are the concepts of action regulation models. They share an emphasis on multiple system levels, system history, goals and intentions as the underpinnings of projects and tasks, and a tool-task-member construal of the basic elements of groups. They also share an emphasis on dynamics.

Who Does What How: Local Dynamics in the Labor and Role Networks

The two component networks that connect members to tasks and members to tools and resources are often closely intertwined, so we discuss the elaboration of both together. Local dynamics in the member network, which includes links that may have little to do with group projects, is discussed in a separate section. In practice, of course, the member network both is influenced by and has influence on the other networks of ties involving members. The assignment of resources to members, for example, is often guided simultaneously by task considerations, by status considerations, and by relationships among members. The extent to which elaboration and change in the member network follow or drive the formation and adjustment of links in the labor and role networks should depend in part on whether the members of the newly formed group are strangers or have preexisting social ties. In this section, we focus primarily on new groups of strangers. In the social network section, we discuss new groups in which some or all members already know one another.

In a group, members are both "clients" and "resources." On the one hand, for a group to be effective in the long run, it must accomplish group projects by drawing on member resources. During formation, each member is matched with some of the tasks the group has identified and will expect to complete those tasks with some of the tools available either to the member individually or to the group as a whole. Members of a newly formed baseball team, for example, will expect to use some of their own personal equipment (shoes, gloves) as well as some equipment that belongs to the team (bases, balls) to play the game.

On the other hand, as it carries out its project-directed activities, the group must fulfill members' needs at least to a minimum level or else be able to quickly replace members who leave. We presume that individual members are reasonably well informed about their own skills and resources. We also presume that members have expectations (both implicit and explicit) about what they will receive as benefits from the group and what they are willing to contribute in exchange for these benefits. The members of the newly formed baseball team, for example, are likely to have preconceptions about what position they want to play and how much playing time they will have.

The extent to which members are well informed about the resources, desires, and cost-benefit calculations of other members, however, varies both across groups and within groups. In a group formed of complete strangers, members will not generally have advance knowledge about one another or preexisting social ties. This is typically the case in experimental groups formed in the laboratory. Circumstantial groups and clubs may also be formed among strangers who either find themselves in a new situation together or seek one another on the basis of common interests. Self-organized groups that form out of a new class of students entering college or graduate school, for example, may consist of people who are aware of their common status but know little else about one another. Members of a large organization may find themselves together for the first time on a task force that draws together people from different departments or plants. Juries, another kind of task force, are typically composed of strangers.

In crews, the clearly defined jobs and the advance training of members make the assignment of members to jobs obvious, and any elaboration of the job and role networks should simply follow the pattern already established on the basis of each member's position in the group. In groups where initial assignments of members to tasks and tools are less clearly related to defined roles, elaboration depends on how members assess the collective array of group-relevant attributes and group-relevant member needs, communicate their own preferences, and negotiate the specifics of who will do what using which resources. Alteration of ties should be driven by the information generated by interaction, which allows members to update their assessment of others' attributes and needs. Actual group work may also change members' preferences for different tasks and tools because they become bored doing the same thing or discover that what they thought would be satisfying is not so rewarding after all.

Whether the process of elaboration and modification is guided by an assigned or emergent leader, constrained by outsiders who supervise or direct the group, or negotiated among all members, the assessments that members make about one another can be problematic. In the following pages, we discuss how strangers in newly formed groups assess one another's attributes and needs and how these assessments shape the developing role and labor networks.

For a specific project or set of tasks, the member attributes—skills, attitudes, knowledge, and personality traits—that are relevant to task performance may be obvious to a group, or the group may find out what is needed by setting to work and discovering by trial and error what does and does not work. A newly formed group may survey its members' attributes before elaborating the tasks and a plan for a project that connects those tasks. Alternately, group members may elaborate the task network required for a particular project in some detail and then assess the capabilities of the membership to complete these tasks. An established job network may require that people performing particular sets of tasks have particular clusters of attributes—a combination of technical knowledge and social skills, for example. When the latter path is followed by concocted or founded groups, needed skills and other attributes can serve as criteria when recruiting, selecting, and training group members.

Assessing Members' Attributes

As noted above, the following attributes are often relevant to task activity, effective group process, and strong interpersonal relations:

1. Knowledge, skills, and abilities (KSAs)
2. Values, beliefs, and attitudes (VBAs)
3. Personality, cognitive, and behavioral styles (PCBs)

How the creators of a group and the members themselves assess these attributes depends on both the ease with which they can be directly observed and the degree to which group members make assumptions about the likely covariation of attributes within individuals. Implicit personality theory (Lord & Maher, 1990), past experience, and stereotypes guide people's assumptions about which attributes are likely to cluster together in a given person.

As a group of relative strangers works together, easily observable attributes, such as skill at performing specific tasks, should be evident. Alteration of existing ties in the labor and role networks and elaboration of these networks as new tasks are identified or new tools become available should be influenced by members' assessments of how well the initial matches between members, tasks, and tools are working. As long as these initial assignments are satisfactory, elaboration is likely to strengthen and mirror existing links. In this way, the mix of tasks performed by each person in the group becomes more differentiated, reinforcing differences in roles, jobs, and status between members.

The membership of work groups formed by managers within organizations may be restricted by employment laws that constrain selection practices. Members of a new work group may have been chosen on the basis of information obtained from tests, résumés, recommendations, and past performance records, and this information may guide the initial links established when the group is formed. Even in formalized and regulated evaluations, this information (e.g., a test of a certain cognitive ability, or acquisition of a formal degree or certification) may not bear directly on the likely level of specific, needed attributes, of course, and interpretation of the information may also be biased by unstated assumptions and conditions. Rarely does this information provide useful guidance about how well particular people will work with one another in a group. When a founder or outside manager determines the composition of a group, information about group members is likely to be secured in a personnel file and not directly available to other members. In some cases (such as recommendations), members may not even have access to information about themselves that guided initial task assignment.

Instead of or in addition to this formal information, members can use more implicit heuristics to evaluate one another's underlying attributes. In evaluating strangers, members may be strongly influenced by expectations based on demographics. In part because they are easy to assess, people often attend to demographic characteristics such as sex, race, and age as proxies to infer what another person might be like. This is especially likely when little direct information is available about underlying attributes such as personality or ability.

Several theories address the use of demographics or other easily assessable proxies as heuristics for inferring underlying attributes (see, Berdahl, 1996, for a review). For example, Kanter's (1977a, 1983) theory of tokenism in organizations suggests that evaluations of tokens are based on their solo status (a solo has a salient characteristic that no other group member has) rather than on their actual task-relevant characteristics. Outcomes of being a solo appear to be largely negative, including being negatively stereotyped by group members (Crocker & McGraw, 1994), being incompletely socialized into the group (Kanter, 1977a, 1983), and being denied opportunities to demonstrate one's true abilities (Berlew & Hall, 1971; Rosenthal & Rosnow, 1969).

Other theories suggest that diffuse status characteristics shape group members' evaluations of one another (e.g., Berger, Conner, & Fizek, 1974; Ridgeway & Berger, 1986). Diffuse status characteristics are salient demographic attributes that have strong status implications in the broader social embedding context. These characteristics are laden with social meaning, defining the distinct opportunities and social roles of people in the larger society. In most cultures, sex, race, age, and socioeconomic class are assumed to signal the presence of a host of KSA, VBA, and PCB attributes, plus other demographic characteristics such as organizational status. Stereotypes based on demographic cues are well elaborated and shared within cultures and tend to be relatively persistent, reflecting the persistence of the differential opportunities and roles afforded members of different demographic groups (Williams & Best, 1990).

Expectation states theory (Ridgeway & Berger, 1986) and social role theory (Eagly, 1987) suggest different ways in which group members may use demographic characteristics as proxies for underlying attributes. Expectation states theory suggests that salient demographic characteristics serve as diffuse status cues among strangers, providing a basis for the ordering of group members in a status hierarchy. Individuals with high-status characteristics are assumed to be more competent than individuals with low-status characteristics and are therefore more likely to be assigned important tasks and elevated to positions of leadership and power within the group.

Thus begins a cycle whereby high-status members are given higher status in the group and more important responsibilities, enabling them to hone their task-relevant and process skills, thereby justifying initial assumptions. Low-status members are relegated to lower-status positions within the group and assigned less significant tasks. This prevents them from gaining experience with or exhibiting competence in important task and process skills, again justifying initial assumptions. Expectation states theory suggests that group interaction over time will reinforce initial job and role assignments, clustering members, tasks, and tools on the basis of status and desirability—as long as these cues also guided the initial links established during formation. If the initial links were based on actual job competencies, however, as should be the case when concocted groups are formed using more objective data such as past training and work records, expectations based on demographic cues should have a weaker effect. However, this theory apparently presumes that groups are formed primarily by internal forces, not by actors in the embedding context.

Social role theory (Eagly, 1987) agrees with expectation states theory that salient demographic characteristics are used to infer underlying attributes among strangers in stereotypical ways. In the early life of a group, members may expect one another to behave in stereotypical ways according to their salient demographic attributes. Over time, however, as members get to know one another, social role theory holds that the use of stereotypes wanes to the degree that they are inaccurate. More accurate, experience-based assessments of members' attributes should guide the adjustment of task and tool assignments over time. Unlike expectation states theory, social role theory suggests that the use of salient demographic characteristics to infer underlying attributes will have initial but short-term effects for the group and its members. Adjustments in the labor and role networks should establish new patterns as members absorb and apply more accurate information about who is best matched with what sorts of tasks and tools.

Berdahl (1998) proposed that theories in this domain differ in four fundamental ways. The first distinction is whether a theory presumes that demographic attributes are or are not actually correlated with underlying task-relevant attributes. Although the theories described above presume that demographic proxies are uncorrelated with task-relevant skills, abilities, and values, the alternative assumption of a strong correlation is possible and in some cases widely held. The second distinction is whether (according to the theory) group members believe that particular demographic proxies are correlated with particular underlying attributes. The third distinction is whether the theory presumes that underlying attributes are relatively stable or mutable. For example, expectations states theory implies that performance attributes are highly mutable; social role theory implies that they are not. The fourth distinction is whether (according to the theory) group members see underlying attributes as relatively stable or mutable. These four distinctions define a four-dimensional theoretical space of possibilities for how the relationship between demographic cues and underlying attributes plays out within a group (see Berdahl, 1998, for a fuller treatment).

Assessing Members' Needs

Along with attempting to carry out group projects, members also attempt to fulfill their own needs for affiliation, achievement, power, and resources. Members' needs and goals should determine which tasks and tools they find most attractive. When member preferences cannot all be accommodated, this can cause conflict in elaborating the coordination network. If current group members are very achievement oriented, the elaboration of member-task links may be a sensitive issue as members compete for the most satisfying tasks. If needs for affiliation are high, then member preferences for different tasks may be based on who they will work with most closely. If group members are power oriented, then tasks and tools perceived as carrying higher prestige may be a focus of conflict. If the need for resources is a primary attraction for members, then how valued resources are allocated should be highly important. Because of the tendency for people to project their own needs and desires on others, members of newly formed groups who do not know each other very well are liable to assume that others have priorities and behavioral tendencies similar to their own, a version of the "false consensus" effect (Hansen & Donoghue, 1977; Orbell & Dawes, 1981).

As members get to know each other better, they may discover the ways in which their needs differ and may create new links based on this understanding. Where member needs are in real conflict, decisions about who gets to complete coveted tasks or has priority use of resources are likely to be based on a combination of criteria—the appropriateness of a match based on task-relevant skills and demands, the status of competing members, and the political skills of contending members in forming alliances. The degree to which a group is willing to make sacrifices to meet a given member's needs should depend on the group's commitment to that member. Group commitment is determined by the expected value of a member's contributions to the group's projects (Moreland & Levine, 1982).

If members do not directly communicate their needs and preferences, other members may rely on easily assessable attributes, such as demographic characteristics, to infer their needs. The four-dimensional theoretical space used for member attributes can be applied to the assessment of member needs as well. The first two dimensions are the actual correlation between demographic attributes and member needs and the correlation that members perceive. One may assume that member needs for material resources are in reality unrelated to gender, for example, but that the stereotype of men as primary breadwinners may lead group members to presume that women have less need for economic rewards.

The other two dimensions are the actual mutability and the perceived mutability of member needs. To extend the example for the proxy variable of gender, one might theorize that needs for affiliation, achievement, and power are in actuality relatively fixed and that members will also perceive them as fixed. Drawing on well-documented stereotypes, this theory might suggest that whereas men and women in a particular group may not really differ systematically in needs, work group members are likely to assume that women are high in need for affiliation and low in need for achievement and power and that men are low in need for affiliation and high in need for achievement and power. These assumptions might lead group members to delegate low-status interpersonal tasks and supportive process tasks to women and high-status project tasks and leadership process tasks to men. Of course, this presumes that group members will not speak up to correct false assumptions based on stereotypes or that stereotypes will override expressed preferences in guiding the elaboration of task and resource assignments.

The actual and perceived mutability of member attributes and needs should set limits on how much a group will modify its initial coordination network. When mutability is low, we would expect adjustments designed to improve the fit of member skills and preferences to the network to tail off after the fit has been improved. If mutability is high, however, members may continue to make changes as their skills and preferences change and as their expectations for what they want from the group change and evolve.

Combining Group Member Contributions

Past group research has devoted considerable attention to how the task contributions of individual members are combined into a group product. Steiner (1972) distinguished among different ways that member task contributions could be combined into a single score for a specific group product for *unitary* tasks. Unitary tasks are group projects for which *every member is doing the same task.* Steiner's distinctions among additive, disjunctive, or conjunctive tasks refer to how these parallel individual contributions are combined into a quantity or task product quality score.

Both Davis (1973, 1982) and Laughlin and Ellis (1986) have used some features of Steiner's analysis of tasks to examine social decision schemes for different types of projects. A social decision scheme is the apparent decision rule used by the group (e.g., majority rule) to choose a single alternative from distributed member preferences. Laughlin and Ellis (1986) emphasized the study of what they called intellective tasks—tasks for which there is a demonstrably correct answer. Davis (1982) emphasized the study of judgment tasks, which require groups to reach consensus in the absence of a demonstrably correct answer. Much of Davis' work has dealt with jury verdicts.

That body of research indicates that task type affects the combination rule, or decision scheme, used by a group. Davis found that juries seem to follow a "strong majority" decision scheme—contrary to their instructions that they must attain a unanimous verdict. Laughlin and Ellis found that on tasks for which there is a correct answer, groups seem to use a "truth wins" or "truth supported wins" decision scheme, depending on how demonstrable that correct answer is within the operating conditions of the group. When members all perform the same task, such as forming an opinion about a problem, but come to different conclusions, we see the emergence of complexity from an initially simple repetition of links. The selection of one of these opinions as the "group" solution further distinguishes among members, marking some as superior to the others. Just as elaboration orders tasks by temporal priority and tools by priority of use, the combination of member contributions into group products orders the links between members and the tasks they complete as more or less valuable to the group.

McGrath (1984) developed a classification schema for group tasks that incorporates the key ideas in these and other treatments of group task differences and extends them to cover a broader range of tasks, including negotiation tasks, brainstorming, and tasks involving physical activity. But that schema, along with all of the others noted above, deals with unitary tasks rather than divisible tasks, in which members do different tasks as part of a larger project. We believe that extant groups engage mainly in projects that include tasks of many or even all of the varieties of tasks discussed by Steiner, Laughlin, Davis, McGrath, and other group researchers.

Elaboration of the Member Network

The relations among members that form a group's social network are typically (although not invariably) more complex than the connections among tasks and tools. Even in groups formed according to a well-specified "prefabricated" coordination network, the interpersonal ties that link members are likely to undergo some elaboration and modification as the group does its work. The maintenance of interpersonal ties can also be critically important to effective task performance, especially in long-term groups such as teams and clubs.

Task and tool relations are logical and functional in relation to performance of group projects. Relationships that develop between members may be important to the members over and above their functional or instrumental value for completing group projects. By fulfilling some of the members' needs, these links are part of the rewards members receive from their membership and activity in the group. They may also be the foundation for, or be based on, interpersonal relations outside the group. As the links in the job, role, and labor networks connect people, the emergent links of friendship and rivalry enrich and deepen the complexity of the coordination network.

When members of a newly formed group are strangers, the elaboration of the member network should be shaped by proximity, perceived similarity, complementarity of needs and preferences, and the unmet needs of members for social contact. Members who work together on closely linked tasks, or who must coordinate their use of a common tool, are more likely to develop additional social ties. Members who perceive one another as similar in attitudes, skills, and behavior are also more likely to be attracted to one another socially. Among relative strangers, of course, demographic cues are frequently used to infer whether a person is more or less similar to oneself. Similarity in member needs—such as high need for affiliation—can be a basis for interpersonal attraction, as can complementarity of needs. Members who both want the same task assignments or who have similarly high needs for power may find themselves in conflict, a different type of member-member tie. When one member seeks expert power and another wants guidance and advice, however, the needs are complementary. The member network includes both positive and negative ties.

Zeggelink (1995) proposed that individuals will seek out new relationships until they reach a limit that satisfies their need for social contact, that the desire for relationships must be mutual for a friendship to form, and that members whose needs are already satisfied will not reciprocate the overtures of others. The local dynamics of the friendship network involves extending friendship overtures; accepting, rejecting, or ignoring these overtures; establishing new ties that elaborate the network; maintaining these ties through interaction; and withdrawing ties or transforming them from positive to negative, which occurs when friendly members have a falling out.

In many newly formed groups, social links are imported because members already know one another. If all members of a new work group already belong to the same embedding system, for example, they are likely to have either direct or indirect knowledge about every other group member. Their impressions about what these other people are like and what they might contribute to the group (along with their own preferences) should guide the division of tasks and tools among members, shaping the distinct role of each person in a newly formed team or task force. Demographic cues should play a less important role when members have more detailed individual knowledge about each member's actual attributes and needs. Evidence from Gruenfeld, Mannix, Williams, and Neale (1996) suggests that groups in which at least some of the members already know each other are better at pooling distributed information than are groups of total strangers.

New groups may be composed of people who all know each other about equally well or who have varying degrees of familiarity. Crew members drawn from relatively small pools within an organization are also likely to have worked together before with at least some of the other members of a current group, although perhaps not in the precise configuration of the current crew. In groups in which some people know each other and some are strangers, the elaboration and maintenance of the member network are likely to reinforce existing ties. Subgroups of members who know each other may form informal political coalitions that guide the elaboration of the labor and role networks. Members who are distinguished by being relative strangers may find themselves with lower status and less desirable assignments than members who can draw on preexisting social ties, even if these "strangers" have better skills or experience that would warrant higher status on a purely project-oriented basis.

Members who know and like one another maintain those ties through numerous actions that reaffirm the friendship, and many of these actions have little immediate relevance for completing group projects. Sharing a cup of coffee, discussing sports or soap operas or family matters, and contact outside of the group context all serve to maintain social ties. Established ties can facilitate the elaboration of new ties in mixed groups in which some people are already acquainted and some are not. Group members who already see each other outside the group context may draw other members into this broader network of ties, extending the social network within the group as well.

Social networks that develop in this way are likely to mirror job and role networks less closely than we would expect in groups formed of strangers. Thus, we would expect the set of networks involving members—role, labor, and member—to be more highly complex when some social ties are imported, as compared to groups that start out with no preexisting interpersonal ties. The downside of complexity in the member network is that the more intense, intimate, and extensive the social ties between members, the greater the potential impact of interpersonal conflicts in any part of the social network. Less close ties and less densely connected networks should be more robust against the wear and tear of interpersonal friction.

∞ THE INTERSECTION OF LOCAL AND GLOBAL DYNAMICS

This chapter has explored the local dynamics within groups as members attempt to complete projects while meeting both group and member needs. The next chapter explores how global variables that emerge from these local dynamics evolve over time and how they shape and constrain subsequent local dynamics. Patterns of coordinated activity are not necessarily the same from one cycle of task execution to another. At the group level, patterns of activity change over time as a function of experience and in response to adjustments in the interchanges between group and embedding systems and between groups and their members. Those learning and adaptation processes are crucial foci of Chapter 6 on development and Chapter 7 on adaptation.

The outcomes of learning and adaptation are in turn embedded in the expectations and agreements about who will do what, and how, that drive the local dynamics of coordination. Learning and adaptation can result in changes in members' attributes, changes in the task network, and changes in the technology (Argote & McGrath, 1993). These, too, are important foci of Chapters 6 and 7.

∾ 6 ∾

Global Dynamics

Stability and Change Within the Group System

The previous chapter addressed how members, tasks, and tools are combined and coordinated to carry out group projects and fulfill member needs. As group members work together, patterns of interaction emerge and change over time, and the overall group structure is adjusted as tasks are completed, tools are adjusted, and members adapt to one another and to the physical, sociocultural, and organizational contexts in which the group is embedded. Group-level structures and patterns guide and constrain a group's subsequent operations at the local level. Out of this recursive relation, a group's developmental history evolves.

A core aim in the study of dynamic systems is the search for regularities in the evolution of the system over time. *Global variables* reflect the state of the group as a whole. *Global dynamics* refers to patterns of stability and change in the state of the group and corresponds to what the group literature calls *group development*. In this chapter, we present a complex systems view of group development and discuss how global dynamics may differ systematically across different aspects of groups as systems, for groups operating in different conditions, and for different types of groups.

Relations among global variables, such as the quality of group performance, group cohesiveness, overall level of conflict, and confor-

mity, have been the focus of much research on small groups. Research
in the experimental tradition typically examines differences in global
variables between groups operating in different conditions and measures these variables at one (sometimes two, occasionally multiple)
points during the group history, which is typically quite short (less than
a day, often less than an hour). Group development studies, in contrast,
examine patterns of continuity and change in groups over time. This research generally (a) views development as a progression through qualitatively different phases or stages (e.g., Bales & Strodtbeck, 1951;
Tuckman & Jensen, 1977; Worchel, 1994; for some exceptions, see
Gersick & Hackman, 1990; McCollom, 1995b; McGrath, 1991), (b) studies groups with a longer lifetime (lasting weeks or months), (c) measures variables repeatedly, and (d) seeks to identify and characterize
stages by examining changes in the values of these variables.

Few empirical data are available on the dynamics that generate continuity within stages or states and trigger transitions to different states,
although many authors have speculated on this issue. Worchel (1996),
for example, suggested that both success and failure on the task can
move a group into the next stage (p. 271). Another global variable that
changes across the six stages of his cyclical model appears to be shifts
in the relative importance to members of individual needs versus group
needs. In Gersick's (1988, 1989) punctuated equilibrium model, group
members' changing assessment of the relationship between amount of
work to be done and time remaining to do it triggers a shift from one
state to another. Carley (1991) suggested that stability is maintained by
the reinforcing nature of interaction on shared member knowledge and
in turn on interaction. Berg and Smith (1995) suggested that the struggle of group members with inherent paradoxes in group life is responsible for both movement and continuity (which they call "stuckness").

No general agreement has emerged on which global variables are
most important to track in assessing patterns of change, and a wide variety of global variables can be (and have been) used to characterize the
ongoing state of the group as a system. We do not believe there is one canonical set of key variables. Instead, the selection of global variables to
investigate should depend on the investigator's purposes. However, we
surmise that a thorough understanding of group dynamics will entail
studies of global variables that index at least six general aspects of small
group behavior. In the first section of this chapter, we identify some
characteristics of promising global variables to study and provide ex-

amples of global variables for these six aspects of groups that have been of enduring interest to scholars.

Although there are almost as many theories of group development as there are studies thereof (for reviews, see Arrow, 1997; McCollom, 1995b; Mennecke, Hoffer, & Wynne, 1992; Wanous, Reichers, & Malik, 1984), theorists frequently presume a single prototypical pattern of development for all small groups. Some have suggested that the pattern may differ somewhat for different types of groups, but the suggested differences usually involve variations on a single model—skipping a stage, for example (Tuckman, 1965), or starting at a different point in a cyclical model (Worchel, 1994), rather than different models for different groups. Exceptions to this rule include contingency models (McCollom, 1995b; McGrath, 1991; Poole, 1983) that suggest idiosyncratic patterns of development across groups. Most scholars have overlooked the possibility that different patterns of development might apply to different aspects (global variables) of the group (for exceptions, see Cissna, 1984, and the contingency models just cited). In the second section of this chapter, we propose that all developmental models can be classified as variants of a limited number of characteristic dynamic patterns. We presume that these patterns may differ within the same group for different variables and across groups for the same global variable.

The dynamic systems approach to identifying these patterns is to analyze the evolution of global variables toward "attractors" of various kinds. An attractor is a single state or a restricted set of states that a system (as indexed by particular global variables) settles into over time. The regularity in dynamic patterns, according to this approach, is not to be found in the exact path a system takes in evolving toward this attractor or in the exact values (or set of values) to which a system is attracted over time but in the qualitative *type* of attractor toward which the system evolves. Two different groups, for example, may both achieve and maintain a stable level of production, whereas a third group cycles consistently from high to low production levels. The first two groups would be viewed as showing the same dynamic pattern, even if their levels of production were quite discrepant. The third group shows a different dynamic pattern.

After tackling the twin tasks of distinguishing among global variables and distinguishing among dynamic patterns, we consider how specific variables and patterns might match up and how that might vary for different types of groups. As part of this discussion, we suggest some substantive implications of different developmental patterns. The chapter concludes with a section on the circular relation between the evolution of global variables and local dynamics.

In his review of the group development literature, Cissna (1984) stated the core problem for theorists: "Every group is like *all* groups in some respects, like *some*—or even *most* groups in some respects, and like *no* groups in other respects" (p. 25). In this chapter, we discuss in greater detail how we believe the attractor-mapping approach to studying dynamics could be applied to improve our ability to perceive the first two types of regularities in group development without getting distracted by the unique idiosyncrasies of particular groups.

∞ IDENTIFYING GLOBAL VARIABLES

Identifying appropriate global variables to study is a top-down, investigator-driven activity. What aspects of the system are studied depends on the theory, or perspective, by which the group is viewed. One critical function of a theory, of course, is to guide the choice of substantive issues to be examined. The metaphors for studying groups presented in Chapter 2 and the propositions presented in Chapter 3 provide a framework for identifying six classes of global variables that reflect important aspects of groups as systems. Three refer to the group's three main functions:

1. Fulfilling member needs
2. Completing group projects
3. Maintaining the structure and integrity of the group as a system

The other three refer to three main types of group activities:

4. Processing information and generating meaning
5. Managing conflict and developing consensus
6. Motivating, regulating, and coordinating member behavior

Table 6.1 lists some exemplar global variables within each of these six categories. This is by no means an exhaustive list. Instead, it is a sampling of global variables that have been studied in the group devel-

Table 6.1 Six Classes of Potentially Useful Global Variables

A. Global Variables Reflecting Activity at the Group-Member Interchange
   Levels of group-to-member commitment and member-to-group
      commitment
   Degree of disparity between those two indices
   Relative emphasis that members place on group goals versus
      individual goals

B. Global Variables Reflecting the Group's Project Activity
   Quantity or rate of production of group product
   Quality of group products
   Use of time swapping versus time sharing as multitasking strategies

C. Global Variables Reflecting the Group's Structure and Functioning as an
   Ongoing System
   Vertical differentiation of a particular component network
   Horizontal differentiation of a particular component network
   Patterns of participation, affect, and influence in group interaction

D. Global Variables Reflecting the Group's Information-Processing
   Activities
   Proportion of uniquely held and commonly held information that is
      discussed
   Proportion of communication that is task relevant versus
      socioemotional
   Tacit coordination based on members' knowledge of who knows what

E. Global Variables Reflecting the Group's Conflict- and Consensus-
   Managing Activities
   Amount of content (task), administrative (process), and interpersonal
      conflict
   Group's de facto decision rules and degree of consensus
   Temporal features of conflict, such as speed of escalation and de-
      escalation

F. Global Variables Reflecting the Group's Regulation and Coordination of
   Member Behavior
   Discrepancies between member behavior and shared normative
      expectations
   Discontinuities, errors, wasted motion in synchronized member
      actions
   Tightness or looseness of the coordination between members' activity

opment literature or that our theory points to as promising indices of important aspects of the group as a system.

Three important principles drawn from complexity theory and from the group development literature can serve as useful guides in choosing global variables to study. First, although scholars of group development disagree about the number of stages or phases and the content of these different group states, they generally agree that the nature of group interaction is distinctly different when the group is in different states and that the transition between states can be abrupt. This fits the dynamical systems notion of a phase transition (Baron et al., 1994). Global variables that characterize those aspects of the group that alter during a phase transition should thus be good candidates for the study of group development.

Second, good candidates for global variables that underlie phase transitions, according to complexity theory, are quantitative measures that index the pattern of coordination among interacting elements that changes during those transitions (Baron et al., 1994; Kelso, 1995). This type of global variable is often called an order parameter. The degree of vertical differentiation in the status system, for example, can be conceptualized as a continuous variable that underlies distinctly different types of status systems, from autocratic to egalitarian. A range of values from no vertical differentiation (all members precisely equal in status) to some modest level of difference may correspond to the same qualitative state of egalitarian relations, as experienced and enacted by members. Within that range, differences in the global variable appear not to matter. Beyond that range, however, the group undergoes a phase transition into a more hierarchical group, with members clearly differentiating between high- and low-status individuals.

Third, a global variable should be an aspect of the system that genuinely reflects the interdependent relations of elements within the group system. Not all aggregated measures of individual-level properties should be considered global variables. Two types of aggregates constructed from member judgments can provide useful measures of global variables. One is the mean judgment of members about an aspect of the group when member judgments show high interrater reliability, indicating that the construct does have meaning at the group level. Another is the *distribution* of member perceptions and interpretations of the group experience itself, which O'Connor (1998) called *experiential diversity,* and which also can be tracked over time as an indicator of changing levels of affective and cognitive coordination among members.

Some group-level variables of great interest to researchers, such as the quality of group products, do not directly index the coordination among interacting parts but are instead an outcome or result of coordinated activity. Tracking these variables, which may or may not reveal phase transitions, can nevertheless point up dynamic patterns, whose source can then be sought in the coordinated action that resulted in these products.

Activity at the Group-Member Interchange

Key indicators of the state of the group-member interchange are the absolute and relative levels of commitment that group and individual members have to one another. The fulfillment of member needs is largely determined by the outcome of negotiations at this interchange. Moreland and Levine's (1982) group socialization model describes the movement of members into, through, and out of groups as commitment levels change. Transitions between different member states (prospective member, new member, full member, marginal member, ex-member) are driven by the mutual processes of group evaluation of the member and member evaluation of the group. The group assesses the "rewardingness" of having a particular member by evaluating that member's contributions to the fulfillment of group needs. Simultaneously, the member assesses the "rewardingness" of group membership by evaluating the group's contributions to the fulfillment of that member's needs. The outcomes of these evaluations are the group's commitment to the member and the member's commitment to the group.

Member commitment to the group and group commitment to the member together describe the state of the group-member relation (Baron et al., 1994; Moreland & Levine, 1982). Transitions in membership status—for example, from prospective member to new member, or from new member to full member—occur when group and member commitment to one another both pass their respective thresholds for that membership phase transition (see Moreland & Levine, 1982).

The two commitment levels may not "match." Disparity between the group's commitment level to a particular member and that member's commitment to the group can serve as a global variable indexing the relative "power" of the two parties in negotiating contributions and rewards. Relative power characterizes the degree to which a group will support a particular member (i.e., contribute to fulfilling his or her needs) and the degree to which the group can call on that member for additional inputs (of time, effort, and other resources).

Group Project Activity at
the Group-Context Interchange

Most indicators that have been used to describe group project activity involve some combination of three interdependent attributes of the outcomes of this activity: quantity, rate, and quality. Sometimes a group's products, services, or results are assessed in terms of the *quantity* generated within a given period of time. Both total quantity (e.g., a hockey team's shots on goal) and quantity of outputs that meet some minimal level of quality (e.g., successful shots on goal) may be measured. Sometimes outcomes are assessed in terms of the *rate* (averaged across some period of time) at which the group produces or completes units of some kind, whether that means number of products completed in a month, number of people served in a day, miles covered in an hour, new skills learned in a week of training, or lines of code written in a day. Quantity and average rate can be translated into one another. Measures of *quality* may assess the average quality of an outcome (e.g., average quality of ideas produced) or of the best outcome (e.g., best idea) produced within a given period.

The fit among the elements and component networks of a group's coordination network and the smoothness with which the group uses the network to tackle its project(s) should affect both the quantity and quality of the group's output. The quantity of group production is shaped by the group's efficiency in performing its tasks, which is influenced by the fit of the task, job, and labor networks; by the type and difficulty of the task; and by features of the embedding context that may stifle or stimulate production. For work groups, two important contextual parameters are the level of demand for the product and externally imposed deadlines (e.g., Ancona & Chong, 1996; McGrath & Kelly, 1986, 1991; Moore-Ede, Sulzman, & Fuller, 1982). The time pressure that deadlines create should vary depending on the length of time remaining and the negative costs of failing to meet those deadlines.

The quality of group products is determined by the type of project the group is working on and by the group's effectiveness in performing its tasks. Although *quality* is often used as a generic term for how "good" a product is, the quality of any given product must be reckoned in terms of criteria particular to that project. The nature of quality assessments varies widely across kinds of outcome, depending on whether the group produces artistic performances, solves the problems of members or clients, competes in sports events, makes decisions, moves furniture, manages themselves or other people, builds things, strengthens a community, climbs mountains, or does any other of the myriad projects that groups can perform. Quality for a mountain-climbing team might involve not only how personally rewarding a particular climb is but also success in avoiding injury and accidents. Quality for a group of mathematicians might mean generating a proof with as unrestrictive a set of assumptions as possible.

Quantity and quality are often considered to be competing requisites. But the evidence for negative correlation is mixed. It is clear that a group can deliberately choose to sacrifice either of these criteria in the hope of enhancing the other (Karau & Kelly, 1992; Kelly, Jackson, & Hutson-Comeaux, 1997). What is less clear are the conditions under which groups need to compromise between the two and the conditions under which groups can realistically improve either quantity or quality without sacrificing the other.

For groups that handle multiple projects, the relative use of time swapping (working on one task, then another) versus time sharing (working on multiple projects simultaneously) is a global variable that indexes task coordination directly. Waller (1997) proposed that this proportion should vary depending on member familiarity and feedback from working on tasks, both of which accumulate over time.

Standing and Acting Structures: The Integrity of the Group System

This category includes two types of variables. One set of variables describes the standing structures of the group that emerge from the operation of its local dynamics—the patterns of roles, jobs, and division of labor, for example, that group members establish and then enact over time. The other set of variables indexes the more ephemeral "acting" structures that emerge during interaction as some of the links in the standing structure are activated during group activities. This includes, for example, the distribution of participation and the smoothness of flow of that communication (with respect to interruptions, gaps, repetitions, and redundancies). In groups that persist over time, members appear to develop cognitive maps of standing group structures and are apt to overlook or discount aspects of acting group structures that do not match these maps (F. Bernieri, personal communication, July 1998). Thus, members will continue to think of a high-status group member as high in influence whether or not that member exerts much influence during a particular meeting of the group. Similarly, a group with elaborate, highly developed task structures but sparse interpersonal links may nevertheless, during particular acting group meetings, activate the interpersonal links and not attend to other group tasks.

In our discussion of global variables in this section, we will concentrate on the structure of links and interaction patterns. The content (as opposed to the structure) of group interaction is discussed not in this section but later in the chapter, under the three process categories.

Structural Features of the Standing Group

All of the component networks of the group structure have some degree of horizontal and vertical differentiation, can be characterized as relatively dense or sparse in number of links, and may show patterns of clustering such as a center-periphery or polarized distribution.

Among the three component networks that link elements of the same type, the member network typically includes the greatest number of different relations. Member-member relations can be considered in terms of friendship links, patterns of advice seeking and giving, sharing of information, agreements and disagreements on issues important to the group, and many other dimensions. The structure of one member-member relation will not necessarily match the structures of other member-member relations. The task and tool networks are typically structures of lower dimensionality.

Among the component networks that link elements of different types, the job network is most easily characterized by a single relation—which tools and procedures are used for what tasks. Horizontal differentiation in the job network is the degree to which specific tasks are uniquely matched with specific tools, whereas vertical differentiation indicates that some procedures (performance of specified tasks in a specified way) have higher priority than others.

In characterizing the role and labor networks, which involve the mapping of members to roles and tasks, global variables characterizing multiple relations may be useful. Member access to hardware, for example, may show a different level of vertical differentiation (some members have access to more tools than others) than the status hierarchy, which differentiates members according to power and influence. Both are aspects of the role network. The former may be determined largely by job assignments, whereas the status hierarchy reflects the emergent result of power struggles among members.

In the labor network of member-task links, the degree of horizontal differentiation indicates how *specialized* the group's division of labor is. Horizontal differentiation can range from every member performing a unique task or set of tasks to every member performing the same (or every) task. Horizontal differentiation in the role network involves differential access by members to different kinds of tools and resources and qualitatively different sets of prescribed and proscribed behaviors for different members. A role network consists of the interrelated patterns of behavior that are expected of, produced, and reproduced by particular members, using both hardware and software. Role expectations include the *how* of member behavior as well as the *what* of it.

With respect to the hardware and software of communication, for example, norms regulate who uses what channels of communication, in what way, and for what purposes. Members may have exclusive use of certain tools—for example, Maria may be the only one who uses the chainsaw, whereas Jenny always drives the van, and all tasks requiring integral calculus go to Shawna. Similarly, Kahlil may always play the role of optimist, whereas Sean points out risks and envisions disaster scenarios. Links specified in the role network may drive the division of labor (Maria does jobs involving cutting because she is the chainsaw woman), and member-task assignments may also determine roles (Sean is the official pessimist because balancing the group budget is his job).

Vertical differentiation in the labor network measures variance in the importance and the prestige of tasks assigned to different members. This is a *control* aspect of the group's division of labor. Many group projects include "drudge" tasks that are considered low-status activities (e.g., entering data, typing letters) and "prestige" tasks that involve more visible, high-status contributions (e.g., writing up results of a study for publication, deciding what projects the group will undertake next). Tasks also vary in how critical they are. Cooking and serving food, for example, may be critical to the work of a restaurant, whereas critiquing the performance of the cooks and wait staff is not. The latter, however, may be considered a higher-prestige task.

Tasks can be assigned so that some people do only low-importance tasks and others focus on critical tasks, or each member may complete tasks of varied importance. Drudge and prestige tasks can also be regularly assigned to different subsets of members or shared via rotation or division. When some members supervise others (i.e., monitoring, instructing, assigning work to, and/or evaluating the work of other group members), this indicates vertical differentiation in both the labor and role networks.

Vertical role differentiation reflects the leadership, influence, and status hierarchy of the group. Members at the top of the hierarchy, for example, may have access to all group resources and use all channels of communication, with few restrictions on when and how they send messages. Members at the bottom of the hierarchy, however, may make very restricted use of the communication system and have access only to tools they must use for the defined tasks they perform.

The density of member-task links may vary among members in that some members do a greater variety and volume of tasks than others. New members, for example, may initially have a light workload and gradually take on more tasks. Differences in volume may also indicate social loafing by some members or marked differences in task difficulty in the assignments of group members. The number of different roles each member plays is a measure of density in the role network, and members may differ in how varied their roles are. The global variable of role density is an important indicator of the level of coordination needed among members as well as the potential for role overload and role conflict.

Clustering in the component networks will have a different meaning depending on the network, but in general, the clustering of links indicates closer coordination among some members and tasks than others. Clustering in member-member relations may indicate friendship cliques, whereas clustering in labor networks is likely in groups using a time-sharing strategy, in which different subsets of members work simultaneously on different projects or on closely linked sets of tasks within a larger project (Waller, 1997). Clustering within the role network may indicate that subsets of members play similar roles, which is likely to occur when the group is large or when a class of members have a distinct status, as would be true for a cohort of newcomers.

High levels of differentiation across the component networks of the coordination network, with little overlap or redundancy among the links, tend to make groups both more efficient in stable situations and more "brittle"—less flexible and robust—in the face of external or internal stressors that may weaken or break some of the links in the system. Lower levels of differentiation, though perhaps associated with less efficient processes, may allow more effective handling of a wide range of projects in dynamic environments.

Group cohesiveness, a popular variable that indexes the structural integrity of the group, is often assessed by measuring interpersonal attraction—the strength of ties in the member network (see Cartwright, 1968; Henry, Arrow, & Carini, 1998; Hogg, 1987; Markovsky & Chaffee, 1995; and Mudrack, 1989, for reviews). Interpersonal attraction has been linked to the similarity or complementarity of members on relevant attributes, such as shared or complementary knowledge, skills, and abilities; agreement on important values; complementarity in personality and behavioral styles; or similarity on salient demographic attributes. Its development can also be affected by features of the group's technology, such as the interplay of (a) norms for politeness, (b) norms for degree of intimacy/impersonality, and (c) the level of intimacy/impersonality that is fostered by the intragroup communication medium.

Other scholars take a broader view of cohesiveness, distinguishing, for example, between social cohesion (interpersonal attaction) and task cohesion (member attraction to group tasks). The Group Environment Questionnaire, a measure of cohesion widely used in sports psychology (Carron, Widmeyer, & Brawley, 1985), further distinguishes between individual attraction to members and to tasks, on the one hand, and member perceptions of group integration or unity in both social and task domains, on the other. Similar variables involving the structural integrity of a group are solidarity, which has been defined structurally as high reachability (all members are connected through strong and direct bonds) and unity (structural homogeneity) within the coordination network (see Markovsky & Chaffee, 1995; Markovsky & Lawler, 1994).

Structural Features of the Acting Group

Indicators of the coordination involved in a group's recurring pattern of interaction include the pattern of participation among members
(both acts of communication and other kinds of behavior), the pattern
of affective relations among members, and the pattern of influence relations among members during given sessions of interaction. Global variables of this nature measure the structure of interaction in the acting
group. This observable structure is based on the selective and sequen-
tial activation of those links in the coordination network that are relevant to the current activities of the group. In a given session of interaction, for example, the relative participation of members may vary from
standing norms because not all members are present, because guests or
observers who do not belong to the group (including experimenters) are
present, because the task requires the special expertise of a low-status
member, because preferred tools are not working, or because of other
transient conditions, such as the group's "cheerleader" being grumpy
and uncommunicative due to a head cold.

The pattern of participation among group members has been studied
quite a bit in past group research, mainly with respect to verbal communication. One robust finding is that as group size increases, communication tends to become more centralized, with one or a very small
number of group members contributing an increasingly high proportion of communication acts while other members account for a small
and decreasing proportion (Bales, Strodtbeck, Mills, & Roseborough,
1953; see McGrath, 1984, for discussion). That disproportionality has
been associated with status relations in the group. Differences in the
degree of centralization have also been linked to task differences, technology effects, and member attributes (e.g., Borgatta & Bales, 1953;
Diehl & Stroebe, 1987; Straus, 1996).

Global variables indexing the affective relations among interacting
members include mean level of affect (the positivity or negativity of the
mood in the group), the degree of emotional variance within the group,
and the influence of the most emotionally extreme members of the
group (Barsade & Gibson, 1998).

The pattern of influence among members is related to, and both generates and results from, the status structure of the group. But the patterns will differ in some respects because a member's influence is also
affected by that member's presumed and actual expertise with respect

to the current tasks, his or her position in the group's communication network, and the normative constraints affecting how, what, and when members can and should communicate with one another. Influence of Member A on Member B also depends on the abilities, expectations, and status positions of B, as well as on those features of A already noted.

In the next three sections, more specific aspects of the patterning of group interaction are described that take into account the content of interaction.

Processing Information, Generating Meaning

In this realm, one global variable of interest is the relative contribution of information by members to the group's task performance activities; another is the degree of overlap in information held by different members; another is the proportion of information contributed to the group that is held in common among members or uniquely held by a single member. Studies of information processing in groups frequently manipulate the second of these global variable and observe the values of the first and third (e.g., Hollingshead, 1998; Larson, Foster-Fishman, & Keys, 1994; Stasser & Titus, 1985; see Hinsz et al., 1997, for a recent review of this literature). Tracking these variables under different group conditions has helped researchers determine why groups often fail to make use of the "best" information they potentially have available.

Another global variable of interest might be the proportion of the group's communications that contain information relevant to completing group tasks or contain socioemotional information about either group members or other people outside the group. The overall volumes of information processed by and generated by the group may also be worthwhile global variables to measure. Studies of transactive memory (Wegner et al., 1991) focus on the degree to which members know what information other members possess; transactive memory is believed to be important for tacit coordination (see Wittenbaum & Stasser, 1996, for a review), which is coordination by group members in the absence of any explicit discussion.

The degree to which members attribute similar meanings to information and develop shared and distinctive interpretations can be considered a measure of group culture, which is often defined as a set of thoughts that group members share (Levine & Moreland, 1991, p. 258). More detailed studies of group culture variables might distinguish among shared knowledge about the group, about group members, and about the work the group does (Levine & Moreland, 1991). The notion of overlapping interpretations can also be conceptualized as the degree of overlap between the mental models or scripts of group members.

Conflict and Consensus

Global variables reflecting group conflict include the amount and distribution over members of conflict involving (a) task content, (b) procedural issues, and (c) interpersonal friction (Jehn, 1997). Conflict may be localized, involving just a few members, or may involve the whole group. The relative amount of conflict experienced and conflict expressed among members (O'Connor, Gruenfeld, & McGrath, 1993) could serve as an index of how "hot" or "cold" the conflict is, with high levels of experienced but unexpressed conflict being the cold pole and matching levels of experienced and expressed conflict being the hot pole. Along with the level of conflict, the rate of escalation and de-escalation of conflict is an important dynamic feature of conflict.

Regarding group consensus, useful global variables might include the level of consensus achieved on the group's task products and the degree of consensus on the group's operating procedures and reward structure. Also useful would be indices reflecting the group's implicit or explicit decision scheme, which specifies the amount of agreement necessary for a group decision to be reached. This varies from no agreement needed (leader decides, with or without consultation) to plurality to majority (simple or strong) to unanimity.

Behavioral Regulation

Some global variables reflecting behavioral coordination have already been mentioned in the "Structural Features of the Activity Group" section, including the distribution of participation among members. Other indices of the group's activity in this domain might include indices reflecting the amount and distribution of group activity with respect to task, process, and interpersonal matters; indices of the extent to which member behavior matches group norms with regard to task, process, and interpersonal activity; and indices reflecting errors in group-coordinated performances. In the case of groups doing projects that involve a physical performance as product (e.g., an orchestra, a sports team), such errors would reflect incorrect actions or wasted movements. In the case of groups doing projects dealing primarily with cognitive products, such errors would be incorrect choices or the application of incorrect or ineffective procedures.

The tightness or looseness of coordination among members, from the split-second timing of athletes in team sports to highly independent activity among members who simply pool the results of their efforts by a common deadline, is another global variable that measures behavioral regulation. As suggested by the examples, this often reflects the particulars of the group projects.

Connections Among Global Variables

Along with variables that fit into the six general categories presented above, global variables may also measure the distribution of group activity and attention across these domains. This is an important issue because stage theories of group development often propose that the focus of group activity shifts from one stage to another and because time spent on different activities is ipsitive.

A strong focus on activities aimed at fulfilling member needs, for example, may affect the quality and quantity of group project results, not only because time and energy devoted to satisfying member needs are not being directed toward completing projects, but also because activities aimed at member need fulfillment may either conflict with or facilitate the execution of group projects. Attending to the socioemotional needs of a member who has outstanding skills applicable to group projects, for example, may greatly increase that member's task performance motivation and effort. When a professional sports team extends and enriches the contract of its star player in midseason, adding "bonus" clauses for attainment of particular performance goals, it may reap a large increment in effort, hence in performance quantity and quality, from that player. At the same time, such enhanced arrangements with one player may enhance or detract from the motivation of other players. The overall point here is that *all of the activities of the group as a system,* not just those directly connected to group project activity, may have consequences for the quantity and quality of project results and for the development of other global variables that measure other aspects of the group system.

The next section uses the concept of "attractors" to distinguish among different characteristic patterns of continuity and change in the group as measured by one or more global variables.

∞ MAPPING THE EVOLUTION OF GLOBAL VARIABLES

In the preceding discussion, we identified six theory-based categories of potentially useful global variables and discussed some exemplar global variables within each. Repeated measurements of global variables over the life of a group can be used to trace the pattern of group development. A high volume of observations, evenly spaced in time, acquired using reliable measurement systems and meaningful metrics for each variable, are ideal for constructing a fine-grained picture of global dynamics. (These methodological requirements are discussed in more detail in Chapter 9.)

In complexity theory, patterns over time are examined to detect the movement of the system (measured by one or more global variables) toward one or more attractors. Attractors are system states that can be conceptualized as locations or regions in *phase space* (the space defined by possible values of global variables) toward which the system tends to evolve under a given set of contextual conditions.

To track the evolution of the system and discover the attractors that shape the dynamics, global variables can be plotted in time series or in phase portraits. A time series plots the value, X, of a single global variable on one axis and increments of time on the other. Thus, each point shows a value of X, and the overall plot shows the pattern of X over time. A phase portrait plots the state of the system in two or more dimensions, with each point representing the state of the system at a particular time. Time is not, however, one of the dimensions (axes) of the plot. Rather, time points are connected in sequence by a line. That line shows the "path" of the system over time. This is like plotting the path of a hiker by showing a time series of altitude over time—which shows position on one dimension only—as compared to drawing the path of the hiker as a series of points on a two-dimensional topological map or on a three-dimensional model of the landscape.

In the physical systems whose dynamics are commonly modeled using this approach—a rocket taking off, for example, or the movement of a pendulum—the axes in this space might represent position and velocity. In a study of small groups, however, the relevant variables are more likely to be factors selected on the basis of theory or determined by factor-analyzing a host of measurements made on the system of interest. Dunphy (1968), for example, in an early study of change in the social structure and culture of groups, found a two-factor solution (strength/weakness and anomie/normative structure) that reduced a huge number of categories into which he had classified member comments into two orthogonal dimensions. He then showed change over time for the two different groups studied by plotting the position of each group at the six time points measured and connecting the dots (labeled 1 to 6) with directional arrows for each group. (This was, essentially, a phase plot).

Phase portraits facilitate the qualitative comparison of patterns between different individual systems. Multiple phase portraits can also be used to compare the dynamics of global variables that measure different subsystems—for example, information processing versus cohesiveness and commitment—for the same group. We presume that patterns of change over time may differ for different global variables for the same group and for different groups on the same global variables. The construction of multiple phase portraits is one strategy for exploring this possibility.

Next, we describe some qualitatively different patterns in the evolution of global variables and connect these patterns to theory and research on group development. These patterns correspond to different types and configurations of attractors.

Robust Equilibrium:
The Dynamics of a Stable Point Attractor

The simplest developmental path, and the one most often assumed in social psychological theories, is for a system to move quickly toward a stable state and then maintain itself in this state. We call this pattern

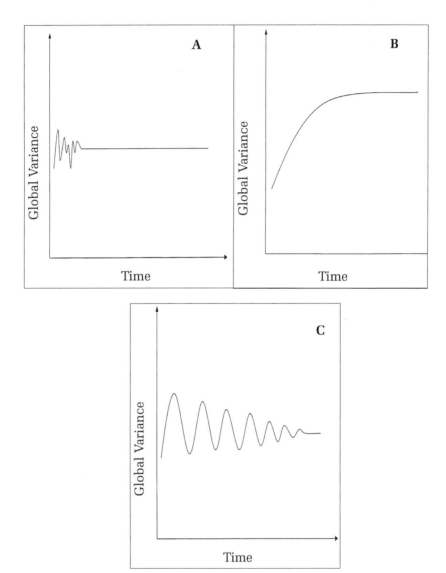

Figure 6.1. Three exemplar time-series plots for robust equilibrium (a point attractor), showing patterns of changes in production volume levels over a group's development. **A:** relatively short initial period of change, followed by settling down to a steady state. **B:** steady movement from a starting value to a different, persistent end value. **C:** fluctuation between an exhausting, unsustainable pace of production and a sluggish recovery pace until a steady, sustainable pace is achieved.

robust equilibrium (Arrow, 1997), and it is the pattern assumed by many treatments of group variables, including the development of group task strategies, leadership structures, patterns of communication, and levels of productivity (e.g., Bales, 1953). This pattern starts with a relatively short initial period of change at the outset of group interaction, after which the group then settles into a stable state—a fixed value or narrow range of values for the global variable in question. In dynamical systems terms, the group moves from its initial state toward a single, stable point attractor.

The trajectory toward this attractor might show random fluctuations that die out as the system stabilizes, in which case a time-series plot of the global variable measured would show a short, squiggly line that quickly became, and remained, straight (see Figure 6.1a). In the early life of a work group, for example, the volume of products per week might jump around unpredictably until the group stabilized at a normative level, which it maintained with little variation thereafter. Alternatively, the trajectory might show steady movement from a starting value to a different, persistent end value. The time series for this would show a rising or falling line that flattened out as it hit the attractor (Figure 6.1b). Continuing the example of production volume, a group might have low product volume at first, then improve up to a point, and then maintain this higher level over time. A third variation would be a cycle that dissipated into a single point, which would appear in the time series (if the time resolution of measurement were sufficiently fine grained) as a wave that flattened, as if the system were "captured" by the attractor (Figure 6.1c). A two-dimensional phase portrait for the latter would show a spiral that curved inward toward the point attractor. This pattern might correspond to production when a group was trying to zero in on a steady, sustainable rate of production but varied at first from an exhausting, unsustainable pace to a sluggish recovery pace until it found a happy medium.

Alternative Equilibria and Multistability:
The Dynamics of Multiple Attractors

Dynamic systems may also have multiple attractor points or regions. A diagram of such a phase space would show multiple basins of attraction with ridges between them. A system that starts out on a "ridge" in the attractor space—at an intermediate value between the two "attractor" values—may end up in either of the attractor regions that borders the ridge, depending on small differences in initial conditions. It is unlikely to remain in the state represented by the ridge, for fluctuations will push it in one direction or the other, and once this begins, the system will continue to move toward the attractor. If the trajectories of multiple groups are plotted in the same space, different groups will end up at different attractors. But any one group will show a developmental pattern that corresponds to robust equilibrium, provided that conditions in the embedding context remain relatively constant.

Other patterns that might characterize the path of global variables include cases involving two or more attractors that a system can visit sequentially. The simplest case would allow for an irreversible move from one attractor to a second attractor, and then perhaps to a third, and so on. A phase space corresponding to such stage models might show successive basins of attractions, like a series of mountain lakes at different altitudes. With the passage of time and accumulation of history, the system moves from one attractor basin to the next, like a leaf carried over a series of waterfalls from one lake to the next. This type of model fits many theories of group problem-solving phases (Bales & Strodtbeck, 1951) and group developmental stages (e.g, Tuckman, 1965; Worchel, 1994). Tuckman and Jensen's (1977) five stages of forming, storming, norming, performing, and adjourning, which probably constitute the best-known life cycle model, involve a fixed sequence of five different group states. Within a stage, the group remains stable, but after some time in a particular stage, the group progresses to the next state. This can be restated as a situation in which the system moves progressively through five attractor regions in the course of the group's lifetime. Attractors that are stable at first become unstable with the passage of time, and eventually the system moves on to the next attractor.

Gersick's (1988) model of punctuated equilibrium is another example of a multistable model. Gersick observed that task forces working against a deadline quickly developed a robust strategy for approaching their tasks and continued using that strategy until they reached the midpoint between when the group started and the deadline at which the project was due. At the midpoint, the groups abruptly switched to a new, equally robust, strategy (Gersick, 1988). This model attends to the

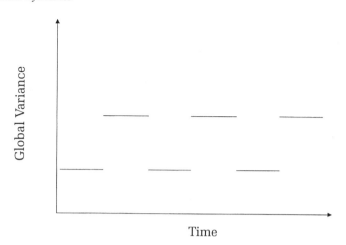

Figure 6.2. Exemplar Time-Series Plot for a Multiple Point Attractor

sequence of shifts in the group's general task strategies, division of labor, and use of resources inside and outside the group.

A more complex pattern involving two or more point attractors allows for reversible switching. Gersick and Hackman (1990) suggested that groups can have multiple habitual routines (multiple equilibria) and that switching between states is possible. They gave the example of crews whose members have trained both for normal situations and for crisis situations. When a trigger (such as a fire bell) goes off, the group switches quickly to the appropriate crisis operating procedures. When the crisis is contained, the group switches back to normal procedures.

This crisis contingency pattern fits into a broader category of contingency models (McGrath, 1991; Poole & Roth, 1989a, 1989b) that Arrow (1997) termed *adaptive response models* because changes between states are triggered by events at the group-embedding context interchange. This pattern is discussed in more detail in the following chapter. However, shifts between attractors based on developments within the group—crises created by interpersonal or task conflicts, for example—are also quite plausible. A time-series plot of global variables that follow a switching pattern would appear as a discontinuous function that would "jump" from one relatively stable line to another relatively stable line and back again (see Figure 6.2). A phase portrait of this pattern would appear as two or more attractor points that the global variable visited, with no intermediate states.

When the location of the system depends on the value of a contextual parameter such as the presence of emergency conditions, a full portrait of the dynamics includes the relevant contextual parameter(s) as an added dimension. Catastrophic bifurcations illustrate the dynamics underlying discontinuous switching (Abraham et al., 1990). At some values of the control parameter, one attractor may be present, whereas at other values, this attractor will vanish and another attractor (or attractors) will appear. *Bifurcation* refers to the change in number or type of attractors; *catastrophic* refers to the discontinuity of changes that are involved.

Cycles and Oscillations
as Periodic Attractors

Instead of reaching a single stable point or moving from one relatively stable point to another, an attractor may be a cycle of values through which a global variable moves in a directional, repetitive sequence. This is known as a *periodic* attractor. Bales's (1953) equilibrium model of group interaction process embedded the notion that groups oscillate between instrumental (or task) activity and expressive (or socioemotional) activity in a recurrent and more or less rhythmic way, with the buildup of activity in one domain increasing the "pressure" for the group to adjust the balance and emphasize the other domain instead. Another example might be conflict that ebbs and flows, gradually building and erupting, then damping down to a low level until the cycle repeats.

An even more complex pattern would be a global variable that had two or more cycles that it repeated, as in the case of multiple point attractors, only now it would jump between cycles rather than between fixed points. A time-series plot of a periodic attractor would be a sine wave; a time-series plot of a global variable that jumped between multiple periodic attractors would look like a sine wave that ended abruptly with a discontinuous jump to another sine wave and back again (see Figure 6.3). A phase portrait of a global variable following a periodic attractor would show a closed loop. A phase portrait with more than one

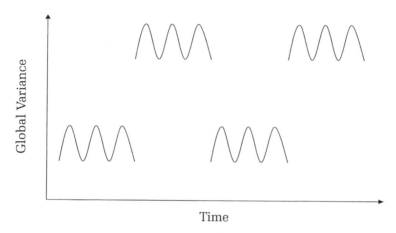

Time

Figure 6.3. Exemplar Time-Series Plot for a Multiple Periodic Attractor

such attractor would look like two or more closed loops with a connection designating the path between them.

Instability and Chaos

Readers familiar with chaos theory will note that we have not described the strange attractors that are characteristic of systems that have chaotic dynamics, in the mathematical sense of the term. Although it is certainly plausible that the dynamics of small groups follow chaotic patterns (see, e.g., Fuhriman & Burlingame, 1994), the requirements for precision, resolution, and volume of data points needed to distinguish between chaotic dynamics and random behavior make us skeptical about the value of searching for chaos in the group research domain. Thus, we have focused instead on the simpler patterns that match extant theorizing on group development.

However, some of the characteristics associated with chaotic patterns—unpredictability and sensitive dependence on initial conditions—should be expected when multiple attractors are available. With bounded ranges of values that fall within the "basin" of attraction for each attractor, one can predict which attractor the global variable will move toward. Within these ranges, the system exhibits equifinality—multiple possible paths that nevertheless lead to the same end point.

Outside these ranges are regions in which the future movement of the system is unpredictable. When a global variable is in a boundary region (such as a ridge between two attractor basins), it is not possible to predict which attractor the system will move toward and when. Groups whose initial conditions are in such border regions will show sensitivity to initial conditions, so that small changes in the group's elements, in their local dynamics, or in surrounding conditions may lead to highly similar starting paths' diverging to end up at one or more different attractors in a multiattractor phase space.

We now consider what particular developmental paths would mean, in substantive terms, for the evolution of particular global variables in different types of groups. Drawing on the small groups literature and basic principles of dynamics, we suggest what kinds of conditions could give rise to particular patterns of global dynamics and how these might differ in crews, teams, task forces, and clubs.

∞ DIFFERENCES IN DYNAMICS AMONG AND WITHIN GROUPS

Different global variables may show different developmental patterns within the same group. For example, the cohesiveness of a group of mountain climbers may follow a spiral pattern that moves toward a single stable attractor, whereas the leadership structure of that same group may switch between two point attractors, depending on whether the group is setting up camp or hiking toward the summit. Which model fits a particular global variable should depend on the local dynamics of that group. As discussed in Chapter 5, adaptive structuration theory proposes that groups continually adapt their components to one another and to the context in which they are embedded. Some of those adjustments at the local level maintain the group in a relatively constant state; some change it.

First, we discuss some basic characteristics of systems that promote stability and change and relate these to different types of groups. Next, we suggest what different patterns might mean, substantively, if they were observed empirically for particular global variables.

Sources of Stability and
Change Applied to
Different Group Types

Stability in a system can be promoted by several different character-istics: rigid structure, shared norms, negative feedback loops, and loose coupling. Rigid structure makes it difficult for changes to be imple-mented. Shared norms ensure that members' beliefs about how they should behave converge. Negative feedback loops correct deviations from a norm or standard and thus tend to counteract change (although the correction is, of course, a change in itself). And loose coupling makes it less likely that change in one part of the system will require change in other parts of the system. All of these characteristics help maintain the status quo for a group.

Local-level changes can occur in the form of random fluctuation and via deliberate movement toward desired states (attraction) or away from undesirable states (repulsion). Changes can also occur as a reac-tion to pressure: The greater the pressure, the more likely that it will create change. Competing pressures can hold a system in a balanced state for a short time, but this balance is likely to be an unstable point at-tractor. Local changes are more likely to lead to global change in the sys-tem characterized by flexible structure, positive feedback loops, and tight coupling. Flexible structures change more readily, positive feed-back loops amplify small changes, and tight coupling makes it more likely that changes will propagate from one part of a system to another. Norms can promote change if the group is not in the desired state; they maintain the status quo if the group is in a normative state. Movement toward desirable and away from undesirable states is likely to scale up into large-scale movement if members have the same preferences.

The passage of time and consequent increase in experience also can promote both stability and change. Experience tends to reinforce habit-ual routines, a source of stability. However, experience also leads to learning and new information, which are sources of change, and too much continuity over time can lead to boredom, which makes change for the sake of change attractive.

In crews, standardization and prior training in roles promote a rela-tively rigid structure and clear, strong norms about how members should behave. These promote stability and make robust equilibrium a likely pattern for the evolution of many global variables in crews. The

tight coupling of highly structured crews, however, also provides a resource for coordinating relatively crisp changes from one mode of behavior to another when crew members agree they need to switch to a
different, but also well-recognized, state. This fits the adaptive matching model of switching between multiple point attractors.

In task forces, we expect punctuated equilibrium patterns to be common. In this form of irreversible switching, however, abrupt changes
are not smoothly coordinated in a tightly coupled system but are triggered in response to a buildup of pressure. This may be time pressure
that increases as the deadline approaches, stress based on task feedback, or, in groups that tend to pay more attention to task requirements
than to socioemotional concerns, interpersonal stresses. Flexible structures and competing pressures in task forces can also drive cyclical patterns as the group responds to first one pull or push and then another.

In teams, the development and maintenance of norms and habitual
routines should make robust equilibrium patterns likely. However, experience and learning can drive the movement from one stage to another in an irreversible progression. Flexibility of structures combined
with the demands of multiple projects may also promote cycling patterns as a team shifts its focus from one set of demands to another. In
Worchel's (1996) model of group development, shifting emphasis on
the relative importance of individual needs versus group goals appears
to underlie the transition between successive stages.

In clubs, which give priority to member needs, the dynamics are
most likely to be driven by changes in those needs, which may occur as
members leave and are replaced or as changes occur within members.
When needs are stable, routines for satisfying those needs should be
quite stable too, a pattern consistent with robust equilibrium. In social
clubs, competing pressures for differentiation among members and
unity among members may promote cycles of closeness and distance.

Probable Dynamics for Particular Global Variables

Commitment

The commitment levels of a member to the group and the group to
that member emerge from negotiation and assessment between mem-

bers and groups. In crews, what members and groups have to offer is likely to be quite straightforward and to be stable over the lifetime of the group. In task forces, a punctuated equilibrium of relatively low commitment, with a jump to higher commitment as the group switches into higher gear to ensure that the task is completed, seems likely. At the midpoint transition, members whose commitment does not meet the raised threshold may be dropped from the group. Commitment levels may also change abruptly in any type of group based on salient successes or failures.

In social clubs and in teams, in which the relationships between members are quite important, cycles of closeness and distance (driven by competing pressures within members as well as in the group) can lead to cycling in commitment as well. Members should be most likely to leave the group during a low point in the cycle, when their commitment to the group falls below their minimum threshold, or at a high point in the cycle, when the group's demands for commitment go up. New members should be more likely to join at a low point in the cycle because the threshold for entry will be lower, and groups may look to outsiders as a source of new energy (Worchel, 1996).

Project Output

If a project requires a constant level of production, and the group has a functional set of ties between its members, tasks, and technology, the quantity and quality of production may move toward a single stable point attractor. For example, for a group that produces Product X—given no externally driven changes such as a sharp change in demand for Product X—group production may quickly asymptote at a certain level of quantity and quality of Product X. That may indicate that the group is "satisficing" rather than striving to maximize with respect to that product. It may also suggest that the group has developed and can enforce strong norms regarding production levels—and by implication, norms regarding expected levels of effort and competence by members (Homans, 1950).

On the other hand, if a group exhibits a sudden "jump" (up or down) in levels of quantity or quality of production, that may indicate that the group has suddenly "gotten it together" (or suddenly "lost it") by means of some shift in its routine task operations. In task forces, a sudden increase may occur at the end of a trial-and-error period, after resolving

uncertainty about how to proceed, or after a change in strategy triggered by either time pressure or negative feedback about progress on
the task.

Groups working on projects that do not require a constant level of
production but instead include specific task stages that the group must
go through before producing a final product are likely to display a more
periodic pattern of production of a final product. For example, a team
whose current project is to produce a research publication may first
delve into the literature, then discuss ideas, then plan a study, then
conduct the study, and then publish several papers within a short time
period after that study. If only the published papers are considered the
"product," that group displays a cyclic or periodic pattern with respect
to production quantity. Teams that take up projects sequentially are
likely to show cyclic patterns of quality and quantity as they go through
a learning period at the beginning of each new project.

Time Swapping and Time Sharing

When groups work on divisible projects composed of many different
tasks, they may divide tasks up among members or all work on one task,
then another. In some cases, the nature of the task or project may dictate
what strategy is used. When either strategy is plausible, the use of one
or the other strategy (or a mixed strategy, in which subsets of members
attack single tasks) may stabilize into a single pattern or change over
time. Waller (1997) suggested that the choice of strategy should depend
on whether the group receives negative feedback from the task itself or
from the environment and whether the group has extensive knowledge
of member expertise. In crews, expertise can be inferred from role position; in teams and social clubs, well-developed transactive memory
systems should result from the highly elaborated member network.
Waller suggested that when this knowledge is high, time sharing is
more likely, and we agree with this prediction for work groups. In social
clubs and activity clubs, by contrast, a primary focus of activity is doing
things together and being together, so time swapping is likely to be the
consistent norm unless the activity requires time sharing.

Waller (1997) suggested that when feedback is primarily from the
task itself, groups will take corrective action more quickly than when
feedback comes from the environment (p. 235). Because clubs are more
attuned to success in fulfilling member needs—which can be assessed

immediately—and work groups are more attuned to signals from the embedding environment, this raises the interesting possibility that clubs will be more responsive to internal feedback than work groups. Negative feedback from task performance, according to Waller, should increase the use of time sharing (different people doing different tasks), whereas negative feedback from the environment should increase the use of time swapping (all working on the same task).

In groups attuned to the environment, the adaptive response pattern of reversible switching among multiple attractors seems likely. The simplest would be a crisis contingency model, in which the group time-shares during routine operations but time-swaps during a crisis signaled by the environment. This is the equivalent of "dropping everything" to all rush to whatever task has the highest priority in the crisis.

Differentiation in the
Standing Group Structure

In crews, if the members are experienced and well trained in their tasks, the standing group structure is likely to change little over the life of the group, except for the emergence of interpersonal ties among crew members who have not worked together before. However, if some of the crew are rookies or perform poorly for other reasons, the crew may need to make adjustments and reassign some duties in order to function effectively. Instead of locking on to a fixed attractor immediately, such crews should show more initial fluctuation in the horizontal and vertical differentiation of labor and role systems. Robust equilibrium should, however, be the norm for crew structure.

In other types of groups, horizontal differentiation within a group's labor and role networks is likely to increase over time, up to some fixed level. Task forces, for example, are often formed with no clear plan for who will do what and how. Although the group may have an appointed chair or head, other roles and status positions are often undefined. As the group accumulates experience in carrying out its projects, initial assignments of members to tasks should lead members to specialize in those assigned tasks and increase their skills in them. That will lead to more well-defined task differentiation and specialization within the group. As members become identified with particular aspects of a group's task operations, they become responsible not only for the completion of their particular tasks but often for acquisition, storage, and dissemination of information regarding their area of specialty, including past events and future planning (e.g., Wegner, 1986).

Another plausible pattern for work groups such as task forces and teams is irreversible switching from a low level of differentiation to a much higher level. Note that this change in standing group structure is different from the changes in acting group patterns, which may involve members of highly differentiated groups all doing the same thing at the same time. The group may start out with everyone working on every task and continue in this pattern until some jolt such as poor performance, duplication of efforts, trouble coordinating use of tools and resources, or time pressure spurs the group to "get organized" and divide up the tasks and define jobs and roles more clearly.

Most theories of role development and empirical studies of groups suggest that robust equilibrium is the most likely dynamic pattern for the connection of specific members with specific roles. Dunphy (1968), for example, found "remarkable consistency and continuity" of roles (p. 215), although he had hypothesized change. What changed in the groups he studied was not who played what role but the relative importance ascribed to different roles in the group. Instead of initial fluctuation, change in an aspect of the role network may occur in a single direction until it reaches a fixed attractor. A status hierarchy, for example, may start out relatively flat and end up steep (Ridgeway & Berger, 1986).

Another pattern that seems plausible is a switch from a periodic attractor to a point attractor of fixed roles. In this case, members may rotate among roles that later turn into fixed assignments (Eagly & Karau, 1991); this pattern seems most likely in teams and clubs, which take time to develop, and seems quite unlikely in crews.

Information Sharing

Stasser's work (Stasser & Titus, 1985, 1987) showed that groups are much more likely to mention, and discuss, information that was available to many or all group members before the group discussion than to mention or discuss information that was known to only one member prior to the group's meeting, even when that uniquely held information is crucial to the group's arriving at a high-quality decision. He and his colleagues and others (Hollingshead, 1998; Larson et al., 1994) have explored some of the conditions that lead to a more effective use of potentially available information in groups. Results of that work at this time suggest that types of decision tasks or problems (intellective vs. judgmental), the level of cognitive processing of information required for a decision or solution, and the communication technology available to the group all may alter the effect to some degree but are unlikely to eliminate it (Hollingshead, 1998; Stasser et al., 1995).

We might interpret that body of work, in the terms used here, as indicating that such decision-making groups have a strong pull toward confirming and reinforcing information that is already known to the group, rather than presenting unique information. This is one attractor. In groups at a later stage of development, however, or in which members knew each other before the group was formed (Gruenfeld et al., 1996), the desire to affirm uniqueness and individual difference may create a separate attractor. In groups composed of strangers, the second attractor would emerge only as people got to know each other.

Conflict

Most theories of group conflict propose a cyclic or periodic pattern. This global variable seems especially susceptible to having regions of instability. If group conflict reaches too high or too low a level (e.g., conflict is always avoided or "not allowed," as in the case of "groupthink"; Janis, 1972), the group may not survive as an intact system. Thus, this global variable may have a bounded midvalue, "safe" region beyond which lie catastrophic changes. Worchel's (1994) theory of group development implies a cycle of increasing, then decreasing conflict. After the decay stage of open conflict, conflict cools to discontent, and either the group drifts apart or a precipitating event starts the group on an upswing to high group identification, conformity, and consensus. As the group achieves goals and gains resources, however, the desire for recognition and a share of the resources sparks a new round of conflict. This pattern is very similar to the classic dynamics of a forced oscillation, in which the system gets a little "kick" that keeps it cycling, rather than settling into a fixed point attractor. The "kick" in this case is the precipitating event. If none occurs, the system runs down to a point of neither conflict nor consensus because there is no group.

Regulating Member Behavior Through Norms

Most considerations of the development of group norms regarding member task performance, group process activities, and interpersonal relations suggest that they develop relatively soon after group formation and, once established, are difficult to change (Homans, 1950). In Tuckman and Jensen's (1977) "forming, storming, norming, performing, adjourning" stages, tentative norms are established in the forming stage, challenged in the storming stage, and solidified in the norming stage. In dynamics terms, the group moves quickly toward an attractor, but the attractor is "weak" (has a small and shallow basin), and the system can easily be pushed out of the attractor basin. In small group terms, the norms are weak because members are not yet committed to enforcing them, and thus behavior that challenges the norms is punished inconsistently or not at all.

After the storming stage, in which the system jumps around, "exploring" phase space, it finds a stronger, more stable attractor and stays there. Any violation of norms (movement away from the point attractor) is met with negative sanctions, pushing the system back to the attractor.

Coordinating Member Behavior

The old adage "practice makes perfect"—or, more accurately, practice makes better up to an asymptote—provides a good description of the relation of training and practice on performances involving complex motor skills. As individuals or groups practice (or train) in the performance of complex, coordinated activities, they improve their ability to anticipate the timing, content, and intensity of one another's actions and to deliver their own actions with timing, content, and intensity that matches their teammates' expectations. Thus, errors and "false moves" tend to drop out of the behavior repertoire. That, of course, describes asymptotic movement toward a single stable point attractor.

In many conditions, however, there is a more complex relation between performance and the amount and type of prior task experience. For one thing, if the conditions for success on the task change (e.g., if an opponent uses strategies not anticipated in the training/practice), well-practiced coordinated moves may prove ineffective. Such a group may persist in using well-coordinated actions that no longer provide an effective level of performance. Under such conditions, success requires that the group "break set" and begin to execute the project according to a different strategy geared to current conditions. If this other strategy is also well practiced, the dynamic pattern will be high coordination, a brief destabilization, and then high coordination on a different task. If the strategy calls for an improvisation, the pattern will shift from high coordination to low coordination, then increasing coordination as the group members get into the flow or continued breakdown of coordination if the improvisation does not work.

∞ EFFECTS OF GLOBAL VARIABLES ON SUBSEQUENT LOCAL DYNAMICS

The logic of our theoretical formulation holds that global variables emerge from local dynamics and subsequently shape those local dynamics. But keep in mind that *global variables derive from and relate to the entire system*, not just to one subset of its local variables. As we indicated at the beginning of this chapter, although certain global variables may *pertain to* a certain segment of group functioning (such as its task product results), every global variable *derives from* the interactive dynamics of *all* of the group's local variables, not just those parts that are directly or deliberately related to that segment (e.g., their direct task actions). Similarly, each global variable (or, more accurately, the system that all of the local variables jointly reflect) may have subsequent effects on *all* aspects of the group's local activity.

Why is this true? One important reason is that global variables are not only more visible to outsiders than the detailed interactions of local dynamics but also highly visible to group members. The quantity of products generated by a group, for example, is much easier for everyone in the group to notice than the many small steps and actions—many completed by other members, not oneself—that go into the creation of those products. When members are pleased with the state of the group, as indicated by global variables such as performance, overall level of conflict, and commitment levels, this reinforces whatever actions they are currently engaged in. When they are dissatisfied with the state of the group, or when outsiders notice and comment on problems in the group as revealed by global variables, this is a cue to change something. However, global variables cannot be changed directly— what needs to be changed is the local dynamics that give rise to them. Action identification theory (Vallacher & Wegner, 1987) suggests that when groups receive negative feedback from the environment, they are cued to focus on lower-level subtasks, rather than higher-level group tasks, as a locus for corrective action.

In this way, the pattern over time of the quantity and quality of group project performance, for example, is likely to have pervasive subsequent effects on many aspects of local dynamics. If the group achieves its project goals (i.e., acceptable levels of quantity and quality of its task products), that may lead to receipt of additional resources and/or rewards to the group and its members from the external system and at the same time lead to modifications in members' feelings of self-efficacy, to fulfillment of members' needs for achievement, and to reinforcement of the norms supporting the group's concurrent coordination pattern. On the other hand, if the group has failed to attain its project performance goals, opposite consequences with respect to all of those and other local variables may ensue.

Past patterns of global dynamics become part of the group's "history," hence part of the social context within which all subsequent action takes place (Mantovani, 1996). Some studies of work groups (e.g., Hackman, 1990) show that groups that initially perform poorly on their main projects may never be able to become effective, in part because they acquire a "reputation" as troubled groups in the perceptions of agents in the external context who partly determine that group's rewards. Initially successful groups, in contrast, seem to be able to make use of that initial success to continue and increase effective project performance and thereby further enhance their reputation with and rewards from external agents. However, the generality of this observation may depend a great deal on the stability of the rewards and costs and on demands and opportunities provided by a group's embedding context.

When the context is stable, early success should lead to later success, via positive responses from the group and external actors that reinforce successful behaviors. When the context is unstable, intermittent early failures may result in a group that is more flexible and responsive to the environment (Sitkin, 1992). The reasoning is that occasional failures will prevent a group from getting too attached to what it did in the past, protecting it from the downside of habitual routines and robust persistence when what worked in the past is not, in fact, appropriate to a new present. The process of adapting to a changing environment, by changing the group or by attempting to change the environment, is the focus of the following chapter.

∽ 7 ∾

Contextual Dynamics

Adaptation of the Group to Multiple Embedding Contexts

*A*daptation is the patterning of change at the dynamic inter-change between a group and its multiple embedding contexts. Group members may respond to past, present, or anticipated future changes in the group's environment by altering the group's structure, its goals, and its behavior. A group may change the composition of members, tools, and tasks, change the networks that link these elements together, or change the characteristic pattern of activity in these networks. Outsiders in a group's embedding context may also intervene directly to change the group. Managers in an organization, for example, may add new members to a team, update its technology, or cancel one of its projects. Events in the embedding systems of individual members—for example, family events such as birth of a child or the relocation of a spouse—can alter a work group by removing a member either temporari'y or permanently.

Operating conditions can also change as new opportunities or constraints appear in the environment. These changes may not disrupt the group system directly but may change the outcomes of its activities. The entry of a hot new team into the softball league may depress the records of other teams in the league. An improving economy and new job opportunities may encourage family members to work outside the home, changing the way things are structured within a household group. Corporate restructuring may make the recommendations of a quality task force more, or less, consequential and may alter members' assessment of the probable political consequences of belonging to such a group. Group members may also act proactively to alter aspects of the embedding contexts that affect group outcomes. Members of a work group, for example, may lobby to change how organizational resources are allocated or how costs are shared among work groups.

Faced with a change in operating conditions or an external intervention, groups respond in markedly different ways. Some react with a series of minor adjustments; some alter their structure and behavior quickly and dramatically; some do not appear to respond at all. In some groups, members execute a tightly coordinated response, whereas in others the members resort to frantic but disordered activity or erupt into conflict. Some groups appear to seek out new opportunities proactively, whereas others do not. How can we account for these differences? How, especially, can we understand responses that seriously damage a group's effectiveness? This chapter presents a framework for understanding why and how group systems react to and act on their embedding contexts in such varied ways.

An adequate model of adaptation must attend to multiple factors that affect how a group interacts with its environment. We propose that a group's response to change at a given point in time is shaped by the history of the group, by the current configuration of forces in the group and at the group-context interchange, by characteristics of the triggering event, and by group members' projections of different probable future states of the group.

Adaptation is shaped by pervasive interactions between past, present, and projected future states of the group. The traces of both the past and the anticipated future affect how group members perceive, interpret, and respond in the present to events that occur outside the group's boundaries or that cross those boundaries. Events in natural groups do not proceed in a neat linear sequence, in which a discrete stimulus is followed by a single response. Instead, while a group is attempting to cope with a change in the recent past, it may be hit with a new shock, and members may also anticipate a further disturbance on the horizon. When the receding pull of one wave of changes collides with the onset of new disruptions, the range of plausible actions is harder to map out, and choosing a path to effective adaptation is harder for both groups and theorists. A group's response to change may make things better or worse, and some actions may yield both positive and negative results. In our conception, change need not be effective to be considered adaptation. Just as people can learn bad habits or acquire false knowledge, groups can "adapt" in ways that ultimately damage the group.

The configuration of forces in the group and at the group-context interchange reflect two sets of dynamics, which are never perfectly in synchrony. One set operates at the group-context interchange. The flow of resources, energy, information, and group products back and forth across this boundary is regulated by a structure of rewards and costs imposed on and in some cases negotiated by members of the group. Together, a group's embedding contexts constitute a field of opportunities and constraints that make different courses of action more or less rewarding for a particular group. This cost-reward manifold can be viewed as a *fitness landscape,* a kind of external payoff structure for the group.

The second set of forces that affect adaptation are those that drive the internal dynamics of the group. In Chapter 6, the evolution of group structure and behavior was examined in terms of sets of attractors toward which global variables tend to move over time. This configuration of attractors reflects a set of costs and constraints internal to the group that make some actions more likely than others, regardless of how the environment is apt to respond. Conflicting pressures inside the group boundary and at the group-context interchange shape the sometimes quixotic path of adaptation.

In the next section, we flesh out a model of adaptation as movement in a fitness landscape. Just as groups are formed by both deliberate action and undirected local dynamics, our model includes both intentional strategies and unplanned sequences of actions that affect how a group interacts with the outside world.

Next, we discuss how the configuration of attractors in the global dynamics of the group affects the path a group follows in traversing a fitness landscape. We identify dimensions of change that influence the nature of a group's response, which may be a collective action agreed on by members or may simply be an aggregate of member actions. We discuss the range of responses that may be evoked by a single salient change in context and then broaden the discussion to look at extended sequences of change over the course of a group's lifetime. We conclude the chapter with four principles of adaptation that highlight the frequently unexpected pairing of change and response in embedding context and group. These principles help explain why it is so difficult to predict how a given group will respond to changes in context and external interventions.

∾ ADAPTATION AS MOVEMENT
ACROSS A FITNESS LANDSCAPE

The concept of a fitness landscape (Wright, 1932) has proved useful in theorizing about self-organization in complex biological systems (e.g., Kauffman, 1993) and has also recently been applied to human organizations (e.g., Bruderer & Singh, 1996; McPherson, 1990). Adaptation can be viewed as a sequence of changes both in the fitness landscape and in a group's position in the landscape. First, we explain in more detail what a fitness landscape entails. Second, we discuss the difference between directed and undirected movement by groups across this landscape. Then we expand the model to include multiple embedding contexts and multiple landscapes.

Fitness Landscape:
A Map of the Group-Context Exchange

A group's environment presents sets of opportunities, constraints, and costs that make different courses of action more or less rewarding for a particular group. A fitness landscape is a geometric representation of how particular configurations of global variables—structure, strategy, or performance, for example—"fit" the opportunities and demands of the environment. In a three-dimensional fitness landscape, the vertical dimension (elevation in the landscape metaphor) represents fit, or the quality of outcomes that a group obtains from the environment. Peaks are relatively good outcomes (high fitness), and valleys are relatively poor outcomes (low fitness). In biological models, different points on the surface of the landscape represent different gene combinations, and fitness is reproductive success. Genetic variation distributes a population of organisms across this landscape. As the environment changes, the fitness landscape may also change, so that sets of characteristics that were highly adaptive (good fit) in the past become less successful. As the species evolves, the prevalence of genetic combinations that yield different structures and capabilities also changes, altering the distribution of the population across the fitness landscape.

Applied to small groups, *fitness* refers to how successful a group with a particular structure, set of strategies, or outputs is in its environment. *High fitness* means that the group gains valuable resources that enable it to survive and prosper. *Low fitness* means that the group is unable to access needed resources (by whatever means) at relatively low costs and/or that it suffers high costs imposed by the environment. Fitness is always relative to a particular setting or context.

In theory, the full fitness landscape may have a very high dimensionality, representing a huge number of global variables that may be related to group outcomes. In practice, however, researchers who adopt this model generally want to limit themselves to a manageable number of factors, either by picking a few global variables of interest or by measuring a great number of variables and extracting a limited number of principal components that can then be related to outcomes for the group. Bruderer and Singh (1996), for example, focused on observable routines as what is constrained or rewarded by the group context. But one could construct a fitness landscape for group design, or sets of norms, or information flow, or group composition, or any other global variable of interest. And, of course, a group's repertoire of available routines generally exceeds what is observed in any restricted time period.

The measure of fitness may be either a single criterion that is related to a host of outcomes—for example, the win-loss record of a sports team—or an aggregated score that represents several outcome criteria. The fitness of a string quartet, for example, might be measured as a composite of critical acclaim, concert fees, number of concerts, and number of albums recorded (Murnighan & Conlon, 1991). Note that the concept of fitness refers explicitly to benefits and costs bestowed by the environment outside the group. It does not include outcomes such as member satisfaction or enjoyment, which may contribute to a group's well-being and survival but are internally generated resources or outcomes.

In the biological model of evolution, individual organisms cannot change their genetic makeup. However, members of small groups can and do change the group's structure, develop new group strategies, alter the effort given to producing group products, and alter other variables that affect the group's cost-benefit relation with the environment. Returning to the sports team example, if the fitness score was the win-loss record, position on the landscape might represent different sets of offensive and defensive strategies. The highest peak on the landscape would correspond to the strategic repertoire of the team with the best record, and the lowest point would correspond to the strategic repertoire of the team with the worst record. A group with a dismal record might very well develop new plays and change its set of strategies to resemble more closely those of the better performing teams. In our model of adaptation, this would be represented as a deliberate move from one location in the landscape to another. For any particular team, of course, some strategy sets (positions on the landscape) will be inaccessible because of the limitations of team members or some other missing resource. A strategy that relies on having outstanding team speed, for example, may be possible only for a few teams in a league. Other sets of strategies may be theoretically possible (they exist on the landscape) but in practice are never used. The fitness of these points on the landscape will be unknown to both researchers and teams.

Landscapes can vary from relatively smooth to rugged (Kauffman, 1993). Points close together on the landscape (similar sets of strategies) might have very similar fitness scores, creating a gentle slope in a smooth landscape. In a smooth landscape, the impact of change in the global variables of interest on fitness will be more or less proportional, with small changes altering outcomes a little and big changes altering outcomes a lot. In a rugged landscape, high points and low points can be close together. Here, a small change in the configuration of global variables may correspond to a big change in fitness.

When a key element of the environment changes, the fitness landscape for some global variables may be transformed. In the sports team example, a change in the game rules may render some strategies illegal or dramatically change the outcomes of a particular set of strategies. Alternatively, a group's position in the fitness landscape may change because of a deliberate intervention. For example, direct alterations of a team's coordination network caused by a change in the roster because of a player trade, or the arrival of a new defensive coach, may cause a change of strategies that is not initiated intentionally by group members. As a group adjusts to the imposed changes by training new members and practicing new routines, its position in the landscape is likely to change again. All of these changes are included in our model of adaptation.

Two Forms of Change:
Undirected and Directed

We propose two basic forms of group adaptation—undirected and directed. At the level of local dynamics, small changes that are themselves responses to the environment but are not part of any overall strategy for change can accumulate into a substantial movement for the group across a fitness landscape. As part of normal variation in behavior, groups (or subsets of their members) may do similar tasks a little differently from one iteration to another. Those actions that members associate with better rewards and fewer costs will tend to persist and become more frequent, whereas those associated with poor outcomes will not persist. Over time, the concatenation of changes based on positive and negative reinforcement can alter the group's global structure and routines. For example, a writers' group that normally meets weekly at a particular restaurant may go elsewhere one week because that restaurant is closed for the day. The new place may turn out to be quieter and cheaper. Although the group may still meet at the old place occasionally, the new place soon becomes the favored spot. Over a group's lifetime, numerous small changes like this can add up to a substantial change in group structure and behavior.

In the example just given, no internal or external actor is deliberately "shaping" the coordinated behavior of group members; there is no overall change strategy and no plan. This process of change over time applies to a wide variety of systems in the natural world. It is the basic mechanism of natural selection in evolution. We call this form of change *undirected* or *emergent adaptation*. It corresponds to what Van de Ven and Poole (1995) called an evolutionary motor and to theories of organizational adaptation that contain features of an evolutionary approach (e.g., Haveman, 1992; Lawrence & Lorsch, 1967; Pfeffer & Salancik, 1978).

Undirected adaptation has three basic features:

1. *Variation*: The structure of groups and the behavior of groups and their members fluctuate over time, as do rewards and costs from the embedding context.
2. *Selection*: On the basis of perceived associations between the states and actions of the group and the outcomes that members and the group as a whole receive, some variants of behavior or structure are experienced as more rewarding than others.
3. *Retention*: These rewarding behaviors or aspects of group structure are retained, stabilized, and routinized, whereas others, perceived as less rewarding, are not.

Another form of change is driven by goals and directed by plans and strategy. It includes the notion of final cause in the sense of goal-directed human activity. We call this *directed adaptation.* Information processing, leadership, conflict management, and motivation, regulation, and coordination of member behavior are all important in directed adaptation. The writers' group, dissatisfied by the level of noise and expense at their usual spot, may decide to try out several alternative restaurants to improve their outcomes. The role of leaders in envisioning possible futures and motivating members to stay the course can be critical. Some theorists have proposed that an important feature of charismatic or visionary leaders is their sensitivity to the environment, which alerts them to relevant changes in constraints and opportunities for the group (Conger & Kanungo, 1987; Sashkin, 1988). This would be change directed from within. Directed adaptation can also be driven by outsiders who hold reward or coercive power over the group (Raven, 1993), and it can involve a struggle between insiders and outsiders who have conflicting goals for the group.

Directed adaptation has four basic features. The simplest version is when change is directed by group members, not outsiders:

1. *Information processing.* Group members construct a shared mental map of the fitness landscape, drawing on their own collective experience and knowledge, and often that of outsiders as well.
2. *Planning.* The group generates ideas for improving fitness by moving to a different point in the fitness landscape.

3. *Choice*. Group members agree on a plan. Ideally, the plan includes both a clear goal (point on the landscape) and a path to reach that goal, starting from the current state of the group.

4. *Self-regulation*. Members coordinate their efforts to execute the plan, which may involve changing from one set of routines to a new set of routines or may involve a sequence of different steps at different points.

Directed adaptation is more complicated when powerful outsiders become involved, especially if (as is usually the case) the goals of outsiders do not exactly match the goals of group members. In this case, each step in the process may involve conflict, negotiation, and attempted manipulation by both parties. Group members may dispute with outsiders about the contours of the fitness landscape (which outsiders may partially control), the choice of a goal, and the path to reach that goal. Often, outsiders are less interested in the nature of group *outcomes* (i.e., rewards and costs to the group) than in the nature of group *output* (i.e., the group's product from the point of view of the embedding systems). The two parties may cooperate to facilitate adaptation, but group members may also coordinate their actions to thwart the plans of outsiders.

Outsiders may also direct adaptation without engaging the group in a process of goal setting or planning. Instead, they may simply alter the fitness landscape for the group and rely on the group to change in response. The management at the restaurant, unhappy because the writers order the cheapest items on the menu and spend a long time at the table, may deliberately seat them in crowded noisy spots and make them wait a long time for a table. This is external direction of change.

If one of the writers knows the owner of the restaurant, a conversation about their joint dissatisfactions may lead to yet another solution. The group could switch the time of their meeting to correspond with a slow time for the restaurant, during which the restaurant also happens to offer discounted meals. In this case, the conversation alerts the writer about an attractive alternative, and the steps that remain are to persuade other group members to make the change and coordinate action so that members all show up at the new meeting time. As is illustrated by this example, directed change can be powered by both teleological (goal-directed) and dialectical (conflict-driven) motors (Van de Ven & Poole, 1995).

Multiple Contexts, Multiple Landscapes

A fitness landscape always represents outcomes for a particular context. In theory, sufficiently high-dimensional "points" on the landscape could represent all of the group's attributes and behaviors that affect its outcomes in that context. However, groups exist in multiple embedding contexts, and a different (and to some degree conflicting) structure of rewards and costs may apply, simultaneously, for different contexts.

A company softball team, for example, may be equipped by and identified with the company (one embedding system) but play in a city-wide softball league (another embedding system). The company may reward the team for providing opportunities for employees throughout the company to participate. In the league, however, winning or losing is what garners prestige, the enthusiasm of the crowds, and other valued outcomes. These two embedding contexts have very different relations to the team. In studying patterns of change, it is important to keep in mind that the constraints in one context may change while the other embedding contexts remain stable (or change in countervailing ways). If only one context is identified by researchers, adaptive responses inspired by a different context may make no apparent sense.

An important distinction among contexts is whether they are relatively *proximal* or *distal* contexts for a group. We generally use the term *embedding system* for proximal contexts that are closely connected to the group and involved in reciprocal exchanges across the group boundary. In a study of East German orchestras, for example, one proximal embedding context was the state agency responsible for artistic policy and management of personnel (Allmendinger & Hackman, 1996). Groups and their proximal contexts often adapt to one another in a series of reciprocal changes termed *coevolution*, which is discussed later in this chapter. Bidirectional coupling is a precondition for this type of interdependent change.

Any group system is affected by events in a wide range of systems outside its boundaries, however, and not all of these systems are interdependent with the group. The weather, national politics, and the economy are usually distal contexts that may (directly or indirectly) have a big impact on a group but are not themselves affected by the group's activities. The political environment for the East German orchestras underwent dramatic changes from the Nazi regime to the East

German socialist regime and then the democratic regime of reunified Germany. These changes certainly affected the overall operating conditions for the orchestras, but the orchestras had little impact on the course of these dramatic events. For the purposes of this book, we use *environment* as a general term for the world outside the group, including immediate embedding systems and also more distal contexts, whose exchange with the group in question is overwhelmingly one-directional.

Barriers to Successful Adaptation

The logic of undirected adaptation suggests that through the process of variation, selection, and retention, groups will move to a different position in the fitness landscape that is better (higher fitness) than their current position. If variations are small and the landscape is smooth, change will be incremental. If variations are more extreme or the landscape is more rugged, the group may greatly improve or worsen its outcomes from one time to another. However, through the processes of selection and retention, missteps should be quickly corrected, so outcomes should also improve over time (or at least not degrade) as the group explores the landscape.

In directed adaptation, new behaviors and structures are chosen according to an overall plan. Rather than climbing to a higher fitness point as an eventual consequence of repeating the kind of choice that improved group outcomes and avoiding the kind of choice that worsened group outcomes, directed adaptation follows a map. The information contained in that map can inspire group members to move *down* a fitness slope from a local optimum en route to a higher peak that has been chosen as a goal.

For example, a group that may currently be quite accurate and efficient in responding to outsiders (a state associated with fitness for the group) may decide that the only way to improve these services further (perhaps in anticipation of a dramatically increased load) is to computerize operations. While the group is implementing the plan, it may move to an efficiency/accuracy point on the landscape that is much lower (worse outcomes, lower fitness) than before it began the changes.

Big changes often follow this pattern because of the need to abandon well-practiced routines and learn or develop new ones. Over the long term, however, directed adaptation is expected to also move the group toward a better and better fit with its environment.

For both forms of adaptive processes, multiple barriers may impede progress. One feature that makes both processes problematic for improving outcomes is a fitness landscape that is changing rapidly and unpredictably. If rewards are inconsistent, the reinforcements of undirected adaptation will not be effective in improving outcomes. If group members are unable to assess what changes might lead to improvement, they have no basis for the strategic changes of directed adaptation.

Another general barrier to progress is that the adjustments that individual members make to improve their own individual outcomes can result in worse overall outcomes at the group level. Up to this point, we have stressed change processes for the group as a unit, which presumes that group members are acting together as members. Adaptation—both undirected and directed—also occurs at the individual level. If group and individual goals are closely aligned, this will not be a problem. When group and individual goals are in conflict, individual and group fitness landscapes will also be different.

Barriers to Undirected Adaptation

Specific barriers to improved fitness via undirected adaptation include (a) too little variation, (b) a forgiving environment that rewards equally a wide range of behaviors (i.e., a flat fitness landscape), (c) selection on the basis of false associations (e.g., mistaking coincidence for causation), and (d) difficulty stabilizing successful routines. If a group has a rigid structure and set of behaviors from which it rarely deviates, it does not generate alternative behaviors from which to select. Carley (1991) proposed that one source of initial variation in groups is the distinct knowledge bases of different group members. Group members may draw on their experiences with other groups to identify potentially successful routines. If group members have very similar backgrounds, however, they may agree very quickly on what to do and how, using consensus as an indicator that they have chosen the "correct" script for the situation (Bettenhausen & Murnighan, 1985). Research in group decision making indicates that when all members agree on an alternative, the group will select it, regardless of whether the answer is correct or even plausible given the available evidence (Laughlin et al., 1991).

Given adequate variation, a forgiving environment can weaken selection (the second element of undirected adaptation) because even though some outcomes are better than others, they may all be satisfactory to the group. A sports team with much better natural athletes than any other team in the league, for example, may consistently win games regardless of its strategy. With a poor strategy, the team may win by a smaller margin, but this may not make much of an impression on the group.

Even when there is adequate variation and meaningful differences in outcomes for the group, groups may select for change on variables that are unrelated to the outcomes, a different kind of selection failure. Group members may select and stabilize irrelevant collective behaviors or structural features. The particular configuration of selection procedures used by the human relations group in a highly successful recruiting year, for example, may become enshrined as part of this group's culture, even if the actual causes of success had more to do with an unusually good pool of candidates, which in turn was related to regional economic conditions.

Even when variation and selection are operating effectively, and group members correctly attribute good outcomes to relevant variables, they may be unable to stabilize these variables into "constants." For example, recruiting bonuses may prove very effective, but the human relations group leader may fail to convince management to provide the funds on a regular basis. A particular sequence of difficult plays may be very successful for a sports team but hard to reproduce because it requires several players to perform simultaneously at the edge of their abilities.

Barriers to Directed Adaptation

Barriers to improved fitness via directed adaptation are (a) errors in the group's collective conception of the fitness landscape, (b) inability to resolve disagreements about how to proceed, (c) trouble keeping group members on track during a temporary worsening of outcomes, and (d) entrenched routines that have become stabilized as part of the group culture.

The first problem occurs when group members agree on a faulty map of the fitness landscape, a failure of collective information processing. Drawing on past experience in either their current group or other groups, members may believe that a particular change in the group will improve outcomes when in fact this is not so. Changes in the embedding system may have changed the fitness landscape, or members may be generalizing from their experiences in groups that operated in a different environment and thus had a different fitness landscape. Members may be unable to resolve differences of opinion about features of the fitness landscape for their own group. Members may also base their model of the fitness landscape on the experience of groups they have observed or read about. Observational learning can provide very useful information about the likely outcomes of different variations in the structure and functioning of a group's coordination network. Once again, however, group members may fail to note and adjust for differences in group type or operating conditions and overgeneralize from what they have observed. Outside consultants may make the same error, advising a group to imitate approaches that worked for some other group or set of groups that actually had very different fitness landscapes.

Given a reasonably accurate map of the fitness landscape, a group may be unable to proceed because members cannot agree about how the group should change. Such disagreements may reflect more pervasive power struggles in the group. Because members differ in what they contribute to the group and what they get out of the group, different action plans will affect member outcomes differently. Although the ultimate improvement in group outcomes could benefit all members, members may disagree about how these projected benefits will be distributed. Consensus may also be difficult when the map of the fitness landscape reveals many different options for improvement and the group members are uncertain about how to choose among them. Paradoxically, a fitness landscape that offers relatively few good outcomes (a small number of peaks) may prove easier to adapt to than a rugged landscape that offers relatively abundant opportunities (numerous peaks).

The third problem—trouble staying the course—arises when an overall strategy for change requires short-term losses and poorer fitness. Under these circumstances, group members need to resist the cues that govern undirected adaptation—feedback about how the group is doing right now—to maintain the process of change. Under pressure from outsiders unhappy with a decrease in performance, members may revert to previous patterns. One meta-strategy for overcoming this barrier is to signal to outsiders that the group is in a transition and ask for patience. Newly hired coaches of sports teams often declare that it is "a rebuilding year." If successful, this may persuade outsiders to withhold "punishment," temporarily altering the fitness landscape to make the transition easier and less painful. If the costs of transition are imposed not by the immediate embedding context but by a distal environment, however, no such negotiation is possible. Leadership is important to keep the group focused on the long-term benefits and to ensure that members stay the course.

The final problem mentioned also arises from a mismatch between the forces of directed and undirected adaptation. The logic of undirected adaptation implies that the behavior of successful groups will tend to become more routinized and less variable (Carley, 1991; Miller & Friesen, 1980; Tushman & Romanelli, 1985). Even without pressure from the outside to revert to the patterns of the past, habitual routines are simply easier to perform than new behaviors (Gersick & Hackman, 1990), possibly because they rely primarily on automatic processing, which requires less effort than consciously controlled action (Shiffrin & Schneider, 1977). If the group is implementing its plan at a time when members feel the group's survival is threatened, the threat-rigidity effect (Harrison & Connors, 1984; Staw, Sandelands, & Dutton, 1981) may also make it especially hard for members to let go of familiar structures and routines because they are comforting and/or low cost.

Because of these barriers, directed adaptation is easier to achieve when some change in the embedding context has either knocked the group out of its normal routines or rendered its normal routines inoperable. Adaptation plans that go against the local dynamics of the group will otherwise be hard to execute because the forces in the fitness landscape and the configuration of attractors that govern internal dynamics are at odds with one another. The next section looks at this conflict of forces in more detail.

∞ INTERNAL FACTORS THAT AFFECT ADAPTATION

Global Dynamics and Adaptation:
The Role of Attractors

As discussed in Chapter 6, attractors are either single states or series of states that the global variables of a system tend to settle into over time as a result of the local dynamics and global dynamics of the system. If we think of consensus and conflict management, for example, the local dynamics of some groups characteristically drive the group quickly toward consensus. Consensus is a point attractor for these groups. In other groups, the interactions among members generate a dialectic in which they come to a tentative agreement, then discover new points of difference, then work toward convergence again before conflict becomes extreme, and so on. In these groups, the attractor is a periodic cycle. In other groups, the relational dynamics are such that disagreements either resolve quickly into consensus or split the group into warring factions. For these groups, there are two point attractors; which of these a particular group discussion leads to will depend on initial conditions for key local variables when the discussion begins. These might include how far apart group members are in their initial views, how important the issue is for the group, and the degree to which the issue relates to values or interests that differentiate the members of the two opposing subgroups.

If there are multiple attractors, data on group patterns under different initial conditions should reveal where the dividing line is between different *basins of attraction*. These basins are like watersheds. In a two-attractor system, there are two watersheds. For the group that either agrees or splits, the level of agreement will head in a different direction depending on the initial level of agreement, which is itself determined by multiple local variables, as described above. For the group with a single periodic attractor, the group will fall into the dialectically driven cycle of low to moderate agreement regardless of where it starts out on an issue; for such groups, complete consensus and extreme disagreement are both transient states.

The configuration of attractors derived from observations of a group thus indicates what states a group will naturally tend toward on the global variable of interest. Just as the fitness landscape represents the relation between some aspect of the group and its embedding context, a corresponding landscape can be constructed that shows where the attractors are for the global variable(s) of interest. The relation between these two pictures can reveal a great deal about barriers to successful adaptation. Fitness peaks do not necessarily correspond to dynamic attractors. It is easy to imagine, for example, that the "fitness" of protracted internal conflict is poor (yields few rewards from the embedding context), yet the dynamics of a group may make it very easy to get mired in conflict, "trapped" in an attractor that is maladaptive.

Particularly bad matches between the two may be obvious both to group members and outsiders. Yet outside pressure on the group to change may have little impact on these vicious cycles, which can be highly stable because they are constantly reinforced by local-level dynamics. The longer the group has been operating in the same way, the more pronounced these attractors are likely to be, with wider basins and a stronger "pull" on the group. A better understanding of how particular local dynamics give rise to the attractors of global dynamics can help group members alter the configuration of attractors by making local changes in the coordination network. When unsuccessful groups fail to improve, or persistently respond in ways that seem to undermine their chances for survival, a mismatch between internal and external forces may well be the culprit.

Although external rewards and internal dynamics are two conceptually distinct forces, conditions in the environment do affect the configuration of attractors via the operation of what we call *contextual parameters* (the control parameters of dynamical systems theory). The values of these variables are typically strongly influenced by circumstances or by agents outside the group system. For the two-attractor system of consensus or serious conflict, for example, member stress levels may affect the critical point that separates the basin of consensus from that of high conflict, by weakening the local dynamics of member support and conformity that maintain the consensus attractor while strengthening the friction between subgroups that maintains the attractor of high divisive conflict. When group members are under a great deal of stress, the consensus attractor may vanish altogether. Collective member stress, which is influenced by many factors in the embedding systems of both the group and the individual members, is thus a contextual parameter.

A change in the embedding context of a group can thus change *both* the fitness landscape and, by adjusting a contextual parameter that governs global dynamics, the configuration of attractors. To gain a better understanding of why groups show such a variety of response to change, we need to keep both landscapes in mind. Without a knowledge of the global dynamics of the group system discussed in the preceding chapter, the effects of environmental change on a group may be very difficult to interpret.

The State of the Group

In this section, we consider the state of the group at the time a change in context occurs or when the group system is directly altered by an external intervention. First, we discuss how past history affects a group's response to change. Then we discuss the impact of a group's current structure and set of routines. Finally, we discuss how the shadow of the future affects adaptation.

The Legacy of the Past

A group's response to change depends in part on the nature of the coordination network, including how tight or loose different types of coordination are and how dense the ties are. This is affected by how long a group has been in existence and under what circumstances. Routines and strategies that have been consistently successful will be quite tenacious, whereas group members will be less attached to behavior patterns that are associated with a mixed record. Groups that have had to cope with failures and problems in the past are also likely to have a wider repertoire of possible responses and may be more open to creative restructuring.

A group's past affects how members interpret current changes in the environment. Past experience with change creates a group script for change that may be overgeneralized. Thus, a group may respond to a new set of changes in ways that would have been ideal for past challenges but are inappropriate for the current situation. Enacting a script that has already been used at least once is always easier than creating a new script, even when the existing scripts are inappropriate. If a group has adapted in the past to many different types of events, it will have a wider repertoire of possible scripts available. The individual experience that members bring from other groups forms the basis for developing group scripts but is often not an adequate substitute for shared experience in the particular group in question.

Differential response to change can be apparent even in the very early stages of a group's time together. When a group forms, member expectations about change and stability can affect a group's openness to adjusting to changes in membership, tasks, and technology. Membership change, for example, should be more difficult for groups whose members expect the group composition to be constant than for groups in which members expect a certain amount of membership change (Hill & Gruner, 1973; Ziller, 1965). We can extend this notion to expectations of change and stability in other features of the group as well—projects, technology, and the type of demands made on the group by its members and its embedding systems.

The longer the group has been together (whether membership is stable or variable), the more complex the coordination network will be, provided the group has been operating as an open system, in active interchange with its environment. In groups with densely interconnected networks, the redundancy of links makes it possible to change a routine by simply rerouting the chain of activities that make up the routine, rather than by changing the network of relations. The type of experience group members have had together will also affect the degree of path multiplicity, the ability to reach the same goal in different ways.

Groups that operate for a long time in very stable conditions may lose complexity and flexibility over time, as the existing structure and routines are constantly reinforced and reenacted. This corresponds to global variables that have settled into single stable attractors. As activity becomes more and more routine, the density of ties in the network decreases. A group that has had to cope with more change in the past is likely to retain more flexibility, more links in the network, and a looser coordination among elements, with a more complex attractor space and a less rigid pattern of action.

Early, consistent success may have the paradoxical effect of making a group less able to adapt to change and less sensitive to the need to make adjustments. Tight coordination makes group behavior and routines more consistent, which is good for efficiency in stable conditions. However, changing components that are more loosely coordinated has fewer reverberating impacts than changing components that have been tightly coordinated. Tight coordination can result from extensive fine-tuning of successful routines or from careful planning, selection, and training in the construction of concocted groups. Whatever the source, tight coordination can make it harder for a group to change unless the needed changes are part of the group's established, planned, and practiced repertoire.

In Chapter 4, we noted that groups are formed by some combination of external and internal forces and vary in the degree to which their structure is planned or emergent. The relative importance of different member needs, a group's temporal boundaries, and the preexisting pattern of ties among group elements also shapes a group's priorities and structure. Members of groups formed primarily by external forces are likely to be more attentive to changes that occur in the external context than members of groups formed primarily by internal forces. Members of groups formed primarily by the activities of members are apt to be more responsive to changes at the member-group interchange.

Groups whose structure is based on a detailed plan are likely to respond quickly to changes that were anticipated by the plan. When operating conditions change in ways not addressed by the design of the group, however, members may initially fail to respond. If the group's architects were outsiders, the group may seek their assistance and advice. If the group was founded, members are likely to expect founders, or other leaders, to generate a plan to address the new circumstances. Either way, these groups are likely to rely more on directed than undirected adaptation.

In contrast, members of groups whose structure emerged via self-organization have more experience in the process of forming and adjusting ties to create a coordinated network. That is how they created the group to begin with. Undirected adaptation is likely to play a greater role in these groups than planned strategies for change.

Current Structures and States:
Position in the Landscape

If we think of a change in context as a change in the fitness landscape and an intervention in the group as a shifting of the group's position in this landscape, it becomes clearer how a small change can have big effects, depending on the configuration of the landscape and where the group stands. A small step off a "cliff" in a rugged fitness landscape will harm a group's outcomes just as effectively as a big step off that cliff.

However, a big change in global variables will have little practical impact if it moves the group from one place to another across a broad plateau in a relatively smooth fitness landscape.

Changes also interact with the landscape of attractors for a group. Take, for example, a group that has several members who have been performing poorly. The group may be actively working to resocialize these members to improve their performance. Following the group socialization model (Moreland & Levine, 1982, 1988), these members have become marginal and will either be resocialized into full membership or be pushed out and become ex-members. Resocialization drains time and energy from group members. If the overall pool of potential new members becomes more favorable, the cost-benefit ratio may shift sufficiently that established members abruptly cut the marginal members loose and turn their attention to recruiting replacements. The dynamical system interpretation is that the change in favorability of the pool of potential members shifted the group toward the basin of attraction leading to member exit and away from resocialization. Because the group was on (or near) the edge separating those two attractor basins, the change set it on a different path.

A change that moves a group across the boundary from one basin of attraction to another can have a major impact, whereas changes of any size that move a group around within the same basin will have less impact because the group will end up at the same attractor. For groups in which all members were performing satisfactorily, for example, a change in the pool of potential new members would have no apparent effect. These groups would be solidly in the maintenance mode (Moreland & Levine, 1988) and thus in a stable state.

Group Types

In general, group members will be more open to adjusting elements and ties that are less central to the group's purpose. For *teams*, changes in projects and associated tasks are expected and normal. Changes in membership, however, are harder for teams to handle than for task forces and crews because the social network of the group is more elaborate.

Major changes in membership can completely disrupt a team's operations. Thus, changes in membership call for more dramatic responses than changes in projects or tools. At the same time, the richness of the

membership system in teams also means that teams have more resources for coping with the loss of a member or the socialization of a
rookie—whether anticipated or not—than do task forces, clubs, or
crews (Arrow & McGrath, 1995). Teams will also resist changes in their
norms for interacting and in member roles, for these become part of the
group's culture and identity. Adjustments based on new projects, however, can often be handled by simply using the existing coordination
network in a different way, without any need for "rewiring" the network. Different combinations of members and tools may be used to
complete a new project, but the ties involved are already in place.

Task forces may be quite amenable to change in their tools and procedures, for they have typically not invested much time and effort in developing the job and role networks. If one set of tools fails, the group
will seek out another set and continue its work. The particular members of a task force are less important to the group than are the members
of a team. A task force may weather minor changes in membership easily, yet be thrown off track by more substantial changes. The most dam-
aging type of change for task forces is not changes in membership but
alterations of the group's project or changes in the time line that task
forces use to pace their work (Gersick, 1988, 1989).

Crews have a carefully articulated job network that links tasks and
technology, and members fit into "slots" within this system. Crews are
relatively insensitive to changes in members, provided the new members fit into the proper slots. A last-minute substitution of one bar-
tender for another, for example, is unlikely to harm performance in a
catering crew (although it may affect member-member relations, depending on preexisting friendship ties). Because the members are
trained to fit the job network and rely on planned procedures, their coordination network often has the least overall flexibility of any of the
group types. Thus, changes that render known procedures impossible
to execute (such as the breakdown of key equipment) are the most difficult for crews to handle.

In *clubs*, changes that threaten member access to resources are the
most disruptive, for this is what drew the members together in the first
place. Changes in the allocation of divisible resources to members are
also likely to be sensitive. In clubs, member needs are closely aligned
with group goals, and club tasks are instrumental to satisfying member
needs. So the role network and division of labor are usually quite flexible. Departure of members and their replacement by new members will

also be relatively easy to handle as long as the club maintains the minimum number of members required to ensure that club goods continue to be provided. This contrasts with more project-centered groups, such as concocted teams and task forces, in which the satisfaction of member needs may be viewed as primarily instrumental to completing tasks.

Group Type, Change Models, and the Shadow of the Future

Just as adaptation is affected by the past and current state of the group, so is it affected by how long members expect the group to stay together. The temporal horizon of the group depends in part on the type of group. Group type is also related to which of the models discussed in Chapter 6—robust equilibrium, punctuated equilibrium, life cycle, or adaptive matching—are most likely to characterize the pattern of group development.

Teams, which have either an extended or an indefinite lifetime, have the longest time horizon, so team members should be more willing to undertake ambitious plans for directed adaptation. If the change is successful in improving fitness, members stand to benefit for an extended period. When teams are characterized by both long-term and intensive involvement by their members, members are likely to identify strongly with these groups, especially after the group has been together for a while (McCollom, 1995b). High commitment to the group should cause members to take the team's successes and failures more personally than they do in groups in which members have weaker commitment, and this should increase motivation to attain and maintain a high level of fitness.

Teams are the group type whose task and socioemotional activities are most likely to follow some version of the life cycle model described in Chapter 6, with a series of developmental stages (see Arrow, 1997; McCollom, 1995b; Mennecke et al., 1992, for reviews). Most stage theories of group development presume a relatively constant environment and thus do not address the issue of adaptation. However, it seems likely that groups following these stages would be more internally focused during the early stages and (for groups at the end of their life course) the termination stage and more responsive to the environment during the stage that is focused on production or performing

(LaCoursiere, 1980; Mills, 1964; Tuckman & Jensen, 1977). (Note that this is the opposite of what is expected for task forces in the punctuated equilibrium model, as discussed later in this section.) For teams whose main activity is socioemotional instead of productive, the emotional climate stage models (e.g., Bennis & Shepard, 1956; Dunphy, 1968) suggest a continuously internalized focus, with little attention paid to the environment. The dynamic contingency model (McCollom, 1995b), a developmental model that incorporates environmental forces as a continuous influence, seems to emphasize gradual undirected adaptation over the planned, strategic changes of directed adaptation. It seems most likely to us, however, that both undirected and directed adaptation operate in teams, although the relative balance between them may vary over the lifetime of the group.

For task forces, the temporal structure is keyed explicitly to the completion of the focal project, and Gersick (1988, 1989) has shown how members of such groups use deadlines to pace their collective work. Groups that fit this prototype best are likely to follow the punctuated equilibrium pattern, with extended periods of work separated by sharp transitions. Gersick proposed that members of task forces are relatively inattentive to the embedding context during the equilibrium phases but that they actively seek information from the environment during the transition, when the group reorients itself to the demands of its environment. (Note that this contrasts with expectations for teams in the life course model, as discussed earlier.) This pattern suggests that during the transition, directed adaptation processes are activated, and the group takes decisive action to move to a better location in the fitness landscape, after which the new set of routines is stabilized. Task forces whose members are contemplating a change in direction or structure should be most concerned about the impact of a change on the group's ability to meet deadlines. Thus, the closer the group is to finishing the task, the more members should resist major changes, even if these would improve the final product and improve group rewards.

The temporal horizon for crews is generally linked to a set time period and a series of tasks. Unlike task forces, however, crews often respond to extended delays by disbanding before their job is done. The next crew takes over where they left off. In some cases, this is mandated by external regulations that limit the time that members of some crew (such as pilots or train engineers) can be on the job. Because crews can generally be replaced with new crews trained to complete the exact same set of tasks, there is less pressure than there is in task forces to finish the job no matter what. The developmental models that crews are likely to fit best are either the robust equilibrium pattern of initial fluctuation followed by stability or the multiple-switching pattern of the adaptive response model. Which of these holds in a given case may depend on how frequently there are major changes in external conditions.

Robust equilibrium occurs early in the life of crews, as the crew members "tune" the structure of their group before beginning work. This formation period is described for a cockpit crew by Ginnett (1990). He suggested that the crew members together import a shared "shell" of structure and procedures and that in the most effective crews, the leader affirms and adjusts this shell at the outset of the group. If circumstances in the embedding context change during the crew's time together, the leader of a good crew will draw on the available repertoire of procedures and adjust the group's activity accordingly. If global variables relevant to the change were plotted, the plot would appear as a smoothly coordinated jump from the high point that had just vanished from the fitness landscape to the new high point that had just appeared. If the change in the environment does not fit the crew's practiced set of routines, however, the group may either not change at all (robust equilibrium pattern) or switch to an alternate pattern that does not match the contours of the altered fitness landscape.

Clubs, like teams, may have an extended lifetime. Members of social clubs, like those of teams, are often strongly attached to their group. Members of activity and economic clubs, however, are less likely to identify strongly with the group, as they are primarily concerned with access to the activities of the club or to the economic benefits that membership confers. If alternative groups offer better benefits, members may be difficult to retain because individual interests are typically more salient that the needs of the group itself. We expect that such clubs will follow the robust equilibrium pattern of change, adjusting to the environment and to member needs when they are formed but resisting change thereafter. If the environment changes in a way that improves member outcomes, the club is likely to continue its current course of action, although it may attract more members. If changes in the environment or an outside intervention degrade member benefits or access to activities, the club is likely to dissolve as members bail out and join other clubs instead.

For example, a group of previously unacquainted single adults who decide to share a house typically join forces because this fulfills individual needs for affordable rent, not to achieve collective goals. If the embedding context for members or for the household changes in a way that makes individual outcomes less appealing, members of this economic club are likely to seek individual remedies by either renegotiating their share of the costs and resources or leaving the group—unless, of course, the club has evolved to emphasize social connections among housemates who want to stay together to preserve these bonds.

In self-organized groups in which social connections are primary, we expect patterns of adaptation to resemble those of teams, although undirected adaptation should play a stronger role than directed adaptation. Life cycle models, particularly those that emphasize emotional climate as a key global variable, should be most useful for understanding patterns of change in these groups. Adaptation to the environment should be based on how that threatens or enhances bonds among the members, and maintaining the group as a social unit should take priority. Attention to member needs should be regularly adjusted in response to the needs of members, which should fluctuate according to the events in their broader environment. When a member's spouse dies or child is ill, other members may be quite willing to set aside their claims on the group for a time to ensure that the more pressing needs of the member in crisis are met. The expectation, of course, is that the group would do the same if any member was in crisis, an expectation that is grounded in long-term commitment to the group.

Although the four models and the six group types make it easier to think about the great variety of patterns in existing groups, it is important to note that actual groups may be similar to more than one group prototype and that any given group may exemplify different group types in a temporally nested pattern. A subset of team members may form a task force for a particular project or may operate as a crew. The change models that describe one set of global variables for a group will not necessarily generalize to other variables, so the matching of different group prototypes to different change models should be taken as a proposition about overall tendencies. Global variables indexing performance quality, for example, will not necessarily show the same pattern of adaptation as global variables indexing emotional climate or interactions between leaders and followers (McCollom, 1995b). A group has multiple fitness landscapes to negotiate, not only because it is embedded in multiple contexts but because the fitness landscape for one aspect of group functioning may be different from the fitness landscape for another aspect of group life.

∞ DIMENSIONS OF CHANGE

Groups do not respond to change as a generic event. Different kinds of change have different meanings to group members and different implications for group coordination and development. The same event can evoke different responses from different groups or from the same group at different times. What group members respond to is the event in context as they interpret it in light of the group's and their own objectives and priorities. Thus, the "same" event (an earthquake, unexpected success, departure of a leader) will be interpreted differently by members of different groups—and often by members of the same group as well. The "same" event at different times is also different because the group and the context will have changed. The response to a second earthquake will depend on a group's experience with the first earthquake, and the meaning of an unexpected success will be different if the group has a pattern of failure than if it has a checkered history of ups and downs.

The focus of this section, however, is not on the differences supplied by the group but on differences in the change events themselves. Big earthquakes and earthquakes that come close together are objectively different from small earthquakes spaced far apart. The planned departure of a team leader is different from the unexpected removal of multiple members after a hostile takeover radically changes the organizational context for a team. We discuss aspects of change that should affect a group's response under three general categories. The first includes attributes of single events that affect how disruptive a change is: location, magnitude, and valence. The second includes temporal features of both single events and series of events. The third includes two features that affect the degree of uncertainty an event entails: how predictable and how controllable it is.

Features of Single Events:
Location, Magnitude,
and Valence

Change events vary in how much and how directly they perturb a group's normal functioning. One dimension that affects this is the *location* of the change. Some changes occur "out there" in the environment beyond the group boundary, changing the fitness landscape without directly altering the group structure or routines. Other events emanating from the embedding context directly alter important features of the group. For a blues band, for example, the failure of a local club where they play frequently or the opening of a new blues club would be an example of the first type of change. Examples of more direct disruptions would be if a talent scout persuaded the bassist to quit the group and move to Los Angeles or if a flash flood carried off the band's van. For a sports team, examples of nonintrusive and directly intrusive events might be an improvement in attendance at games or the expansion of the league (nonintrusive) and a change in eligibility rules that would mean that some members of the team could not play (intrusive).

Events also differ in magnitude and valence. The closure of a club where the band plays once a month is less extreme than the loss of a club where the band plays twice a week, although both are negative (decreasing rewards or increasing costs for the group). A small increase in revenue changes a group's options less than a large increase in revenue, but in this case, both are positive events.

These three dimensions matter because they all affect the likelihood that a group will make adjustments in response. Changes that directly disrupt the group make normal operations impossible, so the group has to adjust in some way, whereas changes in the embedding context that do not directly alter elements of the group can be ignored (whether or not this is wise). Smaller changes are less likely to trigger a response, both because the impact is smaller and because the change is less likely to be noticed. A series of relatively small changes may add up to a big change, but a big event is more likely to grab the attention of group members.

Research on perceptual processes shows that when the magnitude of change in a stimulus (such as heat) falls below a certain threshold, the perceptual system does not register a change. If no change is perceived, no response will occur. The same principle applies to groups, whose model of the environment depends on the perceptions of its members. If a change in costs and rewards is too slight to be noticed, than neither directed nor undirected adaptation can operate on the group's repertoire of routines.

If a group is functioning reasonably well, positive changes are less likely to trigger a response than negative changes, which may threaten maintenance of the current, satisfactory state. This fits the logic of undirected adaptation. If circumstances improve without the group's making any changes, then what is being rewarded and reinforced is the status quo. This prediction of greater sensitivity to negative events is also in line with theory and research in ecological psychology, which proposes that people are more sensitive to negative information that might indicate a threat than they are to positive information (Hansen & Hansen, 1988; McArthur & Baron, 1983).

Temporal Features: Abruptness of Onset, Rate, Frequency, and Patterning

Whether positive or negative, the onset and rate of change can range along a continuum from gradual to sudden and from slow to fast. Changes can be frequent and regular, frequent and irregular, or rare. Cycles of change may vary in periodicity from decades-long business cycles to weekly, daily or even shorter ones. The abrupt loss of multiple members poses a different challenge to a group than having the same number of members transferred or removed one by one over a longer period. A group's ability to adapt to change will be affected by the rate and frequency of change, especia lly if the group is reacting to rather than anticipating that change.

Adaptation is made easier if these changes are part of a recognizable pattern. Taken together, a series of membership changes can add up to a net gain or a net loss in group size, for example. This would be a *trend*. A series of changes can also even out, either because they change direction in a repeating *cycle* (seasonal changes in sales volume for a sales team would be an example) or because they are generated by a process that is more or less random. We call changes that are unpredictable in magnitude and frequency and have no particular direction over time *fluctuations*. The patterning of change affects the nature and likely success of adaptation, especially when it allows some measure of prediction and control.

Uncertainty, Prediction, and Control

Changes vary in how unexpected they are. Changes that are part of a pattern—a trend or cycle—can be predicted once the pattern is discerned. Other events may be predictable because group members have been informed directly about an impending change in the embedding context. In their analysis of environmental circumstances that cause human stress, McGrath and Beehr (1990) distinguished stress-potential environmental circumstances (SPECs) according to the two factors of predictability and controllability. In general, adaptation is easiest when interventions or other meaningful changes in embedding systems are high on both factors and hardest when SPECs are low on both factors.

A household may be informed months ahead of time that they will not be able to renew their lease when it expires. The nature and timing of the change are not at all mysterious, and the meaning is perfectly clear: The group will need to find a new house or apartment to rent or to buy. Negotiations with the landlord might allow the renters to exercise some control over when they must move. At the other extreme would be an earthquake that renders the house structurally unsound. Once again, the group will need to find a new place to live, but this is a dramatically different change compared to the expiration of a lease because earthquakes are both unpredictable and uncontrollable.

Predictable but uncontrollable events are SPECs whose occurrence cannot be influenced even though the timing is known, sometimes with great precision. Examples relevant to our blues band might be the arrival of New Year's Eve, when bands are in demand and highly paid, or the end of the tourist season, when jobs become scarce. The final, somewhat paradoxical category comprises events that are controllable but not predictable. A community can construct a levee to control future floods without being able to predict when such floods will occur.

The predictability and controllability of events affect the nature of a group's response, our next topic. In particular, they constrain the temporal aspects of a group's response to change.

∞ TYPES AND PATTERNS OF GROUP RESPONSE

In this section, we first discuss the temporal matching of a group's response to changes in embedding context. Next, we discuss responses that may all have the some goal—improving the group's outcomes by changing the values of some global variables—but that exhibit different dynamics. We distinguish between responses that act to restore or preserve the status quo and those that respond to change in ways that transform the group. We close by discussing series of interdependent changes that transform both the group and the embedding system.

Temporal Location of Response

Although linear models of cause and effect suggest a neat sequence of stimulus and response, closely paired in time, adaptation does not necessarily work this way. A group can respond to an outside intervention or other change in the embedding system before, during, or after it occurs. McGrath and Beehr (1990) distinguished between responses to potentially stress-producing events at five temporal locations. Preventive coping is response to an SPEC long before it occurs. Anticipatory coping is response to an SPEC before it occurs. Dynamic coping is response contemporaneous with the stressor. Reactive coping is response after the event. Residual coping is response long after the event.

Because it focuses on stress, the McGrath/Beehr typology presumes that change events are generally negative. We generalize the model here to include positive changes that either improve outcomes directly or open up new opportunities for a group. Instead of preventive coping, a group may instigate a potential positive event by actions long before the event, facilitate a positive event by actions concurrent with it, or exploit the opportunity presented by a positive event after it has occurred.

Preventive action can be taken either to block an event from occurring (if it is controllable) or to mitigate the expected effects (if it is not controllable). This type of response is triggered by foreseeable negative events of moderate to high impact and is especially likely when the onset of these events is unpredictable and sudden. Preventive action need not be efficacious. Especially when a dreaded event typically occurs with low frequency, members may have little basis for evaluating the effectiveness of their actions.

Groups whose members expect to be together long enough to experience a particular stress-producing event are more likely to take preventative action. However, even short-lived groups may take preventive action for events that are unlikely but potentially catastrophic. Designers of concocted groups can build preventive action into groups in the form of standard procedures or prescribed routines. Crews, for example, may have a series of routines intended to ward off or mitigate the effects of undesirable developments in the environment. Although any one crew may be together only for a brief period, many crews are recurrent entities staffed by members from the same pool. Sooner or later, a catastrophic failure of key equipment may befall some crew that is staffing a particular technological system.

Not all developments in the environment, fortunately, have a negative effect on a group. A group may take instigating actions to set in motion a chain of events that will, group members hope, bring about a desirable change. Instead of waiting for favorable opportunities to open up and then responding, groups can attempt to shape events in the embedding system. Breeding animals (or plants) to create a herd (or crop) with particular characteristics would be an example. In effect, instigation encourages an embedding context to adapt to the group.

Anticipatory and facilitating responses are taken when group members notice the early signs that an environmental change or intervention is impending. If the change is negative, anticipatory responses can counteract or cushion the effects. A self-organized task force of bankers designing a new account, for example, arranged to deflect anticipated interference by top management by drafting a letter that would "answer people's questions and let them in on the story—without jeopardizing the team's discretion to plan policy" (Gersick, 1990, p. 119). If the expected change is positive, the group may take action to speed its arrival or to prepare to exploit the benefits. An anticipated increase in resources, for example, can spur group members to make plans for how to use these resources. Of course, a positive event can trigger maladaptive responses as well, such as power struggles among members over how new resources will be allocated. The congressional and presidential pronouncements regarding allocation of anticipated U.S. federal budget surpluses throughout 1999 illustrate this case.

Dynamic responses are those taken to cope with the event or shape the situation as it unfolds. The crew of a sailboat in a race may make constant adjustments to their course as they assess the changing wind and the position of other sailboats in the race. This is dynamic, real-time adaptation. The tight coupling between developments in the environment and the actions of the group make the stimulus-response model inadequate for understanding this type of activity. Instead, it is best thought of as a series of synchronous developments, a recurrent, circular chain of causation in a field that includes the group (Runkel, 1990).

Responses that occur shortly after an outside intervention or change in the environment fit the traditional stimulus-response model of linear causation much better. In a longitudinal study of groups that met for 13 weeks, for example, McGrath and colleagues (McGrath et al., 1993) looked for evidence of reactive group responses to external interventions that altered the groups' communication media and membership composition. They found that groups reallocated their time to spend more time on task when their membership was altered (Arrow & McGrath, 1993) and that groups showed increased conflict in response to the change in medium but decreased conflict in response to membership change (O'Connor et al., 1993). These studies expected and found immediate responses to external interventions. When changes directly disrupt the existing patterns of a group, reactive responses are indeed very likely. However, when the change is less intrusive, the response may be delayed. Residual responses either may be "delayed"—that is, not immediate—or may be later developments that a more immediate reactive response leads to over time. Researchers are less likely to detect the relationship between changes outside and inside the group when the response is residual (Kelly & McGrath, 1988), for two reasons: (a) The response may not even occur within the time period studied, and (b) the longer the time between external and internal events, the more time there is for other factors to influence a group (Campbell & Stanley, 1966).

One study of flight attendant teams documented pervasive residual responses to critical events in two teams' early histories (Cohen & Denison, 1990). These were teams instead of crews because at People Express, flight attendants were organized into long-term groups that always flew together. In one team, an early opportunity to prove themselves on a difficult assignment—starting up a new city station for the airline—led group members to view their embedding system as filled with opportunities. Proactive attempts to take advantage of these opportunities can also be seen as residual responses that became embedded as part of the group's pattern. In the other team, the abrupt firing of a teammate by outsiders after the remaining team members had worked together successfully to help him improve his performance led to a very different pattern. Eight months later, the remaining team members continued to respond to their embedding context through the filter of this discouraging and disempowering event, seeing the environment as lacking in opportunities for advancement.

Whatever the temporal relation of group response to external change or intervention, the response may act to dampen or magnify the impact of the change on the group. Negative feedback loops dampen, and positive feedback loops magnify.

Negative Feedback Loops: Preemption, Buffering, and Repair

Negative feedback loops help maintain a system within a preferred range of states. If the system is pushed away from the preferred range, it returns to the preferred state. As discussed in earlier chapters, shared group norms provide a standard that all members can reference in noticing when norms have been violated. Corrective actions can be taken automatically by members—the undirected path—or members may consult and agree on a collective strategy for action—the directed path.

We classify negative feedback responses as preemptive, buffering, or repair depending on whether they occur before, during, or after the external triggering event or intervention. The bankers' task force described in the previous section took preemptive action to lessen the potential impact of interference by management. This action was triggered by warning signs of heightened attention to the group's work, including frequent phone calls to group members by the bank president (Gersick, 1990). Dynamic buffering responses would include the corrections that a sailboat crew makes to keep the boat on track as the winds and currents shift during a race. Without these corrections, the boat would be pushed or blown off course. Repair responses attempt to restore the group to the status quo ante as much as possible. When the composition of established teams was disrupted by removing one established group member and substituting a guest member (Arrow & McGrath, 1993), some groups simply reassigned the duties of the lost member to the guest member, minimizing the amount of change in the social structure of the group and allowing the group to maintain its habitual routines as much as possible.

Negative feedback responses fit the notion of change as disruption (Hollingshead, McGrath, & O'Connor, 1993). They are most likely when (a) the external event or intervention is seen as negative and (b) group members are satisfied with the current and projected future state of the group. Even apparently positive events that improve the fitness of the group on some dimensions can be treated as negative and counteracted if the group anticipates negative consequences on other dimensions that are more important to group members. In the Western Electric bank-wiring studies, for example (Homans, 1950), incentives for improved performance that management considered positive had no impact on performance because the group regulated member behavior to ensure that the group maintained its usual standard. Because this study was carried out during the Depression, it is reasonable to infer that workers valued having their jobs more highly than earning a bonus, and a possible disastrous consequence of higher productivity could have been layoffs or a sharp increase in production expectations by management.

Some groups have members who take responsibility for buffering the rest of the group to minimize disruption by external events. Sometimes the group leader plays this role, protecting the group from the impact of outsiders. Alternately, a group sentry (Ancona & Caldwell, 1988) may monitor and control the information that enters a group. By restricting or filtering information about outside developments that may disturb the group, the sentry blunts the impact of such events. Ambassadors who provide favorable information about the group to outsiders can also help protect the group from unwanted interventions.

Positive Feedback Loops:
Switching, Disorder,
Innovation, and Collapse

Positive feedback loops magnify the impact of an external event or intervention. Like negative feedback loops, they can be activated before, during, or after the triggering event. Unlike negative feedback loops, the result is not to preserve the current state but to change it, sometimes radically. This section highlights several very different responses that are included in this category.

Vicious cycles are an example of positive feedback loops at work. Such self-reinforcing cycles can also be beneficial, virtuous cycles. The long-term effects of events in the early history of the flight attendant teams, for example, showed the operation of positive feedback loops in both groups. In one case, these loops magnified the impact of a positive event; in the other case, they magnified the impact of a negative event.

Switching is when a group changes, often abruptly, from one coherent, organized structure or set of routines to another. This type of response can occur before, during, or after the external event. Anticipatory switching occurs when a group changes to a different mode on the basis of early warning of an impending change. The change from routine operations to crisis mode by an emergency room crew preparing to receive casualties from a recent disaster would be an example. In this case, the switch occurs before the arrival of the casualties and is designed not to prevent the sudden increase in workload (a negative feedback loop) but to facilitate the hospital's ability to handle as many patients as possible.

The case study of flight attendant teams provided an example of dynamic switching. During an in-flight medical emergency, the team reorganized their division of labor to handle the new situation "with a minimum of conversation; yet eye contact and other nonverbal communication suggested that they had jointly determined this approach" (Cohen & Denison, 1990, p. 388). Reactive switching occurs when there is a time lag between the external event and the response. This may result when the group needs time to interpret the event and classify the new situation as calling for a particular alternate pattern. The flight team, for example, might show reactive switching in response to a developing emergency if the scenario did not fit their past experience and training and thus was not recognized at first as an emergency.

Disorder in response to a disruption counts as positive feedback when the level of disorganization or uncoordinated action goes beyond what is caused directly by the disruptive event. This indicates that the group's response is magnifying the impact of the event. A sports team that almost always wins, for example, may lose unexpectedly when playing a particularly able opponent. If the loss sends a good team into a losing streak, this suggests a loss of their usual coordinated patterns. When a group's patterns of action become destabilized, its behavior becomes less predictable and increased conflict is likely.

When there is extreme destabilization, group behavior becomes unpredictable not only to outsiders but to group members themselves. All apparent coordination is lost, members work at cross-purposes or dissipate their energy in multiple disorganized activities, and confusion reigns. One possible outcome of such instability is collapse; the network of relations that forms the group unravels and the group dissolves. This outcome is discussed in more detail in Chapter 8. Another possible outcome of extreme disorder and destabilization is creative restructuring and innovations in strategy. In this pattern, some triggering event throws the group into a period of confusion, from which it emerges with a transformed structure and set of behaviors. This response is different from switching because it involves a breakdown in existing routines before a new set of behaviors emerges to replace them. Switching is also typically reversible—when the crisis is over, the group reverts to routine operations. Transformed groups, in contrast, remain transformed.

One way to understand the process of creative restructuring in dynamic system terms is by using the model of simulated annealing (Carley & Svoboda, 1996; Kirkpatrick, Gelatt, & Vecchi, 1983), in which the elements of a structure are disrupted from their current state and then settle again into a new state. The physical science analogue of annealing is that of repeatedly heating and cooling a solid until it "freezes" in a good (i.e., low-energy) configuration. If we think of a group as having a structure and a repertoire of expressed behaviors that are a reasonable match to the fitness landscape, then when the fitness landscape changes, the fit is apt to worsen. The trigger of an external event can lead group members to try out alternate responses, attempting to find a new good fit. However, if all group members do this independently, the result may be quite disorganized, as the fit of the group as a whole requires that the activities of members be linked together in a workable coordination network. Eventually, both by chance and by local adjustment of links, group members may hit on a set of coordinated activities that both fit together and have a reasonable fit to the new demands of the environment. Then this structure will need to be stabilized. In some ways, this can be considered a return to processes active during formation, when the group is first developing a coordination structure. Whether such a change is considered a major adaptation of the "same" group or a metamorphosis into a "new" social entity—the topic of the next chapter—is a matter of interpretation by the researcher.

No Response

The simplest response a group can have is no response. A group may fail to respond to a change in the environment for a wide range of reasons. First, the group may be unaware of the external event because members are internally focused and not attending to the outside environment. Other constraints on information flow may also prevent adaptation (Hannan & Freeman, 1977). Selected members of the group may be aware of the event but fail to alert others. The group may also fail to respond because the change does not alter the fitness landscape for outcomes that the group values highly.

A group that has been together a long time with little change may become trapped in a set of mutually reinforcing behaviors and structures (Miller & Friesen, 1980). This corresponds to Hannan and Freeman's (1977) notion of history as a constraint on adaptation at the organizational level. Existing structures are maintained via powerful self-regulatory feedback loops that make it hard for the group to change, even when members are aware of an event in the group's embedding context that makes change desirable. Adaptation is difficult in this case because a whole set of structures and behaviors would have to change simultaneously to prevent the group from sliding right back into the standard pattern.

Even when coordination problems do not make change especially difficult in a practical sense, other political and psychological factors may prevent a group from responding. Hannan and Freeman (1977) proposed that organizations fail to adapt in part because of sunk costs in equipment and personnel. Although small groups are unlikely to accumulate a similar weight of investment, commitment to an established course of action and to other members can cause great reluctance to change, even if the group's current position in the fitness landscape is unfavorable (Staw, 1976). Internal political constraints (Hannan & Freeman, 1977) can prevent adaptation if members believe change would upset the current balance of power and allocation of resources within the group.

What looks like "no response" may also be the result of looking in the wrong place temporally. A group that has anticipated and adjusted to an event in advance may appear to have no response to an observer who looks only at the period right after an event. The same can be true for a delayed response that does not occur until after the time period of observation. Finally, dynamic responding can be difficult to interpret as adaptation if the observer is using the frame of "stimulus, then response" or "independent versus dependent variables," looking for the (dependent) reaction of the group to the (independent) external action. In dynamic responding, the feedback loops that govern action are loops, not unidirectional arrows connecting a sequence of independent and dependent events. It may appear to the observer that the group is simply acting as part of its normal operations, not reacting or responding to external events.

When the actions of a group are interdependent with actions in the embedding context such that events in both are shaped by the other, we call this *coevolution* or *mutual adaptation*—the topic of the next section.

Coevolution as Mutual Adaptation: Coupled Series Over Time

When the immediate embedding systems of groups are themselves complex adaptive systems, groups can develop mutually reinforcing feedback loops with their embedding systems. Systems that are functionally interdependent change together via constant adjustments in both systems. When these feedback loops include changes that are critical to the operation of both systems, they can lead to a mutual adaptation process termed *coevolution* (Goerner, 1994; Kauffman, 1993). In ecosystems, predator-prey systems can get into an arms race in which

improvements in prey defense evoke improvements in predator of-
fense, and vice versa. This type of dialectic can also drive mutual adaptation among groups that compete with one another, either in a formal
game structure (sports teams, for example) or because they are situated
in the same embedding context with fixed resources, such that gains by
one group worsen the fitness landscape for the other groups.

At a meso time scale, groups may adjust their repertoire of actions on
the basis of the outcome of games they play and also games between
other teams that they observe. After one team introduces a successful
new offensive formation, the other teams need to adjust their defensive
strategy. As other teams in the conference adopt the new offensive formation, the team that introduced it will also have to adjust *their* defense
to combat their own innovation. This creates a long-term coevolutionary process. Note that what looks like an "external" event from the
perspective of one team (the innovation by another team) is itself a response to the embedding context of *that* team, which includes the first
group.

Both negative and positive feedback loops govern the dynamics between group and context. When a negative feedback loop is operating,
changes in the group's embedding system are damped out by the group,
so that the impact of a change on the group is weaker than would be expected on the basis of the magnitude of the event in the embedding system. If managers make demands that fall heavily on a single group
member, for example, the group may temporarily adjust the division of
labor to cushion this change. Group leaders can also negotiate to
lighten the demands by "pulling strings" (we can think of these strings
as links between group and embedding system) or decrease its contribution to the embedding system on other tasks.

When a positive feedback loop is operating, changes in the embedding system can be exaggerated and magnified by the group response,
which triggers a further response from the organization, and so on.
When interconnections between group and embedding system are
dense, conflicts can spiral quickly out of control. This dynamic can
also lead to a spiral of beneficial changes. A new incentive system can
inspire a big increase in production, which brings extra bonuses to the
group, which inspires further improvements. Whether the group
dampens or magnifies change depends both on the state of the group
and on the joint history of the group and its embedding system. What

makes this a coevolutionary cycle is that the actions of both group and actors in the embedding context are linked to one another. This contrasts with adaptation in response to events in a more distal context (such as the economy) that is either unaffected by the actions of the group or so remotely and trivially affected that mutual entrainment cannot occur.

∞ FOUR PRINCIPLES OF ADAPTATION

Knowledge about the nature of a change in context—including its magnitude, predictability, and so on—is insufficient to predict with any confidence how a group will respond. We also need to know the nature and current state of the group, the configuration of attractors that govern its internal dynamics, and how the imprint of the past affects group members' collective interpretation of the event and its likely effect on the group. Groups respond differently to the same event. Sometimes that response precedes the event, sometimes it follows it, and sometimes action at the group-context interchange changes them both simultaneously. What is common to all groups is the desire of members to attain and maintain preferred states; the interchange between group and context that makes some activities and strategies more rewarding than others; and the internal dynamics that determine which states are easy to maintain and hard to change, which states are accessible but hard to stabilize, and which are nonplausible for a group. To conclude this chapter, we propose four principles that highlight the paradoxical nature of adaptation.

The Principle of Nonproportionality

Groups do not follow Newton's third law of motion: Events in a group's environment do *not* result reliably in equal and opposite reactions. Large events may inspire minor adjustments or no response at all (at any temporal location), and apparently tiny events may trigger dramatic change. The relation, in other words, is nonlinear.

The Principle of Unintended Consequences

Adaptation is an uncertain affair. Groups are complex adaptive systems whose members are complex adaptive systems. They are also embedded in multiple systems that are themselves complex. When complex systems interact, modeling one another's behavior, neither will predict the other's behavior with perfect accuracy. Changes that have unanticipated (or anticipated but unintended) side effects can provoke further adaptive changes, which may in turn have a range of consequences, some foreseeable and some not. In this way, the principle of unintended consequences can lead to chains of successive adjustments in group elements, network structure, and patterns of coordination.

The Principle of Temporal Displacement

Directed adaptation is based on the ability of groups to create models of their embedding systems, set goals, and anticipate the future. Directed adaptation allows for responses that make no sense on the basis of the current configuration of the fitness landscape. Group members may agree on a plan that is based on a model of what the fitness landscape is projected to look like in the future.

In this way, directed adaptation can twist temporal sequence around like a Mobius strip so that groups appear to respond to events before they happen. Groups may also respond to events that never happen except in their faulty model of the future. Of course, all models of the future are faulty (see previous principle!).

The Principle of Spontaneous Innovation

The patterning in time of group behavior displays regularities that are both an expression of and a precondition for coordinated action. The range of *possible* behaviors for a group, however, is vast. Members are only partially embedded within any one group. They all belong to other groups and have a range of experiences and are familiar with many possibilities that a particular group may never have explored.

Members themselves only express a subset of possible behaviors within the context of a particular group. The range will be wider in long-standing, highly involving groups such as families and much narrower in more constrained settings such as short-lived crews or task forces.

When a group changes, a new structure and set of routines may seem to appear out of nowhere if one thinks of a group as a closed system. Groups are open systems, however, and their members, who are themselves open systems, are a rich source of new ideas and unexpected behavior. They can spontaneously "recruit" new activities that were not previously apparent in the group's behavior (Kelso, 1995).

CONCLUDING COMMENTS

As this chapter as a whole and the principles in particular make clear, the variety of adaptive behavior in any particular group is vast. Among the many responses possible, one that we did not discuss at length was the termination of the group as a distinct entity. The extrinsic dynamics of adaptation are not always the cause of termination, however. The following chapter discusses the many ways in which groups disband. It also covers transitions in which a group undergoes such dramatic changes that its members no longer consider themselves members of the same group, even though some continuity links the old group to the new.

8

Metamorphosis

Endings and Transformations

Some groups are ephemeral creations that form, operate briefly, and then disband. Other groups are expected to last indefinitely, with new members replenishing the group as established members are expelled, resign, or die. Many of these groups also dissolve eventually. Some groups are created, expire, and are resurrected in cycles. Some groups go through a long decline before disbanding, whereas others cease operations while operating at their peak. The first section of this chapter discusses some characteristic patterns of death and transformation and identifies underlying dimensions that help distinguish, for example, between dissolution and collapse, expiration and completion as ways that groups come to an end. We then turn to a detailed exploration of the dynamics underlying these varied patterns of metamorphosis.

Chapter 4, the first chapter in Part II of this book, discussed the emergence of a new group as a coherent, functionally coordinated set of links among people, tasks, and tools. This final chapter of Part II discusses the disappearance of this coordinated set of links or its transformation into a new set of links that is different enough that the current members (who may overlap partially or not at all with the prior set of members) perceive it to be a new group. In such cases, ending blends into a new beginning. This is not the only connection between formation and metamorphosis, however. Although ending is not formation in reverse, any more than the process of divorce is a wedding in reverse, endings are sometimes implied in the creation of a group or may result from problems or design characteristics inherent in a group's initial structure. Relations between formation and metamorphosis are discussed in the first section of the chapter.

Chapters 5, 6, and 7 discussed the operations of a group, focusing on three different levels of analysis: the local dynamics of coordination, the global dynamics of development, and the contextual dynamics of adaptation. Continuing the strategy of linking the dynamics of endings to dynamics already described, the next sections discuss (a) coordination breakdowns and other features of local dynamics that contribute to metamorphosis, (b) endings and transformations that occur as part of the global dynamics of development, and (c) metamorphosis as a response to events in the embedding context. These are followed by a section that summarizes typical patterns for the six exemplar group types (teams, task forces, crews, and the three varieties of clubs). We end the chapter with a section on the consequences of decline and impending termination on other processes within small groups.

Relatively little existing theory and research on small group termination is available to guide our theorizing. For many groups, the ending of the group is planned and expected and thus raises few interesting questions. This is certainly true for the majority of groups studied by social psychologists. The duration of groups they study is typically determined by the researchers themselves. Even in extended field studies such as the Robbers Cave (Sherif et al., 1961) or semester-long studies carried out by McGrath and colleagues (McGrath, 1993; McGrath & Arrow, 1996), groups disbanded at a predetermined time—the scheduled end of the summer camp experience or the end of the semester. In the group development literature, Tuckman and Jensen (1977) added adjourning as a final stage to what had previously (Tuckman, 1965) been a four-stage model, but this failed to spark much interest in studying the endings of groups. There has been some interest in endings in other areas of psychology (e.g., Albert & Kessler, 1976; Kramer, 1990; Van Steenberg LaFarge, 1995). Otherwise, our primary source of reading has been in the field of organizational decline and death, which flourished beginning in the late 1970s and early 1980s (see Cameron, Sutton, & Whetten, 1988, for an excellent collection). We draw on that literature plus our own theorizing in earlier chapters to identify four dimensions of metamorphosis that help map out the space of possibilities for endings and transformations.

As noted above, Tuckman and Jensen (1977) added a termination stage ("adjourning") to Tuckman's (1965) previous four-stage theory. Wheelan's (1994) formulation also contains a completion phase, as does Worchel's (1996), and Gersick (1989) also discussed some special features of the ways in which her task forces completed their work. In much of the work exploring stages of group development, though, the focus regarding the final stage has been mainly on the group's completion of a given project rather than on the termination of the group as an intact system. In the case of task forces and of experimental laboratory groups, of course, the end of the project is the end of the group's life course as well. Our concept of metamorphosis of groups is broader in three ways. First, it encompasses both cases where the group simply ends and cases where the group becomes transformed into a new social entity. Second, it deals with cases in which the group's expected life course is not coextensive with its work on a given project as well as cases where they are coincident. Third, we focus on aspects of the group beyond its work on the tasks at hand. So although metamorphosis overlaps with the final phases of all the schemas cited above, it is not the same as any one of them.

∞ DIMENSIONS OF METAMORPHOSIS

Metamorphosis differs along four dimensions we consider important: (a) the speed with which metamorphosis occurs, (b) the proportion of links in the group coordination network that persist after the group has dissolved or transformed itself into a new entity, (c) the degree to which a termination or transformation is planned or emergent, and (d) the relative contribution of internal and external forces in triggering the end of the group. The first two dimensions are basically descriptive. The third and fourth dimensions, which focus on the forces underlying metamorphosis, are the same sets of forces that were important in defining the general categories of concocted, founded, self-organized, and circumstantial groups set out in Chapter 4 on formation. The first and fourth dimensions have been important in theorizing about organizational decline and death.

Speed and Abruptness of Metamorphosis

Endings and transformations differ in how gradually or abruptly they occur. A group may slowly dissolve as contacts among members become less frequent and members put less energy into the group. Or a group may abruptly cease to exist. A task force, for example, may be working at full capacity one day and be canceled by someone in the organizational hierarchy the next day. Endings that are sudden and unexpected are often linked, as this example suggests, with an abrupt loss of resources necessary for the group to function. Loss of a critical member can also precipitate the end of a group if the remaining members decide it is not worth the effort to find a replacement and no current members are able or willing to take on the duties of the departed member. For example, Butterworth (1990) described a long-standing string quartet that decided to disband after one of its members moved away. Loss of a key project may also trigger a precipitate ending. More positively, the success of a group may put it out of business, as might be true for problem-solving groups who complete their task successfully. In such groups, the timing of completion may be unknown in advance, but group members will anticipate the end of the group as they see the project come to completion. Of course, such groups may decide not to disband on achieving success and may instead cast about for another project to tackle.

Transformations that take place more gradually are more likely to be keyed to developmental processes in the group or to gradual changes at the member-group and group-context interfaces. As noted in the previous section, members in a voluntary group may gradually decrease their commitment, or the context in which the group operates may become gradually less favorable. In this case, a period of decline precedes termination.

The smoothness or abruptness of the transition, of course, depends on the scale of measurement. A reasonable yardstick for scaling this dimension would be the length of time a group has been together. Another way to measure abruptness might be to compare the rate of transformation with the normal rate of change in the group based on developmental or adaptive mechanisms. Member and nonmember subjective assessment of the rate of change is yet another indicator of the rate of change relative to what is normal for the group.

Degree of Dissolution in the Coordination Network

Some groups dissolve more or less completely as the coordination network that constitutes the group system unravels or is dismantled into disconnected elements. Other groups do not cease to exist but instead undergo transformations of sufficient scope that the members perceive that the new group is not the "same" group. The distinction may be marked by referring to the "old" versus the "new" group, by a new formal name for the group, or by some other marker to indicate a new identity. A sports team may be sold and moved to another city, for example, acquiring a different name, venue, and coach in the process. In some respects, the reconstituted team is the same team; in other respects, it is a new team. A group can also take on a different purpose and redefine what the group is and does, while keeping much of the same membership.

Transformations to a "new" group with a new identity are often associated, however, with a change in membership. Both continuity of links and change of membership occur when an existing group divides into several new groups, either as the result of growth and expansion or due to a conflict that splinters the group. A new group formed by merging two or more smaller groups is another example of membership change defining a transformation.

A high rate of change in membership can lead to a breakdown in transmitting the technology of norms and shared procedures and the content of collective memory that define the culture of the group. The general boundaries and function of the group may remain the same, at least from the perspective of nonmembers. But when the amount of membership change and corollary change in the labor (member-task), role (member-tool), and social (member-member) networks overwhelm members' ability to anticipate and coordinate behavior, the defining structure and identity of a group may not survive. In effect, a new group—new members but also new member, role, and labor net-works—must be formed to fulfill the functions of the earlier group.

Links may also survive without being incorporated immediately—or ever—into a new group. Groups whose members are drawn from a common context may cease operation as a group while many of the links that members developed in the group survive. These links may later be revived in a new group context. Employees who serve on a committee, for example, may develop a style of working together that carries over into other dimensions of the job after the committee completes its work or stops meeting for some other reason. If several members of the committee find themselves on another task force together in the future, they may reactivate the norms and strategies developed from their prior committee work. Thus, the new task force will import a subset of links from a prior coordination network. In this way, group fragments persist and become reincorporated into new groups, even if no one would see the new group as a "transformed" version of the prior group.

Termination, like formation, is often a process with fuzzy temporal boundaries. This complicates the process of determining the degree of overlap in the set of links that exist "before" and "after" the group comes to an end. Interviews with group members may help to determine at least the general time period during which the group disbanded or when the "old" group was supplanted by the "new" group. Degree of overlap can then be estimated by comparing the roster of elements—members, tools, and tasks—and the main connections between them that existed before and after the group's demise. The task is simpler for groups (such as sports teams with a defined season, or admissions committees that meet yearly for several months) that have fixed endings and reincarnations tied to the end and beginning of seasons or other fixed cycles.

Planning and Emergence

The dimension of planning and emergence captures how routine and expected a group's ending is, from the perspective of both members and outsiders, compared to unexpected endings that just "happen" as a consequence of emergent events. At one extreme are groups that have a fixed duration known to all from the start. Many groups are formed with the expectation that they will dissolve when they reach the end of a cycle that governs the activity of the group—a life cycle, a task cycle, or a time cycle. The crew staffing a particular shift of work, for example, knows the beginning and end point of its work together at the outset. For crews performing critical jobs where fatigue is a concern, the maximum duration of a shift may even be fixed by law. Task forces are expected to dissolve when they finish their project, and the deadline for finishing is often established at the same time as the group. In such cases, the scheduled cessation of work together raises few interesting questions.

At the other extreme of this dimension are groups that disband long before their expected termination and groups that are in principle immortal but that nonetheless cease operations. Groups designed to be temporary may end prematurely, before the expected cycle is complete. In this case, the timing—and sometimes the nature—of the ending is unplanned and unexpected. Other groups are expected to survive indefinitely. Fans hope that major-league sports teams, for example, will continue playing in perpetuity, with new members cycling in and more senior members getting traded away or retiring. The demise of such a group—if we consider this the "same" group season after season—calls out for a closer investigation. If we think of each season's team as a separate group, however, the ending of these groups is keyed to the season for that sport. The U.S. Supreme Court is another group that is designed to persist indefinitely and whose cessation would be quite unexpected. Such endings emerge from developing events in the group and its context, rather than fitting into a preestablished plan for the group.

In the well-populated middle ground between endings scheduled at the outset and endings that take all concerned by surprise are the endings of groups whose expected duration is finite but fuzzy. Some groups extend their existence beyond an expected end point or disband earlier than planned. In other groups, no ending or transformation is planned from the start, but members or architects decide at some later time that the group will be terminated.

In work groups that are heavily dependent on a single embedding context, planning and surprise may coexist. Just as decision makers in a parent company may keep plans to close a plant or other subsidiary secret from some or all members of the affected organization, so actors in an embedding context that controls a group may not inform group members of an impending termination. The reasons why powerful out-

members of an impending termination. The reasons why powerful outsiders choose this approach may be similar to those proposed for secrecy about organizational death—concerns about reduced employee productivity, immediate loss of members, and other negative responses in the period between the announcement and termination (Sutton, 1988). We discuss the validity of these concerns in the section on consequences at the end of this chapter.

Balance of External
and Internal Forces

In the scenario just described, the most obvious impetus for termination is external—the planning takes place independent of member input. However, cancellation scenarios do not preclude a contribution of internal forces in the demise of a group. A group may be disbanded because powerful outsiders such as supervisors or managers perceive that it has become dysfunctional—for example, on the basis of poor performance or pervasive conflict. A high-performance group may also attract negative attention by running afoul of politically powerful actors in the embedding context. This dimension is important because group members may be prone to blame outsiders for a group's impending demise rather than analyzing how the group itself contributed to problems, which might yield ideas for how the group might adapt and survive instead of dying. Internal forces include decay of the coordination network, unresolved conflict among members, loss of interest in the group, reduced contributions by members, or increased demands that the group is unable or unwilling to meet.

Groups may also disband because of changes in the embedding context that affect negotiations at the group-context interchange, the member-group interchange, or both. Consumers of whatever work groups produce may lose interest, or competition for these consumers may increase. Competition for members may also heat up, and more attractive alternatives may lure group members away from the group. In such cases, the inability to retain members or replace departing members may lead to a group's demise.

Determining the relative contribution of external and internal forces to metamorphosis can be difficult. Gradual changes in group structure and embedding context are easy to overlook, as they form the "ground" for the operation of the group. The impact of important developments inside or outside the group may not be felt immediately, and thus they may go unnoticed if causes are presumed to result promptly in effects. Especially when termination is viewed as a failure, group members will not necessarily be motivated by accuracy in fixing targets for blame. They may be prone to look outside the group to find a target (especially a person or persons) to blame, or they may scapegoat a single member rather than realizing how the overall dynamic of the group may have contributed to decline.

∞ ENDINGS AND BEGINNINGS

As discussed in Chapter 4, group formation is guided in varying degrees by deliberate planning and by emergent events in the embedding context and the self-organizing activity of members. This section discusses three general ways in which the pattern of formation and early growth affects the metamorphosis of group: (a) The initial plan may include or imply an end point for the group; (b) the formation processes may not fully "take," so the group may never flourish; and (c) the formation processes may encompass "latent flaws" that ultimately lead to group dissolution. We discuss these here in turn.

Planned or Implicit Endings

As already discussed, some blueprints for forming groups specify the end point of a group. A training group may be slated to disband when the members have completed their training, which may be at either a specified date or a specified state—when members reach the prescribed level of proficiency. The members of a training group may also be reorganized into a new set of functional groups performing the tasks they have just been trained to perform. Crews are frequently assembled for a predetermined period of time—either a specific shift or a specific mission such as a scheduled flight. When their time is up, they disband; work left undone is inherited by the next crew.

Note that all of these examples fall into the category of concocted, project-focused groups. Founded groups also fall into the "high" planning quadrant, and founders may create groups designed to be temporary. However, we also expect that founders, because of their greater emotional involvement in the group and their status as group members, will dissolve a group at its logical end point less readily than outsiders who lack this kind of attachment. In general, endings that are logically implied by the purpose of the group require little explanation. Unexpected endings call for a deeper analysis of how group vulnerabilities and both internal and external stressors intersect.

Among groups formed primarily by emergent processes, many circumstantial groups also have an end point implied by the start. Circumstantial groups formed in response to a crisis situation are defined by their common fate. When circumstances revert to normal—the flood waters recede, or the lifeboat is rescued—the group dissolves. Members of such groups often develop what look like strong member-member ties because of the intense interaction, but these ties are usually not durable. Ex-members may honor the bonds by pledging to "keep in touch" after their normal lives resume, but this is often a form of remembrance (Moreland & Levine, 1988), not a continuation.

Failure to Thrive:
The Liability of Newness

Organizational theorists such as Hannan and Freeman (1977, 1984) have argued that new organizations have a higher failure rate than older organizations, reflecting the "liability of newness" for organizations (Stinchcombe, 1965). Whether findings confirming this liability for organizations (e.g., Freeman, Carroll, & Hannan, 1983) hold true for small groups is debatable, especially because small size is also a liability for organizations, and many new organizations are also small. However, the sources of vulnerability cited for new organizations should also apply to many new groups. The source of vulnerability at the group-embedding context interchange is the difficulty in finding and securing a niche in an environment in which other groups are already established. New groups compete with alternative groups that provide similar services, products, or benefits to customers (product-focused groups) or to members (member-focused groups). A new band trying to get bookings faces an uphill struggle against bands that have established relationships with clubs and a network of referrals for weddings and parties. A new social club competes for members with other groups to which prospective members already belong. Because people assume that newness equals vulnerability, potential consumers of the group's products or services may take a "wait-and-see" approach before committing resources, and the fledgling group may fail to survive the waiting period.

The source of vulnerability at the member-group interchange is similar: Members of a newly formed group may make only tentative commitments, waiting to see how involved and committed the other members will be. When groups are composed of people who are unfamiliar with one another, the emerging relationships are fragile. Empirical studies indicate that in new relationships, people often trust one another as an act of faith before they have sufficient experience interacting to know whether that trust is warranted (see McKnight, Cummings, & Chervany, 1998, for a recent review of this literature). Any indication that other group members may not be trustworthy may scuttle the necessary leap of faith.

The liability of newness at the group operations level is that the coordination network must frequently begin operations before it is fully formed and may function poorly at first. If members are unable to reach initial agreement about how to divide up tasks, make decisions, and sort out status issues, the coordination may never become functional. Conflicting assumptions in a founder's vision for the group (Schein, 1983) may impede the coalescence of the group around a shared mission, members of concocted groups may not understand the architect's purposes, and self-organized groups that emerge out of local activities by members may prove to be ephemeral and never stabilize. Hannan and Freeman (1984) called the maintenance of a stable organizational form *structural inertia,* and inertia takes time to develop. A physical analogy is the difficulty in getting a stationary object moving. New groups take extra time and effort at the beginning, and if this effort either is not adequate or works at cross-purposes and thus is wasted, the group will dissolve before it has ever gotten established.

One way to soften the impact of newness is to put a group together using smaller components of linked and coordinated elements. One of the lessons learned by the U.S. military from action in World War II was

that merged fragments of groups performed better and had fewer casualties than did groups cobbled together from individual soldiers with
no prior coexperience (Marshall, 1947). Although the merger was a
new group, the subgroups within it allowed it to function as a more
"mature" group right away. Groups formed primarily by internal, mem-
ber-driven emergent processes may similarly suffer less from the liability of newness because they tend to form among people who know one
another and are already embedded in a larger network of connections.

Structural Weaknesses
Established at Formation

Groups that make it through the vulnerable period of formation and
become coherent, functional collectives may still fail later due to weaknesses that date back to their initial formation. Where a group system is
vulnerable to stress depends in part on features of its design established
at formation. This relates to what Aristotle called *material cause*. If a
plate breaks because someone dropped it, that is the efficient or mechanical cause. The reason the plate splits in a particular place, however, may depend on cracks that developed when it was first created
and fired, an example of material cause. Groups formed in different
ways tend to have fault lines located at different points in the coordination network.

Concocted and founded groups have a special relationship to the
embedding system that spawned them or the founder who got them
started. Their dependence on key people can be a point of vulnerability.
Troubles in the embedding system, or the loss of a key contact in that
system (the person who concocted the group, for example), can disrupt
the bidirectional flow of group support and group production across
the group/embedding system interchange. A possible result is the termination of a concocted group.

In founded groups, the departure of a founder can be the beginning
of the end for a founded group that lacks leadership depth or has never
internalized the founder's vision. If group members are attuned to the
founder and were drawn to the group on the basis of identification with
and affective ties to the founder, the loss of the founder is like the loss of
the metronome that all of the members are using to coordinate their

group activity. Members align with the founder's intentions, and those intentions serve as a stable attractor for identification with the group. When the founder leaves, the attractor becomes unstable or vanishes. A founded group that has attracted or socialized people on the basis of their attachment to the group's purpose rather than to the founder will be more likely to survive the loss of a founder.

Another source of weakness can be conflicts or incompatibilities that were present from the start. In the effort to get a group functional, these may be ignored or papered over. Stresses on the group later on, however, may cause the group to split along these lines of conflict. Groups formed by merging smaller units, as noted above, may be able to sidestep some liabilities of newness. If these groups do not achieve genuine integration among the previously separate parts, however, they may break apart more easily than groups that had to build their coordination network "from scratch."

Partition groups that emerge when a piece of a larger group splits off may have difficulty functioning as an independent whole. The members of partition groups are accustomed to having close links with a parent group, so the group structure is vulnerable in the places where they relied on those links. Members of partition groups that splinter off because of conflict may find that their shared antagonism toward others is a rather weak bond once they are part of a separate group rather than a polarized subgroup. Member commitment is likely to be a weak point, and any loss of members can further fracture these groups. Moreover, such departures may be interpreted politically (by group members or by outsiders) as a rejection.

∞ COORDINATION BREAKDOWNS: THE ROLE OF LOCAL DYNAMICS

How groups fall apart or transform themselves depends, in part, on the nature of the coordination processes that characterize the group. In most groups, some aspects of thought, feeling, and action will need to be highly coordinated among members, and others will be only loosely linked. Elements that anchor members to the group and help them coordinate with one another—whether a person that others follow, a key activity that all members find attractive, or a resource that is essential to much of what the group does—must be supported and maintained. An important though often invisible aspect of local dynamics is the many small adjustments made on a regular basis that correct slight deviations from a desired way of doing things, repair interpersonal friction, and keep tools and procedures working smoothly. Failure to maintain links in this way, whether because they are overlooked or because of the demands of pursuing more prominent group and individual goals, can cause coordination to falter.

Coordination that is too loose leads to difficulty in maintaining efficient collective action. That will have negative consequences for performance of group projects, for system integrity, and indirectly for fulfillment of member needs. The willingness of group members to submerge individual desires for the sake of improved coordination may be influenced by the expectations they bring from the larger culture in which the group is embedded. Members' comfort with stronger or weaker ties to the group may depend in part on where their embedding culture falls on the dimension of collectivism versus individualism, and uncertainty avoidance may also play a role. In highly individualistic cultures such as the United States or Australia (Hofstede, 1983), holding a group together may be more difficult than in collectivist cultures. People who belong to many different groups have less to lose if they abandon a group. High levels of voluntary group membership are characteristic of the United States, Canada, Norway, Sweden, and the Netherlands (which also score high on individualism), and relatively low levels are typical of Japan (which is more collectivist) but also of southern European countries (France, Italy, and Spain), which are quite individualistic (see Curtis, Grabb, & Baer, 1992, for statistics on group membership). Strong uncertainty avoidance (Hofstede, 1980), which corresponds more closely to low group membership on the national level, may also predispose members to be strongly committed to a small number of groups and reluctant to join alternative groups. Individualists, who endorse values such as hedonism more highly than they endorse values such as loyalty to a group, may be more likely to abandon a group to pursue more appealing alternatives or to remain in the group but engage in free riding or social loafing (Triandis, 1994).

Member turnover will directly affect group well-being, although losing members who lack commitment to the group can have beneficial effects on the commitment of remaining members (Krackhardt & Porter,

1985). Social loafing by continuing members should degrade group well-being unless the group has worked out a tacit agreement that members can take turns slacking off. Unless the group is overstaffed for its projects, social loafing will affect productivity as well. If group well-being sinks below a minimum necessary for members to maintain their commitment, social loafing may spread as members withdraw their energy and the coordination necessary for coherent group action dissolves.

Self-organized groups are more likely to have loose coordination and nebulous boundaries than project-focused groups. A self-organized book discussion group or other group that emerges from a pool of people with common interests may handle high turnover without difficulty. Changes at the periphery of such groups make little difference to their functioning. Changes in core members, however—even temporary absences—may cause the group to lose its coordination, even if the members who are present are capable of carrying out the requisite tasks and of leading the group. The weakness of such groups is the looseness of their organization.

At the other extreme, coordination that is too tight imposes uniformity and can leave members feeling stripped of individual freedom of thought, feeling, and action. We expect that this problem will occur more frequently in project-focused groups than in member-focused groups, with project needs serving as the rationale for uniformity. Groupthink involves a tight uniformity of thought—at least of thoughts that are expressed to the group. Imposed uniformity of thought, feelings, or action may seem necessary when the group is under pressure to perform and efficiency takes precedence over effectiveness. Imposed uniformity is, however, a much weaker form of integration than actual unity or consensus. Effective repression of dissent and of expressed conflict can increase the members' experiences of internal conflict and inspire rebellion and sabotage that lead to collapse.

In a group that has a very strong focus on achieving group goals, there may be little room for members to adjust their activities in the group to ensure that they are meeting their own personal goals as well. The tolerance of members for relatively tighter or looser coordination of thought and feeling may also be influenced by cultural background. The tightness or looseness of a culture (Pelto, 1968) refers to how strictly members are expected to adhere to norms and how seriously deviation is punished. This concept can be applied to large cultural groups but also to subcultures such as that of a particular embedding context—an organization or neighborhood.

Adherence to norms, which serves to stabilize a group, can also break down when there are high rates of member change. Much of the socialization of new group members takes place at the level of local dynamics through informal exchanges between new and established members and through observational learning. When most members are new, however, they may mainly observe one another rather than working closely with and learning from established members. In a study of church size, Chapin (1957) found that institutional strength was associated with a balance between the tradition-carrying members and the population of children going to Sunday school, which he interpreted as potential members in the process of being socialized. High rates of turnover and replenishment that maintains group size should also challenge the ability of established members to integrate new members into a coordination network that is constantly losing elements and links with the departure of established member. Instead of maintaining a functional network, a group whose membership changes too quickly may revert to the formation stage of recreating a new group.

⚭ ENDINGS AND TRANSFORMATIONS AS ASPECTS OF GROUP DEVELOPMENT

At the global level, the ending of a group may be the natural outcome of a global development process or may be triggered by a change in global dynamics. An attractor that helps maintain the group may weaken or disappear, disrupting continuity in the group; attractors can also become so strong that the group loses flexibility. Habitual routines, which help maintain stability in local dynamics, can also impair group functioning over time by reducing the flow of information among group members (Katz, 1982). In this case, a fixed point attractor for the job and labor networks may lead to a gradual decline in information flow that links members. Information based on interpersonal links also is a resource signaling the need for change and adjustment at the level of local dynamics. Declining contact among members may disrupt cycles that are driven by close interaction among members, including cycles of conflict and resolution. If this happens, a periodic attractor for level of conflict may disappear, replaced by a fixed point attractor of low or no expressed conflict. Such changes in the nature of attractors governing key global variables are important indicators of underlying alterations in the local level dynamics of the group.

If we look at these patterns across the lifetime of a group, as group development theories do, termination may be seen as a stage in group development, including characteristic behaviors and changes in rhythm and activity that attend endings of groups. Metamorphosis can also be an expected stage in a group's unfolding history. For example, a development team for a new product may expect to be "spun off" from the organizational parent to form a new unit, or a rapidly growing group may expect to subdivide into multiple smaller groups. Eisenstat (1990) described a learning team charged with getting a new manufacturing facility off the ground. As the team completed this challenging task, it metamorphized into a smaller group that would run the plant. This is a case of developmental processes leading to an expected and gradual transformation of one group into another.

Metamorphosis as a Stage or Phase of Development

The stage theory literature in group development generally ignores such transformations. In their follow-up to Tuckman's benchmark work on stages of group development (Tuckman, 1965), Tuckman and Jensen (1977) added a fifth phase, "adjourning," to the earlier four (forming, storming, norming, performing). This adjourning phase presumes termination, not transformation into a new system. Tuckman and Jensen also made clear that the model was designed for groups with relatively fixed membership and an end point defined in advance. The focus is not on why groups end but on the internal group processes that are characteristic at the end of a group's life. We discuss these processes in greater detail in the section "Consequences of Group Termination" below. Classic progressive stage models such as Tuckman's emphasize gradual change over discontinuous change. Adjourning as a final stage

implies a natural "death." Outside forces are typically ignored. Together, these characteristics suggest that the expected pattern of ending
is characterized by project completion.

Gersick's (1988) model of punctuated equilibrium as a developmental pattern provides more insight into why a group might cease to exist
or undergo radical transformation before an expected end point. For
groups with defined task-completion end points, the model suggests
that the initial meeting and the midpoint are both "critical periods"
during which members are much more sensitive to outside influences.
Between these two periods, group behavior is locked into a stable pattern that resists outside influence that might lead to a group's demise or
inspire a transformation. A generalized version of the model, which allows for multiple phases of stasis and transformation, suggests that
there will be periodic brief periods during which a group restructures,
reinvents itself as a new group, or collapses. The punctuated equilibrium model emphasizes change as sudden, not incremental.

Different Patterns for Different Stages

In Worchel's (1994) cyclical stage model of group development,
groups cycle through stages termed (a) discontent, (b) precipitating
event, (c) group identification, (d) group productivity, (e) individuation, (f) decay, and then back to discontent. The overall conceptual
framework focuses on the tension between the drive toward individuation, which stresses individual goals and needs, and group identification, which focuses attention on common group goals and projects. We
see these as centrifugal and centripetal forces, respectively. The model
also incorporates both negative feedback loops, which maintain continuity, and positive feedback loops, which drive change. Because this
model does not presume a fixed duration or a single cycle, and because
it is so compatible with a dynamic systems analysis, it can be used as a
more flexible framework for noting the ways in which groups may end.
We expect that endings and transformations are most likely at those
stages in the cycle in which the centrifugal forces predominate.

At the *discontent* stage, members feel alienated from the group, and
centrifugal forces are dominant. If no *precipitating event* reenergizes

the members, so as to balance the centrifugal force with the centripal force of group identification, members may drift away from the group. To survive intact, groups must be able to counter the forces that pull people away from the group by maintaining a minimum of group cohesion—the bonds that tie people to the projects, the resources, and the interpersonal relationships that make up the group. In our formulation, this implies fulfillment of member needs. A precipitating event may also break the group up, however, if members are motivated to identify with a different group, either one they already belong to that has competing claims on their time and energy or a new group that can replace some of the benefits formerly found in the old group.

In the *group identification* stage, members affirm the existing group. Internally triggered termination and metamorphosis during this stage is unlikely because centripetal forces are strong, members view the group positively, and conformity pressures are high. The greatest danger to the group is that conflict with outsiders may be welcomed as a way to both promote and express in-group identity, and this could endanger the flow of resources and other support to the group from its embedding context. In the *group productivity* stage, attention is focused not on the psychological bond between member and group but on the ties that connect members to group projects and enable the group to accomplish its work. Problems that prevent the group from doing its work are a potentially serious threat to the group's survival at this stage because the main source of cohesion is task cohesion rather than social cohesion.

During the *individuation* stage, the group is vulnerable to losing valuable members because in-group loyalty is reduced and members become more interested in out-groups and what they have to offer. A relatively small shift in the structure of incentives offered in the embedding context may make the group seem less attractive by comparison. Group boundaries are weaker at this time compared to the group identification and group productivity stages. Worchel (1996) suggested that one important trigger for the transition from group productivity to individuation is success—achieving a productivity goal (p. 271). When success results in rewards to the group, this raises the issue of how those rewards will be divided, and members start focusing on what they contributed and what they deserve rather than on what the group needs. Thus, just at the point that the group achieves success and member benefits increase, these members may be vulnerable to recruitment by another group that promises to reward them more richly, and the group may dissolve if too many members leave. In the next stage, *decay,* interpersonal bonds between members weaken, and intragroup conflict—a centrifugal force—increases. If positive feedback loops escalate a conflict beyond what the member network can handle, the group may collapse, even if task cohesion remains intact.

Development at the Member Level

In all the models presented above, the focus is on the group and on patterns of change in global variables such as cohesion, conflict, and (for fixed-duration groups) time pressure. The group socialization model (Moreland & Levine, 1982, 1988), in contrast, takes the dual perspectives of individual members and of the group as a whole. Thus, it provides additional depth in analyzing groups whose members may be in different stages of their relationship to the group at a given time. This is especially likely in groups that have added new members and thus have more diversity in group tenure than a group that is made up entirely of charter members. Where given members are in their own relationship with the group should depend in part on when they joined the group. New members will be working on developing ties to tasks and tools, whereas members in the divergence phase will be letting these ties lapse. Membership ends with reminiscences for the ex-member and a period of remembrance for the group.

Sometimes members join a group to get a set of outcomes and subsequently either lose their motivation for these outcomes or get their needs filled and are ready to move on. In such cases, temporally staggered entry of members will make continuity more likely; groups consisting of charter members who all joined at the same time are vulnerable if all the members decide to leave the group at the same time. However, diversity in group tenure may also make it more difficult for members to stay coordinated. If some members are identifying with the group while others are emphasizing individuation, this could lead to rifts among subgroups and a rise in intragroup conflict that is not a marker of a stage (as it would be in Tuckman's storming stage or

Worchel's individuation stage) but an indication that members are out of synchronization with one another in terms of their relation to the group. Because it is structural rather than focused on a task, or procedural, or even an interpersonal problem, conflict based on different development stages among members should be especially difficult to handle constructively.

ADAPTIVE TRANSFORMATION AND FAILURES TO ADAPT

Groups may be disbanded or dissolved by forces in the embedding context or in response to shocks coming from outside the group. This would include such events as the deliberate reconfiguration of work groups in the course of a "reengineering" of an organization or the withdrawal of resources (such as funding) that the group depends on. The key interchange here is the group/embedding context. For work groups, the level of external demand for a group's output of goods and services is a critical contextual parameter. For clubs, the level of demand among the pool of potential members for the group's output of goods and services to its members is a critical contextual parameter. This section considers the intersection of changes in the fitness landscape and changes in the group as a dynamic that underlies metamorphosis. It also discusses how pressures for adaptation interact with other dynamics such as formation and group development.

As discussed at the beginning of this chapter, the impetus for termination or transformation can stem primarily from internal forces, primarily from external forces, or from an interaction between the two. This section focuses not on direct interventions that cancel or disband a group but on broader changes in a group's relationship with its embedding context that lead to metamorphosis. When the fitness landscape that determines how successful a group is undergoes change, termination can result from a failure to adapt to changes, from a misguided strategy of adaptation, or as an unintended consequence of sensible attempts to adapt. Alternatively, transformation may allow a group to be reborn in a radically new configuration that better fits changed circumstances.

Stasis: Failure to Adapt

Failure to adapt can lead to the demise of a group when a change in the embedding environment either decreases the overall fitness of a group beyond what is feasible for survival or heightens competition that erodes a group's resource base. Inaction can result from a long history of stability in which the group was not called on to adapt. When change is needed, the group has strong forces opposing change and few strategies for coping with change.

Termination due to inaction is most likely when a group is relatively inefficient compared to other groups occupying the same niche, when the population of groups inhabiting the same niche exceeds the carrying capacity of the niche, and when the group is highly specialized. Inaction by groups that are already doing better than others in the population, in contrast, may have no ill effects. Inaction may also be more effective in the long run if the change in the niche proves to be temporary. In this case, groups that have committed themselves to structural adjustments and a change in strategy may find that their efforts were unnecessary. A group that fails to respond to changes in the fitness landscape is, by definition, unlikely to experience transformation.

Excess: Extreme Responses

Rather than failing to act, a group may undertake constant, disruptive changes to improve fit in a changing environment. Groups in organizations that are constantly reengineering themselves may be pressured to change often enough that basic coordination processes begin to break down, affecting global variables related to fulfillment of group projects, fulfillment of member needs, and system integrity.

Too much adaptation to a narrow niche can also make a group vulnerable. Groups embedded in organizations are typically in a symbiotic relationship with that organization—they are created and sustained by that system. Extended coevolution between a group and key features in its embedding context (such as other groups) may lead to canalization: A group becomes very good at dealing with a specified part of the embedding context—a partner, so to speak—but thereby becomes less and less able to work with other partners or different parts of its external contexts. This kind of symbiosis makes a group vulnerable to removal of the customized part of the embedding system with which it has developed the partnered relationship. A band that relies very heavily for employment on a particular bar that provides regular engagements may gradually lose the ability to negotiate successfully for bookings in other settings and will be vulnerable if its client bar loses viability.

Unsuccessful Adaptation

Groups may dissolve as an unintended consequence of their efforts to adapt to a changing environment. The strategy a group adopts may make a bad situation worse, at least temporarily, even if the strategy is sound. If a niche is shrinking, for example, a group may try to compete more effectively against other groups that inhabit that niche or may decide to transform itself to fit a different niche. A consulting group that specializes in managing organizational growth, for example, may find that demand for such services falters in a recession. Instead of competing more aggressively for its share of a shrinking pie, the group may decide to switch to another specialization and focus on managing organizational decline. If successful, this would count as a transformation. The strategy may fail for many reasons. The group may find itself unable to compete with groups that are already exploiting this alternate niche; the group may go bankrupt in the process of making the transition; or the economy may suddenly rebound, shrinking the niche that the consulting group was transforming itself to occupy.

Another cause of death similar to that last problem is anticipatory adaptation. Groups may make strategic changes in anticipation of new environmental conditions that fail to materialize. A sales team that changes its approach in line with a projected fashion trend, for example, may lose sales and customers in both the short term and the long term when the trend does not appear as projected.

Changes in the Landscape of Attractors

Changes in the fitness landscape directly alter the rewards and resources for a particular set of groups. An example might be the contraction of a niche for hockey teams as sports fans develop a greater interest in figure skating and stop watching hockey on TV. Changes in other contextual parameters, however, can leave the fitness landscape basically intact while changing the landscape of attractors for a group. A change in the rules for professional hockey, for example, may have no impact on the enthusiasm of the audience or the financial rewards for hockey teams but may alter the ability of some teams to execute their habitual coordination patterns.

In dynamic systems terms, a change in contextual parameters can weaken or destroy formerly stable attractors and create new attractors. A group may find that effective patterns of behavior are much harder to achieve or to maintain. The fallout from a bitter labor dispute, for example, may make it much harder for work groups to coordinate smoothly with managers because of increased mistrust. The rewards for effective work group functioning remain unchanged, but the same level of performance becomes much harder to achieve. Instead, a group may move toward a new dynamic attractor of protracted conflict that is detrimental to the group but nevertheless hard to resist. The relevant contextual parameter that governs the configuration of attractors may be trust between workers and management.

One technique for examining the impact of changes in contextual parameters is stability analysis. Under normal operating conditions, an ongoing group typically does not have to spend much time and energy maintaining effective coordination. When there are perturbations from the embedding contexts, effort must be devoted to maintaining coordinated action toward the group's intended goal(s). The force of shared intentions can be viewed as a powerful contextual parameter that the group itself can manipulate. Because shared intentions can mold the dynamics of a group, group goal setting can be a powerful device for shaping a group's level of production.

If we could determine the values of contextual parameters at which attractors for critical global variables become unstable or vanish altogether, we would be able to identify points at which a group was likely to collapse (or transform). Which global variables are most important to group functioning depends on what that group has organized itself around (e.g., member-member links, benefits gained through member support, attraction to a leader or project or technology) and what holds the group together (i.e., what forms of integration are strongest at this point in the group's life). Groups held together by members' devotion to the tasks they perform will be relatively insensitive to the disappearance of member-member attraction, provided it does not cross the line into negative member-member relations. Groups held together primarily by members' desire to interact may be able to maintain effective group well-being even if the group is performing unpleasant tasks.

∞ METAMORPHOSIS IN PROJECT-FOCUSED AND MEMBER-FOCUSED GROUPS

Work Groups

Work groups of all types depend on resources provided by their embedding contexts, which allow them to be productive. Disruption in this relationship can seriously threaten a work group's survival, even if group-member relations remain positive. If the niche that a work group fills becomes overcrowded, or disappears because demand for the group's products or services evaporates, the work group loses its primary reason for being. The different group structures in the three prototypes for project-focused groups make these groups vulnerable to different kinds of disruptions, however, and prone to different kinds of transformations. The loss of a project or access to technology, for example, may abruptly end the life of a task force or a crew, respectively, but not cause a crisis for many teams. Task forces may metamorphose into teams but are unlikely to restructure along the crew prototype. These distinctions are discussed in greater detail below.

Task Forces

Task forces typically are expected to disband when the group's project is completed. Because the strong links in task forces are between members and the core project, the labor network holds the coordination network together and is the source of task cohesion for the group. Project completion severs the main ties between members and group. If changes in the environment redefine the project or take the project away from the group, a task force is liable to dissolve. Substituting a new project might give the group a new core, but the group will literally need to rebuild itself around the new project.

Task forces are often cobbled together in an ad hoc fashion. Their member-member and task-technology ties are generally weak unless the group imports these—for example, in the form of prior relationships among members. Task forces composed of relative strangers are less likely to invest in strong member-member bonds. Conflict among members can easily tear these groups apart when they lack the strong interpersonal ties that help teams weather such storms.

Gersick (1988) described a task group that dissolved without ever really getting off the ground: Group members opposed the project presented by their leader and objected to all his plans, at which point the leader simply chose one plan and dissolved the group. Our conception of a task force makes clear why failure to gain commitment to a shared project results in a stillbirth, as members are never linked up to a task network that would allow the project to be completed. On the other hand, successful completion of a project may inspire a task force to continue working together after their "natural" end point—marking the metamorphosis of a task force into a team.

Temporal coordination is critical to the pacing of task forces. Perhaps more than other forms of group, task forces entrain their work to the temporal milestones provided by project deadlines. Major changes in deadlines can also derail a task force. If the deadline evaporates or the core project loses its value, members may lose their commitment to the group and drift away or decide to disband the group. If the deadline is advanced dramatically, the group may be unable to adapt itself to the accelerated pace required and may give up the project as hopeless.

Teams

Teams are generally expected to last longer and to tackle a wider range of projects than task forces. The members are expected to have a long history together, during which they will handle a long succession of projects. They develop strong links among members and between the members and the technology, and the typical group has dense structures in its coordination network. But these structures take time to elaborate and are shaped to the individual members who make up the team. High levels of membership change imposed on the group, either by member attrition or by intervention from the embedding system, may overwhelm the group's ability to reengineer its coordination structures. Too much membership change early on in the team's history may also lead to an early demise because the core role structure that holds a team together never develops. This should be especially true for teams with a high level of member diversity, which need extra time to develop a workable coordination network and become productive (Watson et al., 1993).

Teams, more than task forces, are likely to work on a complex range of tasks and projects simultaneously. Their coordination network is likely to be much more complex than that of groups that work on narrower, more routine projects. The more elaborate network may allow for more path multiplicity and flexibility, but it also means that removing key members is likely to alter many more links and require many more adjustments than the loss of a member from a less complex network. Among teams with stable membership, relationship conflicts can cripple the group. Jehn (1995, 1997) found that although task conflict can be beneficial for groups performing nonroutine tasks, avoiding open conflict may be the best route when the friction is interpersonal. Members who dislike one another on a crew know they will work together for only a relatively brief period and can interact almost entirely on the basis of their formal position. In a team, however, relationship conflict can have a similar effect as losing a member if some team members refuse to work together. In each case, a whole set of ties that may be critical to the group stops functioning.

Teams are unlikely to transform their structure into that of a task force or crew, although subsets of members may operate as task forces addressing particular projects within the larger context of a team working on multiple projects simultaneously. If an established team loses its core sets of projects or its mission becomes obsolete, however, the members may reinvent the group as a new team with a new overriding mission. An example of this occurred when members of the rugby team described in Read's (1974) book *Alive* crashed in the Andes, an emergent external event that transformed the survivors into a new circumstantial group. Drawing on the relationships and leadership structure that existed in the sports team, the survivors reorganized themselves for their new mission of staying alive and contacting civilization so they could be rescued.

Crews

In crews, the termination process is likely to be as brief and routinized as the formation process unless the intensity of interaction between members was high, the members already knew one another before their stint in the group, or the group faced some nonroutine situations that promoted richer interpersonal interaction than was called for by standardized role behavior.

Crew members who are trained to fit into a predetermined niche in the job network are able to achieve coordinated action and work together as a group with a minimum of formation process activity, and they should be able to disengage from the job network to which they were temporarily assigned with the same alacrity.

Crews, of course, can cease operation prematurely. They are vulnerable if their technology fails. If the operating theater is not available or lacks the proper equipment, the surgical crew cannot perform its job. When people concoct crews, they need to craft precision parts that fit together just right so that minimal carpentering is needed. The technology is specifically adapted to do particular tasks, and the pool of people eligible to staff this technology have been carefully trained in its use. If the technology fails to function, or the crew is assigned to a project for which the technology does not work, the crew will often lack the ability to generate new job structures and tools on the spot. It may simply abort the mission and disband.

Member-Focused Groups: Economic, Activity, and Social Clubs

Clubs form to serve member needs, and they dissolve, generally speaking, when they stop fulfilling this function. Member needs may change; members may find another group or an alternate set of relationships that serves their needs better; or the club may find itself unable to provide the goods that members expect. Clubs are often sensitive to group size; if membership drops beyond the point at which the club is able to generate what members care about, whether this is cheaper skiing or enough people to play a basketball game, the remaining members may quickly abandon the group. At the other extreme, too many members can cause overcrowding effects, so that not all members get what they want, or what they get is less satisfying. Below, we discuss how these problems vary for the three prototype clubs—groups focused on economic resources, participation in valued activities, or social connection.

Economic Clubs

The strongest set of links in the economic club prototype is the network that connects members to resources. Members of such clubs must balance direct provision of resources to members with the group need to maintain the integrity of tools and systems used to produce these resources. More members means more contributions toward maintaining the resource base but also more members drawing on the goods the club produces. This makes economic clubs prone to free-rider problems and the depletion of resources. Club members who think they can get a better deal elsewhere are more likely to leave the group than are, for example, team members, who are more likely to invest their energy in maintaining the web of coordinated ties that makes group action possible.

Members of cooperative buying clubs, for example, get lower prices on groceries but also need to contribute labor to keep the co-op running, divide up the bulk goods, and so on. If some members take the benefits without paying this cost, the exchange balance for those who are working more than their share will quickly become unattractive. The irony is that the members most likely to quit in these circumstances are those most valuable to the survival of the club. Screening of members and monitoring of contributions can help defend against this threat to an economic club. Monitoring as an extra cost becomes more difficult to maintain the larger the club grows. The solution for a popular economic club may be to split into two smaller clubs.

Another cause of demise is broader: a change in the cost-benefit ratio for members based on developments in the embedding environment. If a big discount grocery comes to town, members of the food co-op may find that their desire to save money can be met more efficiently by shopping at Cheap Food Co. Revolving credit associations may dissolve if banks become more willing to lend money to members who previously found it difficult to access credit through conventional institutions.

In this case, the decline in niche size makes it likely that only highly efficient clubs will survive. Because fewer potential members will find the clubs attractive, they need to compete successfully not only with other co-ops or credit associations but also with the discount institutions that occupy a different niche.

Activity Clubs

Clubs focused on activities that can easily be pursued by a variable number of members are liable to be more robust than those that focus on activities that are ideally pursued with a fixed number of members. A book discussion group or quilting club, for example, or a weekly writers' workshop, can hold successful meetings with 4 members or 12. A bridge club also has some flexibility because tables of three or four are plausible, but if too few members show up for a baseball game and no one can pitch, the enjoyment members anticipate will be diminished. If way too many people show up, than many members will sit on the sidelines, also diminishing their enjoyment.

If such clubs fail to develop a mechanism for managing these participation problems, the club is unlikely to survive, for members who fail to stay connected to the tasks they enjoy have no reason to stay in the club. One solution is to develop stronger social bonds that can be used to maintain participation; another is to create a role (such as leader) or rely on outsiders (such as parents) to handle the coordination problems and schedule participation. Activity clubs, like task forces, may also end by expiring, when the club is created as a summer activity for children, for example, or the week-long expedition to the mountains is over. Activity clubs concocted by outsiders may also be canceled if the continuing demands for outside support exceed what outsiders are willing to supply or if the number of members interested does not warrant keeping the club going.

Social Clubs

Social group interactions that involve small numbers of members (three to five members) are liable to be more satisfying to members than gatherings that are large enough that close social interaction becomes difficult. Although a social club of friends may be much larger than this size, it may have regular events at which only a subset of people appear.

This allows for a richer set of social connections while maintaining smaller groups for actual interaction. A larger set of members also allows a group to provide social support to members in special need without exhausting the rest of the members. Thus, a social club that has too few members can fall apart if the needs of one or more members exceed what others are willing or able to provide.

Social clubs are also vulnerable to interpersonal conflict. Because the member network connects everyone in the club, conflict can spread and split the club if other members take sides. Members who leave these groups are also, in a real sense, irreplaceable, for the network connects particular people, not members in a generic sense. Thus, a club that suffers high member attrition—from members moving away, finding other friends, or falling out with other members—may dissolve as a result. In this case, the ending is relatively gradual and based on a combination of internal and external forces.

Long-standing social clubs may spawn task forces and crews to handle special events or needs among their membership. Hence, a social group tending to a sick member may organize itself into shifts similar to the structure of a crew to handle needed chores. A subgroup may also take on a specific project, such as organizing a party or trip, and structure itself as a temporary task force. In this case, however, the embedding context for the task forces is not an organization but the social club itself. Although this may look like metamorphosis, we do not consider it an example of transformation. Instead, it illustrates the protean nature of groups with highly complex structures, as are typical of social clubs and teams, which can mobilize subsets of links as temporary groups contained within the larger group.

∞ CONSEQUENCES OF GROUP TERMINATION

Tuckman and Jensen's (1977) addition of adjourning as a distinctive stage of group development was inspired by several studies that noted distinctive features that occurred near the end of a group's life. LaCoursiere (1974), for example, observed a final stage of termination that included sadness and some self-evaluation by group members in a study of three training groups of student nurses. These groups lasted 10 weeks. A study of nurse training groups (Spitz & Sadock, 1973) also noted a final phase of disengagement that included anxiety about separation and positive feelings toward the group leader. What the studies had in common was an emphasis on the emotional aspects of termination, with a secondary emphasis on the tendency to review and reflect on the group's life. All the studies cited were of groups that worked together for an extended period.

The time needed to complete the emotional process of adjourning, and the focus of leavetaking, should vary depending on (a) how long the group has been together; (b) how intensively the members worked together; (c) the nature of ties among members, including the proportion of negative, positive, and neutral interpersonal ties; and (d) whether the members expect to continue working together in the future, either in a reconstituted version of this group or in some other context. It may also depend on another dimension of metamorphosis: the pacing of change in the termination/transformation process.

The group socialization model (Moreland & Levine, 1982, 1988) provides an interpretation for why some members may show more pronounced emotional and cognitive effects (sadness, evaluative review of the group's history) than others at a group's termination. A member who was already on the way out of the group may have already worked through the separation process, whereas full members may actively resent and resist the loss of the group.

In a separate but related body of literature, studies of organizational decline and death also emphasize emotional reactions to the impending demise of a company or agency (see, e.g., Krantz, 1985). This literature typically studies organizations whose expected lifetime was indefinite and thus is most relevant to the endings of teams and clubs whose duration is similarly open-ended. When termination is certain, emotional reactions may follow a sequence analogous to the stages of denial, anger, depression, and acceptance that people experience when coping with the death of a relative or their own impending death. However, the demise of an organization or group is often projected but uncertain, and the efforts of group members may alter the outcome. Thus, the actions members take may be just as important as the emotions they are feeling. Anger may translate into efforts to save the group by mobilizing members against a perceived enemy. Denial may fuel fantasies about the revival of the group in a new form, which can inspire efforts at transformative adaptation. Depression may lead to a decline in productivity and effectiveness, sealing the group's fate.

Sutton (1988) listed the following common managerial beliefs about employee reactions to impending organizational death: Productivity and quality will decline; sabotage, stealing, and conflict will increase, spurred by the dominant emotion of anger toward management; the best employees will leave immediately, and rumors and denial will be rampant among those who remain. In the closings he studied, he found that many of the best employees did in fact "jump ship" and that rumors and denial were common. No support was found, however, for decreases in productivity and quality; on the contrary, these were more likely to increase. Sabotage did not increase, increased stealing was found in two of the eight cases, and conflict typically decreased, contrary to what managers expected. Although some hostility was observed, fear and sorrow—not anger—were the dominant emotions.

Members of both groups and larger organizations can facilitate the final emotional stage of acceptance by enacting rituals that mark the end of the group. Such rituals are a formalized way to complete the termination process, providing a setting for reminiscence and helping members with the transition to ex-member status. In groups in which endings represent a form of completion (e.g., the graduation of a training group), this may be both a final ritual and a celebration. The remembrance process is different for groups with unexpected endings. Their members need to improvise ways to complete termination or may be left with many unexpressed thoughts and emotions and experiences that have not been put into context. Parting ceremonies for dying organizations studied by Harris and Sutton (1986) included the expression of both anger and sadness; they also seemed to help participants accept that the organization really had died.

The distinction between expected and unexpected endings often corresponds to the difference between positive and negative adjourning. Divorce is a negative ending for a household, whereas the disbanding of a group of students who are graduating is a positive adjourning. Van Steenberg LaFarge (1995) proposed that most group members experience ambivalent emotions at the termination of a group, whether the adjourning is predominantly negative—a failure—or predominantly positive—a successful completion of the group mission. In groups that have been successful, members may mourn their impeding separation from the group while simultaneously experiencing a satisfying sense of closure and release. In groups whose performance has been less successful, members may also be ambivalent, seeing the ending as the loss of an opportunity to redeem the group by a success while also feeling relief that their tenure with the group is complete.

∞ CONCLUDING COMMENTS

This chapter on endings and transformations concludes Part II of the book. The presentation of our theory is now complete. The chapters in Part III consider the implications of the theory for conducting research on groups and then discuss in detail some specific strategies for research on groups as complex systems.

PART III

ISSUES AND STRATEGIES

∞ 9 ∞

Implications of Our Theory for Constructing a Research Program

*O*ur theory of groups as complex systems carries with it what Lakatos (1970) might call an implied research program. If we construe small groups as complex systems in fundamental ways, we will have to reexamine many of the implicit and explicit assumptions of past theory and research on small groups. Our approach highlights many issues that have received scant attention in past small group research in the experimental social psychology tradition. It places new demands on but also opens up new opportunities for research on groups.

Treating small groups as complex systems raises substantive, epistemological, and methodological issues. The research program implied by our theory requires that we examine groups as embedded in and interacting with multiple contexts, over time, and under varying conditions. It invites a reconsideration of the nature of evidence, of what constitutes replication and verification, and hence of the practical meanings of validity and confirmation. It challenges premises about randomness and error. To handle these issues, we need to borrow and adapt, invent, and develop new research strategies and methods to expand our current repertoire.

This chapter presents some of the major conceptual and methodological issues raised by our theoretical approach and discusses some problems with standard empirical methods for research programs that follow this approach. The next chapter suggests some ways in which traditional methodological tools can be supplemented with, or transformed into, new data collection, analysis, and interpretation strategies. (We also encourage the reader to consult a recent book by Vallacher & Nowak, 1994, which contains a number of chapters that provide similar critiques of current research on social psychological issues and suggestions for alternative methodological approaches.)

The following discussion considers five sets of assumptions that the logic of inquiry implied by our theory calls into question. These assumptions concern (a) the proper unit(s) of analysis, (b) time and validity in the research process, (c) cause, (d) generalization of results, and (e) measurement and error.

THE PROPER UNIT(S) OF ANALYSIS

Instead of studying static relations between variables that index different aspects of group structure, process, and performance at a given time (e.g., the relation between level of cohesion and level of productivity, or between leadership style and degree of consensus in the group), our conceptualization invites us to study the trajectories of global variables over time. Global variables reflect the changing states of the group as a system. Thus, we might study the evolution of the influence structure in a set of groups (Arrow, 1997; Berdahl & Craig, 1996) or the patterning of group productivity over time (Hollingshead et al., 1993), given a particular set of initial conditions. For the studies just cited, media richness and social presence, possible contextual parameters, differed depending on the type of communication medium that different sets of groups used: a computer conferencing system versus face-to-face interaction.

Our conceptualization also shifts the focus of study because it directs attention to the interchanges between multiple system levels. One of the main principles of our theory is that action at the local level yields emergent structures (i.e., patterns of relations and of actions) at macro levels and that these in turn constrain subsequent action at the local level. Furthermore, the idea of embeddedness and the role of the group-context interchange in driving adaptation imply that we need to study phenomena across multiple levels—member, group, and context—and to focus on phenomena that occur at the interchanges between levels (see Klein, Tosi, & Cannella, 1999). If we take the idea of interchange seriously, we must go beyond input-output models that presume one-way arrows of causal influence and look at patterns of interdependence and exchange as well.

∞ TIME AND VALIDITY
IN THE RESEARCH PROCESS

Although time has played a relatively minor role in theory and research on small groups (and on other social phenomena; see McGrath & Kelly, 1986), temporal factors are crucial to study design and to the validity of findings (Kelly & McGrath, 1988). Time plays a crucial role in the interpretation of research results because it is central to traditional concepts of causality, reliability, and measurement. For example, time is crucial in the logic of inference by which cause (meaning efficient or mechanical cause) is assessed. Effect cannot precede cause. In study design, the passage of time creates several threats to validity and is thus something to be controlled (or "held constant") when attempting to get a clear picture of a phenomenon (Campbell & Stanley, 1966).

Our treatment of groups as complex systems, however, gives time an integral—indeed a profound—role in both theory and research. We believe that theory should be dynamic, tracking recursive relationships among variables of interest over time. To study groups as complex systems, researchers need to develop theories about, and to explore empirically, various temporal cadences among system processes—from split-second coordination of action to long-term developmental patterns. These processes unfold simultaneously, are temporally nested, and are intertwined.

In the remainder of this section, we discuss (a) how traditional conceptions of validity discourage the study of groups over time, (b) the use of within-group designs, and (c) the interplay of multiple temporal

cadences in group processes, a topic that has been largely ignored in
group research.

Internal Validity

Six of the seven main threats to the internal validity of a study—history, maturation, testing, instrument change, mortality, and regression
to the mean (see Cook & Campbell, 1979)—are temporal in nature (see
Kelly & McGrath, 1988). These rival hypotheses weaken our ability to
claim that the variables we attempt to control and isolate in our experiments are alone responsible for the effects observed, and thus they constrain the causal certainty to be gained from a study.

In our view, however, the history of a group (i.e., the sequence of external conditions it has experienced) and its own maturation (i.e., its
own internal development) represent crucial and meaningful facets of
the complex system being studied. Effects of history or of maturation
are indigenous, dynamical features of the group: features to be studied,
not artifacts to be eliminated via experimental control or rendered
moot via random allocation of cases and statistical aggregation. The effects of a group's history and development on the trajectories of global
variables are a topic for examination, not elimination.

Between- and Within-Group Designs

Between-group designs are more frequently used than within-group
designs in experimental social psychology and small group research
generally. And for good reason! Within-group designs are costly and
pose many conceptual problems. The conditions being studied and
those being controlled, for example, tend to get confounded; this problem is exacerbated in extended longitudinal studies. The research program implied by our theory, however, specifically requires that studies
extend over long enough periods of time to capture the dynamics of interest or to represent the life spans of groups of interest. Depending on
the variables of interest and the type of group, this may be a matter of
minutes, hours, weeks, months, or years.

The problem with using between-group designs to study groups as complex systems is that they tell us very little about how global variables change over time with development within groups and with changes in contextual parameters. Between-group designs tend to study differences in the average level of some variable (collapsed across groups in the same experimental condition) between groups with different levels of some other variable (i.e., different experimental conditions). For laboratory groups, the dependent variables are typically measured at the same point in the brief history of the groups. For naturally occurring groups, however, groups measured at different times in their history may be treated as groups in the "same" condition. Study conditions may correspond to different levels of contextual parameters or to what we would call global variables. Often, only two levels are studied, and the dependent variables are presumed to have a linear, monotonic relations with these independent variables. The dependent variables of interest may correspond to either local or global variables.

The logic of our theory, however, suggests that what we are looking for is qualitatively similar patterns over time in the trajectory of global variables for groups in substantially similar operating conditions—not stable differences in the *values* of these variables between sets of groups in different conditions. A trajectory is a within-group pattern over time. Local details of the trajectories may vary across groups in ways that are not important to our theory, but such differences will show up as spurious differences if a variable is measured only at a single point in time across groups.

Let us take the example of conflict as a global variable. A trajectory that approaches a fixed point attractor over time may approach the fixed point at a somewhat different rate in different groups; the fixed level at which the variable stabilizes may also differ across groups. Alternately, conflict may follow a cyclic attractor, increasing, then decreasing, then increasing again. However, the period of this cycle may vary between groups. From the perspective of our theory, each set of groups would be showing a single qualitative dynamic pattern—fixed attractor or periodic attractor—with some local variation. However, a between-groups design that did not measure the global variable over time would fail to detect these regularities and would instead highlight differences in static levels of these variables across groups, failing to distinguish the two dynamic patterns and misinterpreting surface similarities and differences at a single point in time.

Time itself is a within-group variable. In repeated measures analysis of variance, time (e.g., Trial 1, Trial 2) is a variable that can be analyzed only within groups and can have significant effects only within groups. Given the importance that our approach gives to the temporal unfolding of global patterns within groups, our research program must incorporate within-group designs. It needs to combine within-group and between-group designs, however (see Arrow, 1997, for an example), to study the impact of different fixed settings of contextual parameters. The impact of actual *changes* in contextual parameters, of course, can be studied only as a within-group phenomenon.

The Interplay of Multiple Temporal
Cadences in Group Processes

Individual human behavior follows many temporal rhythms. Some are as short as milliseconds and minutes, some approximate a day's length (the circadean rhythms), some last weeks or months or seasons, and some span an individual's entire life (McGrath & Kelly, 1986; Moore-Ede et al., 1982; Pittendreigh, 1972). Cycles and rhythms also underlie the behavior of groups.

We can regard the group's total developmental cycle in much the same way as developmental psychologists view the life span of an individual. For individuals, the normal life cycle includes birth, stages of growth and development, decline, and ultimately death. Our conception of groups includes formation, operations involving coordination, development, and adaptation, and metamorphosis, which ends the life cycle of that group. Because groups are social entities rather than biological organisms, the analogy has its limits; patterns of development in groups can vary more dramatically and be altered more readily than patterns in individuals that are anchored to fundamental biological processes. We propose that group processes may operate differently depending on where the group is in its life cycle. Moreover, we propose that contextual factors may have different effects depending on when in the group's life cycle they occur.

Some of the temporal patterns that underlie group behavior arise not from features of the group and its developmental stage but from features of the projects that groups undertake (e.g., groups doing short, repetitive assembly-line tasks versus groups doing a year-long project). Some temporal patterns arise out of the relation between the group and its projects, on the one hand, and features of external embedding systems, on the other. Holiday seasons impose strong temporal patterns on the work of many sales groups, postal service groups, and resort service groups, for example, and arbitrarily defined "seasons" impose temporal patterns on the conditioning, practice, and play of athletic teams.

At more micro levels, executing the tasks that make up groups' projects themselves often requires enactment of particular temporal patterns, including temporal coordination of different acts by the same person and coordination of acts by different persons. Temporal coordination includes sequencing requirements, synchronization of start times or finish times of different members' actions, or even a synchrony of all actions involved in the task. Consider the complex temporal patterning required of musicians playing a symphony. The actions of every member of the orchestra must be coordinated down to the level of a sixteenth note!

In individual humans (and many other animals), effective functioning of the individual requires that sets of multiple biological rhythms become "entrained" to one another—mutually synchronized as to phase and periodicity. Moreover, internally synchronized bundles of such rhythmic processes also can become "entrained" to external signals or rhythms (i.e., pacers, or zeitgebers; see Moore-Ede et al., 1982). The body's circadean rhythms, which become mutually entrained to one another and then entrained to the day/night cycle of the planet, are good examples of the entrainment process. A number of recent social psychological studies of individuals and groups (Ancona & Chong, 1996; Karau & Kelly, 1992; Kelly, 1988; Kelly & McGrath, 1985; McGrath & Kelly, 1986; Warner, 1979, 1988) suggest that various social behaviors of individuals and groups also become entrained—temporally synchronized—to one another and to external pacers. Such social entrainment—temporal coordination of multiple actions of group members—may be an important global variable that will emerge from the local dynamics of operation of groups. This offers still another aspect of temporal patterning that needs to be taken into account.

Thus, if we wish to study groups as complex, adaptive, dynamic systems, not only must we design our studies to capture group activity over a meaningful period of that group's life or project activity, but we must attend to multiple temporal patterns (rhythms, cycles) of behavior and disentangle them in our analyses.

∝ CAUSE

Aristotle delineated four types of cause: (a) mechanical cause, (b) final cause, (c) formal cause, and (d) material cause (see Bohm, 1980, pp. 12-13, for a good explication). Mechanical cause requires that targets be acted on from the outside; action is not indigenous. Material and formal cause, however, involve causes of behavior that lie inside the group. Final cause, understood as human intentions and goals, can influence the group from both the inside and the outside because both members and nonmembers may impose their agendas on the group.

Later, Western philosophers settled on mechanical cause as the mainspring for a positivist science. A simple, chainlike unidirectional interpretation of mechanical cause has reigned ever since in the social and behavioral sciences, even though the physical and biological sciences from which we borrowed the paradigm have long since incorporated a more sophisticated treatment of cause. It is time for group researchers to also adopt a more sophisticated approach to analyzing causal relations. We need to expand our conceptions of how mechanical causal relations function over time and pay more attention to the other three forms of causality.

First, our conceptualization (as well as that of many other social and behavioral scientists) holds that human systems have agency or intentionality. Such intentionality implies something akin to the Aristotelian final cause, stripped of the original theological underpinnings. In our view, it is not God's plan but individual human goals, and the coordination and interplay of those goals in collective action, that direct the behavior of humans in group.

Second, the dynamic development of a system corresponds to Aristotle's formal cause. Bohm (1980) called this *formative cause* to emphasize its dynamic nature and defined it as an ordered and structured inner movement that shapes things according to their essential nature (p. 12). In groups, the basic flow of interaction integral to human beings exerts a strong formative influence on groups, constraining their possible structures.

Third, our conception also involves some aspects of material cause. *Material cause* refers to the characteristic way that different materials behave: Glass shatters and wood splinters because of the structural properties of those substances. By analogy, the internal structure of a group can determine what lines members will split along if the group is put under sufficient pressure. Material cause depends on the particulars of a group's composition, including the attributes of elements and the structure of the coordination network; its past history (which leaves a legacy of strengthened and weakened links); and its concurrent state, which includes a particular pattern of activation among the links in the coordination network.

A dynamical systems view also puts serious strains on the traditional unidirectional view of efficient causality. A unidirectional chain or sequence of linear cause-effect relations holds that A affects B, which then affects C, and so on. Even in its more sophisticated multivariate versions (e.g., A and B both affect C, and C and D both bring about changes in E), it is still most often treated as a nonrecursive, directed, chained reaction.

In contrast, treating groups as complex systems presumes that effects originating within and outside of the group are connected via feedback loops so that most effects are recursive and bidirectional. Furthermore, we argue that there are strong dependencies between system levels. Events at the local level lead to global-level changes, and those emergent global-level structures subsequently constrain local activity. All of this implies that we need a systemic view of causal processes and that the traditional mechanical causal chain will not suffice.

∞ EXPERIMENTATION, GENERALIZATION, AND THE GOALS OF SCIENCE

Nomothetic and Ideographic Issues

A nomothetic approach seeks universal laws applicable to all instances of the unit of study. It requires that we study a number of cases for which initial conditions are identical in all important respects except for the one or few conditions that are manipulated. The nomothetic paradigm then proceeds either (a) by calculating covariation among quantitative indicators of two or more aspects of those cases or (b) by aggregating quantitative indices of one or more aspects of those cases and comparing average levels on those indices for subsets of the cases that had different levels on independent variables manipulated by the researcher.

The logic of the nomothetic paradigm, as represented in the experimental tradition, makes these presumptions:

1. All cases being treated as alike are indeed alike, in all ways that matter, on all variables except the experimental manipulanda and the dependent variables. Of course, this is frequently not true. The problem is generally handled by the next assumption.

2. Differences or idiosyncrasies that do exist among those cases, on aspects not being studied, will be more or less evenly distributed among experimental conditions, provided cases are assigned to conditions via random allocation, a sine qua non for a true experiment (Cook & Campbell, 1979).

3. The set of cases studied represents a larger population of cases, with a quantifiable margin of error, provided the cases are selected via random sampling from this defined population (a sine qua non for generalization; Runkel & McGrath, 1972). Resulting values for the cases studied (sample means and variance) can be used to estimate parameters (population means and variances) for the population as a whole.

4. The data collection methods used for any study inevitably contain both systematic and random errors of measurement, but steps such as counterbalancing, use of multiple measures, and random allocation of cases to conditions will minimize systematic errors of measurement. Residual errors of measurement are assumed to be random.

5. Random errors of measurement are assumed to be independent of each other and of conditions and to be normally distributed.

This set of assumptions implies that for true experiments in group research, the researcher needs either to obtain or to create a number of identical groups, all starting from the same initial conditions, and to assign those groups randomly to different experimental treatments so that any variations among initial conditions will be evenly distributed across experimental conditions. These groups also need to be randomly selected from a defined population of groups. Furthermore, all groups must be subject to the same sequence (and timing) of subsequent conditions—except for any differentiations that are part of different experimental treatment(s).

Our theoretical formulation explicitly contradicts several of the assumptions required by true experiments. We presume that even small differences in initial conditions for each system can make a difference in the impact of all subsequent events and that a group's particular history can have a major effect on subsequent states. Even when groups start from what appears to the researcher to be the same initial conditions, small differences can have effects that become magnified over time rather than washed out as randomly distributed noise.

Moreover, a careful consideration of the requirements listed above leads to the conclusion that true experiments on groups are in principle impossible. In actuality, most experimental social psychology falls short of the nomothetic ideal of studies that permit the discovery of laws that all human beings follow, because the outcomes of experiments, even those that yield large and statistically robust effects, rarely apply to every single case within the sample, let alone every human being (Runkel, 1990). Furthermore, not only do laboratory experiments using concocted groups not select from a population of groups; they cannot, because they study groups that would not have existed as social entities if the researcher had not created them.

We propose that researchers (a) study each group as a case unto itself; (b) study many groups of the "same" kind because, inevitably, each will be starting from at least slightly different initial conditions; (c) study many groups that operate at different levels of contextual parameters of interest; and (d) study groups in which contextual parameters change in value over the life of the group. We further propose that analyses not focus on the average level of some dependent variable(s) across a set of groups treated alike, compared to the average level of that variable(s) for a set of groups receiving different treatments (different starting points or different subsequent conditions). Rather, we propose that the goal of analyses be *to map the trajectory of each group, over time,* on one or more global variables, given that group's initial conditions and given the series of conditions it subsequently experiences. We construe that trajectory as an outcome of the group's own developmental forces, constrained by a landscape of attractors that is defined by the settings of contextual parameters. This suggests that we need to have an ideographic method nested within a nomothetic intent. It also reinforces the idea that studies must combine within-group and between-group designs.

Prediction Versus Description

This discussion raises a deeper issue, at once both methodological and substantive, of what the goal of scientific inquiry can and ought to be. The dominant goal for positivistic research has been to predict (and, ultimately, control) the behavior of systems not yet studied (but similar to those that have been studied), under conditions not yet extant and in time periods not yet experienced. In our conceptualization, the dominant goal is not predicting the level of some system variable under some specified set of conditions but rather identifying the qualitative pattern or patterns that are plausible for a system variable over time, given specified ranges of values for contextual parameters.

The generalization that we aim for—the conceptual leverage—comes from the ability to deduce the rules of system operation that hold for systems of the particular kinds we are studying and that generate the expressed (and tracked) trajectory of particular global variables under particular sets of circumstances (i.e., rules that "explain" the data of our studies). Patterns in empirical data are expressions, in the particular case (i.e., for particular groups with particular initial conditions, and particular histories), of underlying rules of system operation. Our deeper purpose, then, is to deduce those underlying rules, which is, of course, a nomothetic aim, achieved by ideographic study of particular systems. Our goal is to describe from an empirical inductive standpoint and to understand from a theoretical deductive one.

Among the many dangers that lurk for the researcher who pursues this kind of research is the danger of "going native," a problem well recognized by ethnographers. Researchers can easily become so engrossed in the particulars of a given group, studied intensively over time, that they lose sight of, and interest in, how the phenomena relate to the general case—or, worse, assume that a particular case *is* the general case.

∞ MEASUREMENT AND ERROR

In our discussion of the nomothetic approach, we referred to some basic assumptions about measurement and error that underlie experimental psychology. These include (a) assumptions underlying classical measurement theory in psychology and (b) assumptions underlying parametric techniques of statistical inference. Both involve a theory of error. Our approach encounters problems primarily with the former.

Classical measurement theory in psychology posits that what we want to measure is the essential attributes of static entities (e.g., individual traits or behaviors, group attributes or structural patterns, extant conditions of an environment). Classical measurement theory assumes that each measure captures some part of that essence being assessed and that the covariance of all of the measures, taken together, will capture the "true score" of the essential feature being studied. The scale on which the feature is being measured is quantitative. In contrast, our conceptualization calls for measuring the trajectories of variables that index the state of the group. In that approach, our interest is not so much in a fixed quantitative level (i.e., average magnitude) of a given variable as in its pattern of values over time.

The value of a measurement, in classical measurement theory, is assessed in terms of two important properties:

1. *Reliability.* A perfectly reliable measure is one that would give the exact same results if used to measure the same property of the same object twice at the same time and with the same measuring instrument (but independently).
2. *Construct validity.* A valid measure provides, as nearly as possible, an isomorphic representation of the entity, or at least of its essence.

Reliability can be estimated only by techniques such as test-retest, alternate forms, or the intercorrelation of multiple items (internal consistency), each of which involves procedures that only partly fit the strict definition of reliability. That is because the strict definition of reliability, given above, involves mutually contradictory requirements (i.e., for the two measurements to involve the same actor, behavior, instrument, and time but nevertheless to be independent). Construct validity, ultimately, can be attained only by definition—either via conceptual fiat or via consensus of the scientific community—although predictive, convergent, and discriminant validity can provide support for that judgment.

Our research program requires measures of global variables over time. Such measures face the same reliability question as do static measures. But the assessment of reliability is even more problematic. Global variables are liable to be selected, not as attempts to mirror the essence of the system isomorphically, but rather as reflecting relatively observable features of the system that are of interest to researchers. The researcher expects to find substantial variation in these global variables over time because the systems under study are regarded as dynamic systems, not static entities. When a variable changes over time, it is difficult to separate "true variance over time" from "unreliability of measurement over time."

In classical measurement theory, error in measurement can have both systematic and random components. Researchers and designers of instruments are responsible for assessing and removing the effects of systematic measurement error; residual error variance is treated as random error or noise. Large numbers of items on tests help ensure that this residual error contributes relatively little variance compared to the covariance among correlated items, each of which is an imperfect measure of the attribute of interest.

More recent theories of measurement, such as multivariate theories and latent function theories, treat these matters in a more sophisticated and much less simplistic manner. But they still rely on aggregation of scores over items, or over cases, at a given point in time, to estimate various measurement parameters. So they still pose the same kind of problems for our perspective, which calls for tracing the qualitative patterns of global variables over time.

In all of these measurement theories, the meaning of each measurement is, in effect, submerged by aggregration with, and averaging over, multiple measurements of the same variable at different points in time or on different systems (i.e., cases). Our interpretation of complexity theory implies a theory of measurement that does not assume that each measurement consists of a true component and an error component. Instead, every measurement is to be taken at its face value. Its meaning is not to be attained by aggregating and averaging it with other measurements taken before and after it or on other systems. Rather, its meaning is to be interpreted by its placement in the context of a *sequence of measurements of the same variable on the same system, over time.*

When applied to experimental research, using a large number of cases and aggregating the results helps minimize the relative contribution of residual error variance in somewhat the same way, with the large number of cases serving the function of the large number of items. This practice implies that if we have enough cases, what we don't know won't hurt us—much. This works if errors of measurement really are small and really are normally distributed across cases, hence cancel out. In this view, small differences in initial conditions that our measures fail to detect will not matter much in the long run.

A complexity theory view, in contrast, is that small differences in initial conditions may matter quite a bit in subsequent system dynamics, both with regard to the quantitative value of variables at particular times and with regard to the qualitative pattern of trajectories. However, if small groups are like other complex systems, this sensitive dependence on initial conditions should hold only within particular ranges of values of key contextual parameters. Within other ranges of values, small groups are likely to be quite robust against differences in initial conditions. Studies that map the ranges of values in which a system is sensitive or stable are essential to research on groups as complex systems.

∾ CONCLUDING COMMENTS

Taken together, the issues raised in this chapter call for a substantial rethinking of a number of conceptual, substantive, and methodological features of our past approach to small group research. They suggest that we cannot pursue research on the new conceptualization of groups offered here—as complex systems—solely via laboratory experiments, or at least not via the kind of experiments traditionally used. We must put more emphasis on supplementing this approach with other research strategies.

Our new conception raises questions about many features of traditional group research methodology: what phenomena are studied, how studies are designed, how measurement is construed, and how we think about causality. Several research strategies that have been relatively underused in past group research can help us plan and carry out the kind of research program envisioned here, while taking into account the issues raised in this chapter. These strategies are the topic of Chapter 10.

∞ 10 ∞

Some Research Strategies for Studying Groups as Complex Systems

*I*n light of the difficult issues raised in the previous chapter, it is clear that we need to rethink our theoretical and methodological preferences and practices as group researchers and identify which strategies will be most useful for studying groups as complex systems. The first section of this chapter identifies three underused research strategies that we think are potentially helpful for our quest to understand groups as complex systems. The next three sections discuss in more detail these three research strategies that hold special promise for research along the lines suggested by our theory: experimental simulations, comparative field studies, and computational modeling.

∞ RESEARCH STRATEGIES USEFUL FOR THE STUDY OF GROUPS AS COMPLEX SYSTEMS

Most researchers pay homage to the idea that we need to make use of multiple methods, at both strategic and tactical levels. All eight of the strategies in the Runkel and McGrath (1972) circumplex are represented in past group research. Nonetheless, most past group research in social psychology has followed the experimental tradition. That work emphasizes research strategies that maximize precision and control in the measurement and manipulation of variables, notably the laboratory experiment and the judgment study. In their review of group research appearing in the most prestigious social psychology journals between 1975 and 1992, Moreland et al. (1994) found that 76% reported data from laboratory experiments. Although high in precision and control, these studies are relatively low in generalizability and very low in contextual realism (Brinberg & McGrath, 1985; Runkel & McGrath, 1972). The naturalistic and theoretical traditions, which maximize contextual realism and generalizability, respectively, have received much less emphasis from such researchers.

The naturalistic tradition has been represented somewhat more strongly by group researchers publishing in organizational psychology journals, however. Sanna and Parks (1997) found that 21% of articles on groups in this literature reported data from field studies, with 7% using field experiments and 10% using surveys. Laboratory experiments (50%) still were the most popular research strategy, however.

Although all research strategies can be valuable, all have serious limitations. Research programs that draw on work from all three research traditions—experimentation, naturalistic studies, and theoretical formulations—provide a richer and broader contribution to our understanding. In examining and exploring any given domain, however, including that covered by our theory of groups, some of the strategies within each tradition are more useful than others.

Our theoretical perspective places special importance on a group's relation to its embedding contexts. This requires research strategies that emphasize contextual realism. Our focus on the pattern of a group's global dynamics over time (rather than on the level of particular variables at particular times) and our emphasis on a group's initial conditions and its developmental history suggests that we seek generality across systems with regard to qualitative patterns, at the cost of precision in controlling variables not being studied at specific values. Precise measurement of system variables does matter. Controlling variables not being studied by isolating the system from its embedding systems, however, conflicts with our interest in naturally occurring dynamics.

Rather than settling exclusively on a single research tradition or on a single research strategy within that tradition, we propose that a research program combine strategies from each of the three research traditions. In the rest of the chapter, we discuss three research strategies, one from each tradition, that we think are most useful for examining our theory of groups as complex systems. Because of the strong need for contextual realism and for studies over time, experimental simulation is the most useful research strategy in the experimental tradition. From the naturalistic tradition, comparative case studies is the strategy best suited for our research program. The general verbal theory presented in the first eight chapters of this book can best be complemented by the use of computational modeling, a research strategy that falls within the theoretical tradition.

Naturalistic Research Using Comparative Case Studies

A crucial methodological implication of the perspective offered in this book is the need for relatively detailed (precise) information about the group as a system over time (i.e., the global variables of interest). It is essential that our empirical data be on groups that continue to function as systems over time. Moreover, the importance placed on initial conditions and past history makes it valuable for the researcher to be able to follow groups from their inception.

Ideally, the groups that supply the empirical evidence for our theory ought to be natural groups, which emerge and function as systems independent of the research enterprise. That calls for extensive use of field studies. But the need for multiple sets of comparable groups—to escape the system uniqueness trap—suggests the use of comparative case studies rather than single-case field studies. Unfortunately, it is usually difficult to obtain repeated access to natural groups for data collection purposes, and to some extent frequent data collection renders these groups less natural. It is also very difficult to obtain access to *sets* of natural groups that are somehow comparable to one another—in size, structure, projects, past history, and so on—so comparative case studies usually have to lump together groups that have differing initial conditions. Furthermore, almost by definition, it is hard for the researcher to arrange to be present at the creation of natural groups. Thus, it will be hard to study those groups from formation through metamorphosis, with a temporally rich body of empirical data.

One feature that makes such naturalistic comparative case studies more feasible, though, is our focus on tracking the evolution of emergent, global variables, descriptive of the overall system, instead of studying the microlevel relations of a system's local dynamics. Such global variables, assessed at frequent intervals over the system's life span, are just the kind of indices available in many archival databases. So archival studies, taking advantage of richly articulated databases, offer a good option as a form of comparative case study to examine groups as complex systems.

Experimental Research
Using Experimental Simulations

In contrast to naturalistic studies, the laboratory experiment solves both the "present at the creation" problem and the multiple comparable groups problem elegantly. Unfortunately, it is difficult in principle (and even more difficult in practice) to run experiments on a given system over extended periods of time. For one thing, the very logic of analysis accompanying laboratory experiments calls for both *experimentally independent* cases and experimentally independent "trials" (or X-Y sequences, where X is a manipulated cause and Y is a measured effect). Independent cases are required because that logic of analysis, based on inferential statistics, requires multiple independent cases that can be considered comparable or equivalent in all respects except for the manipulated conditions. Independent trials are required because that logic of analysis seeks directional causal inferences *at the most micro level possible* (i.e., it is reductionist).

The second session of a given group, however, is not independent of the first, nor will the third or fourth session of that group be independent of the first and second sessions. Instead, the course of a single group's life can be conceptualized as a single trial. Moreover, true experiments require stringent control (or randomization) of variables not being studied, including contextual variables in the system's embedding contexts that affect the system. But our theoretical perspective requires a full consideration of the continuing, dynamic interchange between the group and its embedding systems (as well as between the group and its embedded members). So the usual experimental strategy, of isolating the unit of study from all outside influences except those provided by the experimenter, would be counterproductive.

Experimental simulations overcome some of the difficulties posed by both field study and laboratory experiment strategies—though at a cost in contextual realism relative to field studies and in precision relative to lab experiments. In experimental simulations, researchers *create* multiple instances of the kinds of systems they wish to study— for example, product development teams—and do so in a way that reflects as nearly as possible the conditions that would prevail if they were natural groups of the same genre. In contrast to naturally occurring groups, however, these groups allow easy access to empirical data about interaction and performance over time from their moment of creation to their ending. For such studies to have contextual realism, the groups must be working on projects that have consequences for the group and its members.

So experimental simulations have the potential to offer (a) quasi-realism with respect to both the functioning of the system and its dynamic interaction with its embedding contexts; (b) some precision and control in the measurement and manipulation of crucial system variables; and (c) the opportunity to study multiple comparable groups as systems from their beginning through whatever period of time is appropriate for the type of group being simulated.

Theoretical Studies Using Computational Models

Computational modeling has not been used much in social and behavioral science research, including social psychology, until recently. Only in the past decade have the necessary computational resources become widely available. Now computational modeling has become eminently practical and is gradually becoming a more widely used research strategy in social science.

With computational modeling, researchers create a computational analogue of a given class of systems. This allows them to generate a large number of simulated groups having particular characteristics and then to run those groups, symbolically and computationally, under particular sets of conditions.

Computational models allow researchers to move beyond some of the pitfalls of traditional verbal theories in building more dynamic, complex, and precise theoretical formulations. It is difficult or impossible to derive predictions about complex systems that include multiple interacting variables and stochastic processes with verbal theory alone, yet computational models can handle this quite easily. In addition, the proper interpretation of terms and the exact nature of relations are often unclear in verbal theories. To be used at all, a computational model must be expressed precisely, in assumptions, algorithms, and, ultimately, computer programs. So the researcher is forced to clear up the ambiguities of verbal theories when translating them into mathematical terms. In contrast to the tradition of formal mathematical models, however, this translation into mathematical language is instrumental and not an end in itself. Computational modeling also enables a researcher to explore multiple different interpretations of a given theoretical point that was ambiguous or purposively flexible in the verbal theory by building different algorithms for each of the interpretations and testing them.

Computational models predict what researchers can expect to observe if the theories informing the model are correct, so they can be used to guide the design of experiments and the collection of empirical data. A computational model can run hundreds, even thousands of groups, on inexpensive PCs, exploring many different sets of combinations of conditions. The researcher has data on the initial conditions of groups and can assess key variables at whatever frequency is desirable and continue groups' "lives" as long as desired. Furthermore, the computational model can run groups under combinations of conditions that would be impossible to implement empirically—for ethical, or legal, or practical, or even logical reasons. So computational modeling permits us to extend the range of possible conditions and kinds of groups that can be studied, beyond the range that exists among extant groups or that we can create in our labs. In this way, researchers can efficiently explore the effects of various factors and conditions on thousands of groups and home in on experimental designs that test the most interesting or pronounced results suggested by the model.

Concluding Comments

Thus, in terms of the research strategies and traditions available, our theory of groups as complex systems calls for (a) more use of naturalistic strategies—field studies and especially comparative case studies; (b) a shift in the strategy of choice for the experimental tradition from laboratory experiments to experimental simulations; and (c) more reliance on theory, including verbal theory (which our theory of groups as complex systems represents) and computational modeling. Together, these provide a strong combination of generalizability and contextual realism and a reasonable level of precision and control. By drawing on research strategies from each of the three traditions, we aim to finesse some of the limitations of each strategy via triangulation. The next three sections discuss studies that exemplify each of the three strategies.

∞ EXPERIMENTAL SIMULATIONS OF GROUPS

Probably the most familiar forms of experimental simulation are the driving and flight simulators used in studies of individual (and sometimes team) performance in human-machine systems. A long tradition of experimental simulations in social psychology goes back to the classic Lewin et al. (1939) study of boys' clubs. Those clubs were created for research purposes, and events were manipulated for research purposes, but the experience of being in a boys' club was doubtless quite real for the participants. Work using such experimental simulations includes the Sherif et al. (1961) Robbers Cave study in which competitive groups of boys were created in a field camp setting. These groups were then induced to cooperate by experimental arrangements. Newcomb's (1961) acquaintance process study can also be considered an experimental simulation. That study arranged for a set of men to be assigned to a campus housing unit organized for research purposes. Various events were manipulated experimentally to become data collection occasions. Although the students would have lived in some campus housing even if the research had not taken place, they would not have experienced the experimental manipulations of that study. Many board games played by groups could be used for experimental simulations as well, such as Monopoly and Risk, very simple abstractions of the real estate industry and of international political and military relations, respectively.

These examples differ in at least three important ways. First, they differ in the degree to which the simulation is a highly abstract representation of the concrete system being studied or a richly articulated representation with high contextual realism. Board games are the most abstract; the Robbers Cave study and Newcomb's housing setting are among the most concrete. Second, they differ in the degree to which the people being studied are a population appropriate for performance in the real-world system being simulated. The pilots-in-training often used for flight simulators are a highly appropriate population. Third, the examples differ in the degree to which the simulated systems reflect the actual difficulty and complexity of performance in the real-world system and carry the same kind of serious performance consequences as the real-world counterparts of the simulated systems. The consequences for players of board games are relatively trivial. The consequences for pilots-in-training in the flight simulators are important but clearly (and fortunately!) less serious than consequences in actual planes, especially when things go wrong. These simulations—like computational models—allow operators to explore combinations of variables that would be far too risky to experiment with in real aircraft. The consequences for the boys who took part in the Robbers Cave study, and for the college students in Newcomb's acquaintance process study, however, were comparable to those faced by boys in nonexperimental summer camps and those faced by college students in standard housing, respectively. In some cases, however, the more real the consequences are for participants, the more ethically questionable the experimental simulation may be (e.g., the Stanford Prison Experiment by Haney, Banks, & Zimbardo, 1973).

The essence of such simulations is as follows: The researcher creates a set of conditions that to some degree emulates those of some referent real-world systems. Then a population of people, presumably similar to those who would ordinarily inhabit the referent real-world system, are formed into groups in ways presumably reflecting the selection processes of the referent real-world groups. Those groups are provided with the resources and technology that would presumably be available to groups operating within the referent real-world systems and are given the opportunity/requirement to carry out projects similar to those indigenous for the referent real-world systems.

In flight simulator research, for example, individuals (or crews) "fly" an aircraft simulator on assigned missions in which they encounter conditions that also occur in the real world (e.g., environmental perturbations). In the Lewin et al. (1939) study, the researchers organized after-school activity clubs for boys, and the participants became part of a group being studied over a series of meetings.

The key features here, for studying groups as dynamical systems, are that (a) the individuals act within a context that is, psychologically, much like the context within which the members of the real-world referent system would act; (b) the context is structured so that particular actions lead to results similar to those that ensue from those same actions in the referent real-world systems (i.e., the "cause-effect network" is veridical); (c) the activities have some meaningful consequences for the participants; and, above all, (d) the simulation continues over an extended period of "system operation time," so that the system's dynamic processes unfold as they would in the real-world referent system.

Some Examples From
Our Own Research Program

We have conducted two major and related studies of tasks, technology, and groups over time that qualify as experimental simulations. We discuss them here not because we regard them as exemplary but because we know them in detail. Thus, we can point out, from our own experience, both some strengths of this strategy for studying complex systems and some serious limitations.

The first of these studies was a semester-long (13-week) study of 22 three- and four-member work groups within an undergraduate class on the social psychology of organizations. Half of those groups communicated with each other via a computer conference system; the other half worked face to face. All groups switched communication medium for 2 weeks near midsemester. We also rotated one member from each group into a different group for 2 weeks in the latter part of the semester. The second study was a quasi-replication, with 30 groups working together for the first 7 weeks of the semester and 30 new groups, reconfigured from the same class of students, working together for the final 7 weeks of the term. Half of the first batch of groups worked via computer conference, the other half face to face. All participants switched communication medium as well as group mates for the second half.

In both studies, groups were asked to suppose they were consulting groups working for an organizational consulting firm. Each week, during a 2-hour lab session, they were assigned problems appropriate to such a premise and to the content of the course. Tasks varied widely from week to week—including problem-solving, decision-making, policy selection, negotiation, brainstorming, and planning tasks. Each group performed the assigned task (which sometimes included an individual task segment and always included a group task) and completed a 15-minute questionnaire. Next, participants completed both an individual and a group essay and then completed a final 5-minute questionnaire. The essays addressed the question of how that week's assigned task related to the concepts in the lectures and readings of the course. Although quality of performance on the experimental task did not affect student grades, quality scores on both the individual and group essays formed a major part of each student's course grade. It was presumed, therefore, that students were motivated to do well on the essays. All group activity in the face-to-face groups was videotaped; all messages sent on the computer conference system were logged to a file.

Thus, we collected considerable and relatively fine-grained data. We had detailed questionnaire responses on a standard set of questions from each member of each group for each of 14 weeks. Those questions asked about individual reactions and feelings about the group, its members, its task performance, and the individual's own and other members' contributions. We had group task performance measures and, for many weeks, individual task performance measures as well. We had quality scores and other scores on both individual and group essays for each week. We had a record of all text in the computer groups and of both spoken and nonverbal interaction in the face-to-face groups, for all group interaction for all 14 weeks.

Many results of those studies appear in special issues of two journals. In those publications, the two studies are referred to as JEMCO1 and JEMCO2 (JEMCO was the name of the organizational consulting firm that the students were ostensibly working for). Several studies from the first experiment, JEMCO1, appear in *Small Group Research* (Arrow & McGrath, 1993; Gruenfeld & Hollingshead, 1993; Hollingshead et al., 1993; McGrath, 1993; McGrath & Arrow, 1996; McGrath, Arrow, Gruenfeld, Hollingshead, & O'Connor, 1993; O'Connor et al., 1993). Several studies from the second experiment, JEMCO2, appear in *Computer Supported Cooperative Work* (Arrow et al., 1996; Berdahl & Craig, 1996; Bouas & Arrow, 1996; Cummings, Schlosser, & Arrow, 1996; Lebie et al., 1996; McGrath & Arrow, 1996; Rhoades & O'Connor, 1996). The results of these studies allow us to make several points about studying groups over time as complex systems (McGrath & Berdahl, 1998).

Two features are worth noting about the results that we have published so far. First, most of these studies use conventional statistical techniques for analyzing quantitative data (e.g., ANOVAs, correlations, path analysis, regressions). The findings, however, are quite complicated. Most significant results involve two- and three-way interactions rather than "simple" main effects, most with significant effects for time. Interpretation of such complex results using those conventional analysis techniques can be problematic.

Second, we also collected a large body of "qualitative" data from three basic sources: (a) field notes made by each experimenter each week; (b) the recorded conversations of groups—on video or in the computer logs; and (c) the content of the individual and group essays. In the course of connecting the week's activities to concepts in assigned readings for the class, these essays often offered valuable insights about the group, its members, and its ongoing processes. This qualitative information helped us enormously in our efforts to make sense of the complex quantitative findings. However enlightening that qualitative information might have been, though, standard methodological practice in our field relegates it to the pejorative status of "anecdotal information." It is perhaps analogous to the status of "hearsay evidence" in a courtroom: It may well be true, but you can't use it as evidence.

Those two points taken together constitute a double bind for researchers interested in studying complex systems such as groups. On the one hand, quantitative results stemming from the operation of complex systems are likely to be too complicated for definitive analyses by conventional techniques and in any case far too complicated for definitive interpretation. On the other hand, the rationale supporting these conventional techniques has also led many researchers to view rich qualitative data as illegitimate or inappropriate as evidence. Clearly, some of those "conventions" are going to have to change before this type of research on groups as complex systems will be readily accepted by the field.

Several key points about the design and "independent variables" of those studies emerged as well. In the first study, we intended for every group to keep the same membership and communication medium throughout the study (except for specific manipulations) and for every group to perform the same experimental task in a given week. That design poses several major problems. First, it confounds task and week. We could not distinguish the effect of a specific task used in Week 3 from an effect of "Week 3." Even worse, if that task occurred in one of the weeks during which the communication medium or membership was manipulated, we could not definitively distinguish the task effect from the week effect from the effect of the experimental manipulation.

Such an "activity-by-time" confound is inevitable within studies dealing with complex systems over extended periods of time. A change in design of the second study let us clear up some of that confounding but introduced other confounds. In that second study, instead of shifting groups to new media for a short time and then back again, and shifting group membership for a short time and then back again, we shifted both group membership and communication medium permanently at the halfway point. This helped unconfound week and task type because we used different tasks of the same type in both halves of the study. But it confounded "group life" with week: For example, the second week of life for groups in the second half of the study was really "Week 9" of the overall study and of the semester. That manipulation gave us twice as many groups in each communication medium while halving the life span of the groups. Other alterations of the design would remove some confounds and introduce others. No one design is satisfactory in all respects.

An even more pernicious feature of the design for both studies was that some of the initial participants dropped out of the course, hence out of the study, during the early weeks. Furthermore, members of most groups had unplanned absences throughout the semester. Real-world groups are like that. But experimental groups are not. So all of the problems indicated above, regarding complex quantitative results and inevitable design confounds, are thereby multiplied. One consequence of member drops and absences, and of the other design and data complications noted above, is that although we collected a huge volume of data, for many specific analyses (often involving complex interactions) we often had relatively few "cases" to which we could apply conventional statistical techniques.

These groups only partially met the criteria for effective simulation stated in the earlier discussion. These were not "real" work groups. The population of participants was only a weak match to the populations of people who might inhabit such organizational consulting groups. The study did provide motivational conditions that were far stronger than most laboratory studies but certainly not as strong as those that would obtain in real groups. Moreover, the psychological situation for the participants was not real; indeed, some of the participants' behavior might have been in reaction to being in an experiment. Finally, the groups existed for 7 weeks or 13 weeks, meeting for 2 hours each week, which provided a poor match for the temporal patterning likely to obtain in real consulting teams. Although the structure of standing groups that take up a series of projects simulates teams, the meeting pattern was closer to that found in many task forces, and the fixed duration of meetings and of the groups' life spans most closely resembled groups that fit the crew prototype.

In extended experimental simulations, every "dependent variable" is confounded with the sequence of events, and every later measurement of a variable is confounded with earlier measures of that same variable for that same group. Such dependence on the unit's own history is characteristic of the operation of a complex system over time, but such time dependence is problematic for our conventional data analysis procedures.

Experimental Simulation
and Complex Systems

Initially, we did not apply much of the thinking, or any of the techniques, of dynamical or complex systems research to the data of the

JEMCO studies (for an exception, see Arrow, 1997). Indeed, our experience in dealing with the complex data of these studies via conventional means of analysis—and in trying to relate the rich qualitative data to the quantitative data—was a major stimulus impelling us to examine more deeply the possibilities of concepts borrowed from dynamical and complex systems theories.

In principle, we could *reconstrue* the features of the two JEMCO studies to make use of the concepts and logic of analysis for complex systems. For example, we could view the quality of the individual and group essays as global variables and track their evolution for *each* group over the weeks (rather than aggregating across groups and time periods, the approach taken by Gruenfeld & Hollingshead, 1993, and Cummings et al., 1996, for JEMCO1 and JEMCO2, respectively). Alternative global variables might include group identity, group-member commitment levels, hierarchical versus egalitarian pattern of member participation, or level of within-group conflict. We could use the two variations of communication medium as different levels of an important contextual parameter. Other potential contextual parameters include sex composition of the group and prior membership stability or change. So it would be possible, in principle, to reanalyze and reinterpret substantially all of the quantitative evidence from those two longitudinal studies in terms appropriate to the perspective formulated in this book.

∞ COMPARATIVE CASE STUDIES OF GROUPS

Comparative case studies collect the same or very similar data from each of a number of different cases, all of which are "alike" in important respects. Depending on the nature of the data available about each case, data analysis and comparisons between cases can be done on the basis of one variable or many, in qualitative or quantitative terms, and for a few or many points in time. Ideally, when studying groups as dynamic systems, the data should be temporally fine grained and should track global or system-level variables over some substantial period of group life.

Comparative case studies are used extensively in some social and behavioral science fields but have not seen much use in social psychology generally or in the study of groups in particular. Examples using archival data are studies that make use of the Human Relations Area Files or similar archives. Some use quantitative data; some use qualitative data; some use both. With any comparative case study, the trick is to get comparable data on groups that are in some sense the same or comparable and to do so over meaningful periods of time.

One good exemplar of a set of comparative cases is the work of Hackman and colleagues (collected in Hackman, 1990). Altogether, the group of researchers conducted intensive case studies of 27 extant work groups. They included several groups of each of seven types, with types classified on the basis of the kinds of projects they were carrying out: (a) top management teams (engaged in policy formulation and policy setting activities); (b) task forces (with a meaning similar to our use of that term in this book); (c) professional support groups (e.g., an airline maintenance crew); (d) performance groups (e.g., a string quartet or a sports team); (e) human service teams (e.g., a mental health treatment team); (f) customer service teams (e.g., a flight attendant crew); and (g) production teams (e.g., an airline cockpit crew).

The investigators gathered a richly articulated body of qualitative data on each of those groups, following a plan that yielded relatively comparable pictures of each (insofar as one can get a parallel picture of groups doing vastly different projects under vastly different circumstances). Results were treated at three levels of analysis and interpretation. First, each was presented as an intact case study of a portion of the life history of that group (see the individual chapters of Hackman, 1990). Second, a comparative integration was made of the subsets of three or so groups of each group type (in the summary chapters at the end of each section of that book). Third, those subintegrations were woven together into an overall integration of findings with regard to all 27 groups (in the final chapter of that book). Together, those studies and their integrative treatment amounted to a partial empirical verification (and revision) of a group theoretic framework that was laid out in the initial chapter of that book. The framework was recapitulated, with extensive revisions, in the final chapter. That final integrative treatment emphasized a series of unanticipated themes and issues that permeate many of the group studies and noted some special risks and opportunities that are faced by groups of the different types. The themes and issues are quite compatible with our view of groups as complex systems, stressing temporal and rhythmic processes, self-fueling spirals, authority and autonomy issues, and work content issues. The different risks and opportunities that the authors identified for groups of each type highlighted the importance of different group projects for establishing the local and global dynamics of those groups.

This example shows both the strengths and the limitations of that strategy. The book provides a rich body of data, mainly qualitative but relatively systematic, about a wide array of extant groups. Though it does not present a literal time series of data points about the groups, it provides information about the temporal patterning of events and responses of those groups over considerable periods of their "lives." Because the project primarily studied extant groups that already existed at the time the project began, the investigators were not in at the creation, so they had only retrospective information about formation processes. In some cases, they provided information about metamorphosis, but in most cases, the groups continued after the research project was completed. The set of comparative studies does provide rich information about coordination, development, and adaptation over a considerable period of operations for those groups and hence about the local dynamics, global dynamics, and contextual dynamics of these groups. Of special importance, in the present context, is that these investigators built their data collection and interpretation plans on the premise that these groups were complex, adaptive, dynamic systems.

∞ COMPUTATIONAL MODELING OF GROUPS

Computational modeling can serve as the embodiment of the complexity theory and a dynamical systems approach to the study of human systems, including small groups. Such systems are invariably complex, and neither verbal theory nor empirical data collection alone can do justice to them (Berdahl, 1998). Computational modeling offers a strategy that can, for half a dozen reasons (for reviews, see Ostrom, 1988, and Harrison, 1998).

First, computational modeling can remove some of the ambiguity from verbal theory by requiring the researcher to flesh out vague verbal statements in the form of computational algorithms. Second, computational modeling lends itself extremely well to the integration of disparate theories addressing the same phenomenon. It therefore can be used as an interdisciplinary tool for unifying complementary theories, testing competing ones, and representing groups as the multifaceted complex systems that they are. Third, computational modeling enables us to explore beyond the one or two iterations usually derived with verbal theory and thus to explore temporal cadences and rhythms of group phenomena and to incorporate multilevel and multidirectional notions of cause into our theories. Fourth, computational modeling can handle the effects of learning and adaptation within groups over time and explore the effects of random initial conditions and stochastic events on groups. Fifth, computational modeling can aid theory evaluation by helping us identify key variables and temporal patterns to observe in empirical studies. Finally, computational modeling allows us to manipulate parameters of interest in ways and to levels that might not be possible or ethical to do experimentally.

Computational Modeling as a Bridge Between Verbal Theory and Empirical Data

Verbal theory and empirical data are essentially mismatched in scope and detail, and we suggest that computational modeling may provide a crucial interface between them. On the one hand, general theory is usually stated in verbal terms, is often equivocal or open to several different interpretations, and usually consists of at best "directional" predictions (e.g., Group A should exhibit more of X than Group B; as X increases, Y should increase, and as X decreases, so should Y). On the other hand, empirical data are usually in quantitative form and very specific. Behavioral and social scientists have developed research methods that allow collection of rigorous empirical data and analysis of such data using sophisticated statistical techniques.

At the same time, verbal theory is often addressed to problems that are very broad in scope, with the intention of giving the theory broad applicability, whereas empirical data, by definition, strictly apply only to the measured aspects of the observed cases under all of the observed conditions and can properly be generalized only to "universes" of cases and conditions of which those are a random sample. Thus, these two main resources available to the researcher—verbal theory and rigorous quantitative data and analyses—are inherently mismatched both in their levels of specificity and rigor and in their scope and generalizability.

Computational modeling can act as a bridge between them by translating verbal theory into specific and quantitative language and providing output on the level of specificity of empirical data. Computational modeling forces the researcher to move beyond verbal descriptions of a theory into specific and rigorous statements that make much more specific and quantifiable (e.g., point rather than directional) predictions (Ostrom, 1988). This process reveals how equivocal or ambiguous verbal theory can be. Output from a computational model provides specific quantitative descriptions of the implications of the theory that informs that computational model. Those implications can be treated as "hypotheses" or predictions made by the theory. Empirical data can then be compared against model data to test the theory that underlies the model.

Computational Modeling Can Go
Beyond Verbal Theory and Empirical Data

Computational models can go beyond verbal theory and empirical data in several ways. First, they allow properties of the system to emerge from interaction—emergent properties that verbal theory would likely not anticipate. In the run of a computational model, in contrast, all results, including unanticipated results, are recorded precisely. Second, they permit the integration of several alternative verbal theories, which may have competing predictions or may present complex combinations of possibilities, the integration of which may pose a task too complicated for a thought experiment or for working out "on paper" in verbal terms. It may be difficult or impossible to identify the implications of such verbal theories, especially those that arise only after several iterations of the system they describe. Computational models can do this relatively intractable intellectual task for us. Furthermore, model output may clarify implications of verbal theory—especially in iterated interaction—that are simply not specifiable using verbal techniques.

Not only can a computational model allow for emergent properties to evolve that verbal theory cannot specify in advance; it also can allow for explanation of emergent properties that cannot be provided by empirical data. It is often not possible to infer how emergent properties (i.e., global variables that describe a system) came about simply by examining empirical data—even if we have very good discrete or continuous time-series data from an empirical system. Empirical data are always overdetermined: Too many possible explanations can account for any given finding. It is impossible to identify which of a very large number of possible "extraneous variables" (and "noise" or stochastic shocks to the empirical system) may have been operating and may therefore account for the patterns observed.

In the case of computational modeling, however, theoretical considerations guide the choice of local variables and the dynamics of the system. The researcher can ensure that different runs of the model begin with identical initial conditions and have identical system dynamics (a desideratum that can only be approximated in experimental studies) and subsequently can track, at every iteration of the model, the values and dynamics of each element and emergent property of the system. Furthermore, the researcher can choose to introduce "noise" or stochastic shocks to the system and can manipulate their duration, effects, and probabilities, allowing the researcher to examine systematically the implications of these stochastic shocks on the system. Thus, computational models represent virtual systems whose dynamics can be decomposed to identify which variables and processes are responsible for emergent properties of the system and how that takes place.

Benefits of Computational Modeling for Studying Groups as Complex Systems

One of the benefits of computational modeling as a method of studying complex systems is that it allows the researcher to integrate several minitheories into a holistic theoretical system (Ostrom, 1988). This is consistent with our treatment of groups as systems, in which we attempt to describe groups in holistic terms, integrating what we identify as the major elements, properties, and dynamics of groups.

In developing a computational model of a system, the researcher must (a) identify primitives, algorithms of the system, and rules of the system; (b) identify possible emergent properties of these primitives and these rules; (c) build in algorithms and measures of these emergent properties and traces of these rules; and (d) consider how these primitives, rules, and emergent properties are affected, constrained, or bounded by parameters extrinsic to the system. In other words, the researcher delves into core concepts of dynamical systems theory, identifying local variables, dynamic rules, global variables, and contextual parameters of the system of interest.

Another central feature of computational modeling that makes it consistent with our approach to studying groups as complex systems is that it is intrinsically dynamic. It allows the researcher to explore implications of a theory over any number of iterations of the system, not just for the single or few iterations usually described or envisioned by verbal theory. In contrast to collecting data on groups in experimental studies, the research can measure variables at every time step without disrupting the unfolding process in any way. Computational modeling also allows aspects of a system to unfold with different time cadences (e.g., long-term developmental patterns, short-interval performance cycles, one-time external events) and allows the researcher to examine the temporal patterning of different aspects of the system. Such multiple temporal cadences are difficult to anticipate when specifying verbal theory and even harder to anticipate when deciding how to collect empirical data.

One further advantage of modeling a system over several iterations via computational modeling is that this strategy allows the researcher to explore nonlinear relations between elements of a system and emergent properties of that system. Furthermore, it allows the researcher to model nonlinear relations between system global variables and the system's embedding environment, or contextual parameters; such relations are ubiquitous in complex systems and self-regulatory systems. This moves beyond the independent variable/dependent variable and input/output models that have dominated research on small groups (and social and behavioral science research in general) by introducing feedback loops between "independent" and "dependent" variables (inputs and outputs) and by introducing nonmonotonic and nonlinear relations between them.

Another implication of the dynamic nature of computational modeling and the introduction of feedback loops within a system is that systems can be programmed to "learn" from their prior states. Such systems can become self-altering, not only with respect to values of system variables from Time X to Time Y, but also with respect to their rules of operation at Time X and at Time Y. Again, this moves the researcher beyond the limitations of both verbal theory and empirical data because the dynamics of such self-altering systems would be difficult or impractical to predict with verbal theory and impossible to track with, or infer from, empirical data.

Finally, computational models allow the researcher to explore the implications of different combinations of variables and rules for the system (Nowak, Lewenstein, & Vallacher, 1994). This gets at the systems theory ideas of path multiplicity and equifinality: Do different combinations of local variables and local dynamics yield similar emergent properties, or qualitative patterns of global variables, for the system? Do systems with different initial conditions arrive at similar states? Similarly, it allows the researcher to explore the possibility of sensitive dependence on initial conditions, a key idea for complex and/or chaotic systems: Do systems with nearly identical initial conditions diverge greatly over time? Finally, it allows the researcher to explore the impact of stochastic or random shocks: Do systems with identical initial conditions diverge greatly if small changes or minor stochastic shocks are introduced to the system?

In sum, computational modeling provides an extremely powerful tool for exploring and understanding complex systems. It not only bridges verbal theory and empirical data but moves beyond them in many ways, allowing the researcher to explore questions and implications of system dynamics that would be impossible to examine with verbal theory, empirical data, or both.

Different Types of Computational Models

Computational models come in different forms. One is a computer simulation that models the global dynamics of a system directly by implementing a mathematical model that specifies initial conditions and rules for system evolution. This is the approach used for modeling large-scale weather patterns, for example, using well-known equations describing fluid flow, heat convection, and so on.

Another form of computational modeling is the study of the emergence of global patterns from local dynamics by modeling local interactions of actors within a larger environment. This is an agent-based approach to computational modeling, using object-oriented programming, and it is the approach we think appropriate for exploring our group theory. Rather than implementing a single mathematical model that covers the global system dynamics, in the agent-based approach one creates a set of individual agents, or miniprograms, each of which follows a set of rules. An ant colony, for example, is simulated by having each individual ant be a program with rules for behavior (Drogoul & Ferber, 1994; Gordon, Goodwin, & Trainor, 1992). The set of equations that govern these models may be the same for every agent or may differ for different categories of agents. They may also incorporate contingencies: For example, agents may respond differently depending on the classification of various potential partners in interaction. In a model of a predator-prey system, for example, predators respond differently to prey than they do to other predators.

In the next section, we describe a computational model of groups that incorporates several aspects of our group-theoretic framework and draws on other group and social theory. It illustrates one instantiation of our group-theoretic approach in computational modeling terms.

An Example of a Computational
Model of Small Groups

Berdahl (1998, 1999) has developed a computational model as a step toward a general, dynamic, and testable theory of small groups as complex systems. As an agent-based model, it simulates for 20 time periods one four-person group whose members remain in the group and do not recruit new members. Several parameters can be manipulated in the model, including group project characteristics and member skills, needs, and demographic characteristics. Different algorithms can also be selected, including the way members initially evaluate each other's skills, whether skills, needs, and evaluations change over time, and the order in which assignments are made in a group. The model makes predictions for group performance, divisions of labor, member commitment to groups, group commitment to members, and member power over time.

Berdahl's model integrates theories addressing (a) group socialization processes, (b) group projects and member characteristics, and (c) the influence of demographic characteristics. Moreland and Levine's theory of group socialization (Moreland & Levine, 1982, 1988; Levine & Moreland, 1991) served as the guiding theoretical framework. Their theory proposes three key psychological processes in the member-group relationship: (a) evaluation, (b) commitment, and (c) role transition. Members evaluate how well the group can fulfill their needs, and groups evaluate how well each member can fulfill the group's needs. The more a member evaluates his or her opportunities within a group to be consistent with his or her needs, the higher the member's level of commitment to that group; the more a group evaluates a member's contributions to the group as fulfilling group needs, the higher the group's commitment to that member. Members' status within the group changes as member and group commitment levels rise and fall, and these changes in status are conceptualized as transitions between potential, new, full, marginal, and ex-membership roles within the group.

Moreland and Levine's model (1982) treats evaluation as the key process guiding the member-group relationship over time but leaves open the particular kinds of characteristics that groups and members evaluate in each other and how these characteristics are assessed. Berdahl's model draws on theories of group projects (e.g., Bales, 1950a; McGrath, 1997) to specify group needs and member characteristics evaluated by a group: Group projects can be defined according to their relative amounts of task, interpersonal, and process requirements, and the group evaluates these three skills in its members accordingly. Theories of member needs (Baumeister & Leary, 1995; Maslow, 1943; McClelland, 1985) are drawn on to specify member needs and group characteristics evaluated by members: members have varying levels of need for achievement, affiliation, and power and evaluate their opportunities for fulfilling these needs in the group.

Theories of the evaluation process itself are also incorporated into the model. Three different evaluation processes were explored in initial runs of the model (Berdahl, 1999): (a) evaluations based on true values of member characteristics that contained some random error normally distributed around those true values; (b) evaluations based on the demographic similarity between members (member sex, race, age, and class are included in the model); and (c) evaluations based on demographic stereotypes. The model also allows the user to specify the skills, needs, and demographic characteristics of group members, as well as whether members' skills and evaluations of each other and the group over time remain the same or change as a function of experience. In this way, the model explores the impact of different assumptions regarding skill differences between demographic groups, how evaluations are made, and how evaluations and skills interact to shape each other over time (e.g., Eagly & Karau, 1991; Ridgeway & Berger, 1986; Tajfel & Turner, 1979).

Several issues arose during the development of the computational model that were not clearly addressed by the theories and the relevant literature informing the model (Berdahl, 1998). One of these issues was how project requirements would be divided among members of a group to create a division of labor. This had to be specified in the model so that member contributions to the group's project could be tracked and used to compute group performance. Three possible options for project alignment were included in the model: (a) a random order of project assignments, (b) assignments made in order of member power (i.e., the most powerful member of the group negotiated his or her assignments first, then the second most powerful member, and so on), and (c) assignments made in order of the group's commitment to members (i.e., the member to whom the group was most committed negotiated his or her assignments first, and so on).

Initial runs of the model simulated groups working on task-oriented projects and systematically explored the impact of the different evaluation rules (accuracy with random error, similarity-biased, and stereotypes), different group demographic compositions, and different orders of making project assignments within groups (Berdahl, 1999). Runs were first conducted on a simple case to verify that model algorithms behaved as expected and to explore the implications of the different conditions on a simple case. Runs were then conducted on simulated random samples of groups to explore the expected effects of the different conditions on large samples of groups randomly drawn from a population. These runs illustrated some interesting dynamics and implications of the model that could not have been derived with verbal reasoning alone.

For example, results of runs conducted on a simple case were generally more consistent with predictions made by the theories informing the model than were results of runs conducted on random samples of groups. This highlights the fact that theories are usually developed with an "average" or simple case in mind and that it is difficult or impossible, using verbal reasoning alone, to make predictions for the infinitely many different permutations found in random samples. Of particular interest was the fact that initial evaluations of member skills had less of an impact than suggested by traditional theories of diversity that fail to incorporate member needs and group processes into their predictions.

Another intriguing result followed the manipulation of the order in which assignments were made in groups. This seemingly trivial and neglected aspect of group process that had to be specified in the model had a large impact on group outcomes. The first interesting observation was that making assignments in random order yielded highly similar results to making assignments in order of member power. This illuminated a strong and potentially problematic equilibrium dynamic in the way that member power was defined in the model.

Both the random and member power orders of making assignments in the group were akin to an "equality" norm of distributing opportunities to group members in that they ended up taking equal turns negotiating their assignments first, second, third, and fourth in the group. Perhaps making assignments in the group in order of group commitment to members is a more plausible scenario: Groups negotiate assignments with favored members first. This order of making assignments, however, yielded significantly worse outcomes than did the other two: Performance was lower, divisions of labor were more centralized, skills decayed more, members were less committed to their groups, and groups were less committed to their members. The disadvantages of this order of allocating assignments and opportunities in the group only grew over time.

This counterintuitive result highlights another advantage that computational models bestow on the researcher: the opportunity to explore the implications of different initial conditions and processes over time that may not be empirically observable. For example, though social theorists have long argued that equity norms serve to disguise and justify inequitable processes and outcomes (Bourdieu, 1977), it is impossible to establish which came first: social inequities or the norms that justify them. A computational model can explore the implications of such a norm given a variety of theoretically plausible initial conditions. This model would suggest that following an equity norm to distribute opportunities within a group may itself produce and reinforce inequalities that did not initially exist.

∞ STRATEGIES, LIMITATIONS, AND PROSPECTS: A THREE-PART RESEARCH STRATEGY

Although none of these research strategies solves all of the problems faced by a researcher who wishes to examine groups as complex systems, together they provide a powerful multiple-strategy approach. Specifically, we recommend a systematic program of research that incorporates and integrates the following:

1. Development and refinement of a comprehensive verbal theory
2. Execution of experimental simulation studies and collection and analysis of comparative data from field studies appropriate to test that theory
3. Development and application of a comprehensive computational model (or series of models) of groups as complex systems

The three facets of that strategy are mutually supportive (see Figure 10.1). The group theoretic framework provides guidance for designing empirical studies and for initial analyses of empirical data (arrow "a" of the figure). In turn, results of those studies challenge and/or confirm hypotheses derived from the theory (arrow "b" of the figure). At the same time, the group theoretic framework provides the basis for developing computational models (arrow "c" of the figure), and use of those models can illuminate and challenge hypotheses of the theory (arrow "d" of the figure). A similar, mutual relation obtains between the body of evidence and the computational model: Extant data from our own and other empirical research studies provide values for initial settings of parameters and distributions used in the model (arrow "e" of the figure), and subsequent results of the model can be assessed against the empirical relations established in our own empirical studies and in empirical studies by other researchers (arrow "f" of the figure).

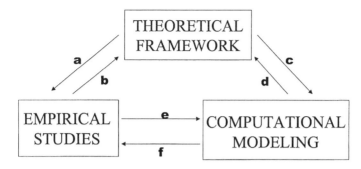

Figure 10.1. A Three-Part Strategy for a Research Program

Yes, carrying out such a research program is difficult and time consuming and requires massive research resources. We do not expect anyone to try to follow the prescriptions we have laid out as a cookbook formulation for how to do research on small groups. We do regard these prescriptions, and our recommendation of an integrated three-part strategy, as a *template* that can be a very useful guide for research on complex, dynamic human systems, including small groups.

Limitations of Our Formulation

In the preceding chapters, we have tried to present, systematically, what we regard as a new way of conceptualizing and studying small groups. It is, we believe, solidly grounded in the theoretical and empirical work of the past. It also recasts past findings and understandings in a new light—in a way that enables us to take seriously the idea that groups are complex, open, adaptive, dynamic systems.

Any reader who has persisted this far is aware of many shortcomings of this book. We have presented a detailed and technically complex formulation that is nevertheless far from complete. We have staked out an enormous domain as our universe of discourse and have examined many specific facets of our object of study: groups as complex systems. We have examined this domain using traditional concepts and substantive topics of the group research field—such things as group composition, norms, interaction process, task performance, and so on—but also using concepts borrowed from general systems, dynamical systems, and complexity theories: ideas such as attractors and fitness landscapes and emergent global variables.

Our treatment of all of those sets of concepts is incomplete. We have cited a number of empirical findings from our own and others' work, but our coverage of the literature is selective and unsystematic. We have examined some thorny methodological and epistemological issues raised by the new concepts we are importing and have discussed how researchers can mount research programs to explore our formulation while taking those issues into account. That methodological discussion, though useful, needs still further development. And taking issues into account is not the same as resolving the methodological problems. Finally, we have posited a number of hypotheses about patterns of relations that we think should develop under particular sets of conditions, but we have not yet formulated a full and systematic set of theoretical hypotheses for that full range of possibilities.

Prospects for the Future

We have taken these ideas as far as we can take them at this time. We hope that they are interesting enough, and explained well enough, so that others will carry out the further theoretical and empirical work needed to advance them to a fuller stage of completion. We view the ideas in this book as a *starting place* for a new program of research on small groups. We hope other scholars will find our formulation interesting enough to undertake theoretical and empirical work to expand it, modify it, even refute it.

As discussed in Chapter 2, for about a century small groups have been the object of research and theorizing within social psychology and a number of related fields. The topic has had several cycles: Interest in groups appears to follow a periodic attractor with heydays followed by periods of low attention, then gradual reinvigoration. Each new incarnation of strong interest in research on small groups has been both similar to and different from previous cycles. In each new reincarnation, theory and research on small groups have tackled more complex issues and have done so with more sophisticated conceptual and methodological tools. Successive cycles have raised and dealt with new substantive issues, as well as reexamining old substantive questions, often in new dress.

Each new reinvigoration of group research has also run afoul of some persistent and fundamental dilemmas underlying research in such a domain. One is the sharp opposition between what seems theoretically valuable and what seems practically feasible. Regardless of intentions, to some extent the practical always wins out. Researchers can only do what they have the tools, energy, time, and other resources to do. So researchers must and do make simplifying assumptions to carry out empirical research—assumptions that often deny or make moot their own theoretical prescriptions, such as ours regarding groups as complex, adaptive, dynamic systems. We do not expect our presentation to precipitate a sudden paradigm shift in practice, no matter how interesting our ideas may be and how clearly we have presented them. What we do hope for, though, is a substantial nudge in the direction of such a fundamental paradigm shift.

Our theory about groups is relatively specific and detailed in conceptual and substantive terms. We specify constituent elements, component networks, forms of coordination, intrinsic and instrumental functions of groups, levels of dynamics, and modes of group life. But the substantive specifics of those conceptions (e.g., are groups "really" made up of people, intentions, and resources?) are not nearly as important as our fundamental presumption that groups are complex, adaptive, dynamic systems operating at and in interaction with multiple levels of embedding and embedded systems. Of course, it is precisely that fundamental presumption that poses the most radical conceptual challenges and the most intractable practical hurdles.

We see this book as a starting point that raises more questions than it answers and identifies more problems than it solves. In accordance with this view, we close by listing some key questions that we think need to be kept continually in mind by those who wish to understand small groups and how they work.

First, we need to broaden our conception of reliability, replication, and robustness. Given an empirical relation, of course, we must continue to ask, "Would this finding replicate if we did the study again?" But we should also ask, "Would this relation have continued, or would it have changed or vanished, if we had studied those groups over a longer period of time?" Then we must ask, "Would this relation, or a different one, have been found if we had done our study with groups of Types X, Y, and Z, rather than of Type W?" and "Would the relation have been same or different if we had carried out our study under Conditions A, B, or C rather than D?"

Second, we need to enlarge our conception of the nature of causation in human systems such as groups. Instead of simply asking, "Does a high level of Y occur when, and only when, the condition X is present?" (or, more often, "Does Y tend to be higher with X than without it?"), we need to also ask, "Does the relation reflect interdependence of X and Y rather than dependence of Y on X?" Moreover, in complex systems such as groups, we need to ask "What system forces (U, V, W) come into play when a high level of X occurs, and do those forces tend to offset, or exacerbate, the change in level of Y that X initially produced?"

Third, we need to examine the shape of posited relations, especially when we extrapolate beyond extant data. We must ask not only "How does Y increase (or decrease) as X increases?" but also "Over what range of values of X does that hold, and how might the relation change beyond those limits?" We need to ask, "Is there symmetry in the amount of change in X and amount of change in Y, and how does that degree of symmetry change over different ranges of X and of Y?"

Fourth, we need to rethink the role of intentionality in human systems. Groups sometimes do things simply because they decided to—which reflects a kind of teleological or final cause rather than efficient cause. We also need to reckon with the impact of planning on subsequent responses to events in the embedding systems. For example, when an event occurs that we believe will evoke a response from the group, we need to be prepared to ask, "Has the group already taken this event into account—by preventive coping actions—so that their lack of contemporaneous response does not imply 'no response'?"

If group researchers take these and similar questions seriously, as matters to be routinely considered in interpreting findings and not just as ideas to throw into final sections on "questions for the future," then the field will begin to reckon with the implications of viewing groups as complex, adaptive, dynamic systems. To deal with those questions, of course, we will need to find new ways to pose them and to explore them. We hope that some of the ideas we have adopted and adapted from complexity theory will prove valuable in this quest. We regard the conceptualizations in this book, and our recommendation of an integrated three-part strategy, as a *template* that can be very useful for guiding research on complex, dynamic human systems, including small groups.

∞ CONCLUDING COMMENTS

We began the book, in Chapter 1, with an example of a specific small group that one might regard as a complex system. There, we posed many questions about factors that one might need to know to predict that group's actions and their consequences for the group, its members, and its embedding contexts. We have now examined many of those factors, and many others, that we think may play a part in affecting group actions and outcomes if one wishes to regard such a group as a complex, open, adaptive, dynamic system.

What can we now say about that six-person group from Minerva— consisting of Sally from sales, Ed from engineering, Manuel from manufacturing, Felicia from finance, Mark from marketing, and Richard from R&D—who have undertaken development of a sophisticated electronic notepad?

If our theoretical formulations are correct, then that group's activities will indeed be affected by all of the forces mentioned and many more (member attributes and needs, features of the project, accessibility of needed tools and resources, and so on). These factors will interplay in the form of multivariate, nonlinear, recursive relations that constitute "local action," from which will emerge patterned system-level (global) variables, which in turn will modify and modulate the functioning of those patterned local dynamics. We argue that we are not likely to be able to predict the direct "efficient cause" relations among particular local variables but that we probably can discern systematic patterns of development of global variables—as a function both of initial conditions and of the group's own particular history. Moreover, that group's activities and its consequences for all constituencies will be affected by changing conditions in the organization, the industry, the units of the organization to which the group's members belong, and many other social systems with which the group and/or its members are interdependent. It is not possible, we maintain, to predict actions of the group without knowing about forces and events in the group's and members' numerous embedding systems to which they must adapt.

Furthermore, if we are going to regard groups as complex systems in a serious way, then we should not expect *all* groups to act the same way under what we as researchers see as apparently "equivalent" initial conditions, for at least four reasons. First, an implicit principle of complex systems theory holds that no two systems have exactly the same initial conditions and that even small differences in initial conditions can lead to major differences in subsequent system states and actions. Second, groups of different "types"—for example, groups with different fundamental purposes, such as families, sports teams, airline crews, friendship groups, and task forces such as Minerva's product design group—are not likely to act in the same or even similar ways because they are trying to *do* entirely different things. Third, even if two groups were of the same type and really had equivalent initial conditions, no two groups would be likely to experience exactly the same series of contextual conditions or events or to react to them in precisely the same way. Finally, in all human systems—including both groups and the individuals who are the group's members—intentionality plays a major role. The actions of human individuals and groups always reflect what they are trying to do, as well as what various features of the situation are nudging them toward.

So, we believe, future research on small groups needs to shift the form of its fundamental questions. We need to change from asking questions such as "How can we predict what groups of this 'kind' will do under such and such conditions?" to asking questions such as "How can we assess what this group did do, and under what conditions, so that we can better understand what 'kind' of group it is or has become?"

References

ABRAHAM, I. D., ABRAHAM, R. H., & SHAW, C. D. (1990). *A visual introduction to dynamical systems theory for psychology.* Santa Cruz, CA: Arial.

ALBERT, S., & KESSLER, S. (1976). Processes for ending social encounters: The conceptual archaeology of a temporal place. *Journal for the Theory of Social Behaviour, 6,* 147-170.

ALLMENDINGER, J., & HACKMAN, J. R. (1996). Organizations in changing environments: The case of East German symphony orchestras. *Administrative Science Quarterly, 41,* 337-369.

ALLPORT, F. H. (1920). The influence of the group upon association and thought. *Journal of Experimental Psychology, 3,* 159-182.

ALTMAN, I., & HAYTHORN, W. W. (1967). The effects of social isolation and group composition on performance. *Human Relations, 20,* 313.

ALTMAN, I., & ROGOFF, B. (1987). World views in psychology: Trait, interactional, organismic, and transactional. In D. Stokols & I. Altman (Eds.), *Handbook of environmental psychology.* New York: John Wiley.

ANCONA, D. G., & CALDWELL, D. F. (1988). Beyond task and maintenance: External roles in groups. *Group and Organization Studies, 13,* 468-494.

ANCONA, D. G., & CALDWELL, D. F. (1990). Information technology and new product teams. In J. Galegher, R. Kraut, & C. Egido (Eds.), *Intellectual teamwork: Social and technological foundations of cooperative work* (pp. 173-190). Hillsdale, NJ: Lawrence Erlbaum.

ANCONA, D. G., & CHONG, C. (1996). Entrainment: Pace, cycle, and rhythm in organizational behavior. In B. Staw & L. L. Cummings (Eds.), *Research in organizational behavior* (Vol. 18, pp. 251-284). New York: JAI.

ARGOTE, L., & MCGRATH, J. E. (1993). Group processes in organizations: Continuity and change. In C. Cooper & I. T. Robertson (Eds.), *International review of industrial and organizational psychology* (Vol. 8, pp. 333-389). New York: John Wiley.

ARROW, H. (1996). *Standing out and fitting in: Culture, gender, and socialization in growing organizations.* Unpublished doctoral dissertation, University of Illinois, Urbana-Champaign.

ARROW, H. (1997). Stability, bistability, and instability in small group influence patterns. *Journal of Personality and Social Psychology, 72,* 75-85.

ARROW, H., BERDAHL, J. L., BOUAS, K. S., CRAIG, K. M., CUMMINGS, A., LEBIE, L., McGRATH, J. E., O'CONNOR, K. M., RHOADES, J. A., & SCHLOSSER, A. (1996).

Time, technology, and groups: An integration. *Computer Supported Cooperative Work, 4,* 253-261.

ARROW, H., & McGRATH, J. E. (1993). Membership matters: How member change and continuity affect small group structure, process, and performance. *Small Group Research, 24,* 334-361.

ARROW, H., & McGRATH, J. E. (1995). Membership dynamics in groups at work: A theoretical framework. In B. M. Staw & L. L. Cummings (Eds.), *Research in organizational behavior* (Vol. 17, pp. 373-411). Greenwich, CT: JAI.

ASCH, S. (1951). The effects of group pressure upon the modification and distortion of judgment. In H. Guetzkow (Ed.), *Groups, leadership, and men* (pp. 177-190). Pittsburgh, PA: Carnegie.

BALES, R. F. (1950a). *Interaction process analysis: A method for the study of small groups.* Cambridge, MA: Addison-Wesley.

BALES, R. F. (1950b). A set of categories for the analysis of small group interaction. *American Sociological Review, 15,* 257-263.

BALES, R. F. (1951). The equilibrium problem in small groups. In T. C. Parsons, R. F. Bales, & E. A. Shils (Eds.), *Working papers in the theory of action* (pp. 111-161). Glencoe, IL: Free Press.

BALES, R. F. (1955). Adaptive and integrative changes as sources of strain in social systems. In A. P. Hare, E. F. Borgotta, & R. F. Bales (Eds.), *Small groups: Studies in social interaction* (pp. 127-131). New York: Knopf.

BALES, R. F. (1999). *Social interaction systems: Theory and measurement.* New Brunswick, NJ: Transaction.

BALES, R. F., & COHEN, S. P. (1979). *SYMLOG: A system for the multilevel observation of groups.* New York: Free Press.

BALES, R. F., & SLATER, P. E. (1955). Role differentiation in small decision-making groups. In T. Parsons, R. F. Bales, & Associates (Eds.), *The family, socialization, and interaction process* (pp. 259-305). Glencoe, IL: Free Press.

BALES, R. F., & STRODTBECK, F. L. (1951). Phases in group problem solving. *Journal of Abnormal and Social Psychology, 46,* 485-495.

BALES, R. F., STRODTBECK, F. L., MILLS, T. M., & ROSEBOROUGH, M. E. (1953). Channels of communication in small groups. *American Sociological Review, 16,* 461-468.

BALL, J. R., & CARRON, A. V. (1976). The influence of team cohesion and participation motivation upon performance success in intercollegiate ice hockey. *Canadian Journal of Applied Sport Sciences, 1,* 271-275.

BARON, R. M., AMAZEEN, P. G., & BEEK, P. J. (1994). Local and global dynamics in social relations. In R. R. Vallacher & A. Nowak (Eds.), *Dynamical systems in social psychology* (pp. 111-138). New York: Academic Press.

BARSADE, S. G., & GIBSON, D. E. (1998). Group emotion: A view from top and bottom. In M. A. Neale, E. A. Mannix, & D. H. Gruenfeld (Eds.), *Research on managing groups and teams* (Vol. 1, pp. 81-102). Stamford, CT: JAI.

BARTON, S. (1994). Chaos, self-organization, and psychology. *American Psychologist, 49,* 5-14.

BAUMEISTER, R. F., & LEARY, M. R. (1995). The need to belong: Desire for interpersonal attachments as a fundamental human motivation. *Psychological Bulletin, 117,* 497-529.

BAZERMAN, M. H., MANNIX, E. A., & THOMPSON, L. L. (1988). Groups as mixed-motive negotiations. In E. J. Lawler & B. Markovsky (Eds.), *Advances in group processes* (Vol. 5, pp. 195-216). Greenwich, CT: JAI.

BENNIS, W. G., & SHEPARD, H. H. (1956). A theory of group development. *Human Relations, 9,* 415-437.

BERDAHL, J. L. (1996). Gender and leadership in work groups: Six alternative models. *Leadership Quarterly, 7,* 21-48.

BERDAHL, J. L. (1998). The dynamics of composition and socialization in small groups: Insights gained from developing a computational model. In M. A. Neale, E. A. Mannix, & D. H. Gruenfeld (Eds.), *Research on managing in groups and teams* (Vol. 1, pp. 209-227). Greenwich, CT: JAI.

BERDAHL, J. L. (1999). *Perception, power, and performance in small groups: Insights from a computational model.* Unpublished doctoral dissertation, University of Illinois at Urbana-Champaign.

BERDAHL, J. L., & CRAIG, K. M. (1996). Equality of participation and influence in groups: The effects of communication medium and sex composition. *Computer Supported Cooperative Work, 4,* 179-202.

BERG, D. N., & SMITH, K. K. (1995). Paradox and groups. In J. Gillette & M. McCollom (Eds.), *Groups in context: A new perspective on group dynamics* (pp. 107-132). Lanham, MD: University Press of America.

BERGER, J., CONNER, T., & FIZEK, M. H. (Eds.). (1974). *Expectation states theory: A theoretical research program.* Cambridge, MA: Winthrop.

BERLEW, D. E., & HALL, D. T. (1971). Socialization of managers: Effects of expectations on performance. In D. A. Kolb, I. M. Rubin, & J. M. McIntyre (Eds.), *Organizational psychology: A book of readings* (3rd ed.). Engelwood Cliffs, NJ: Prentice Hall.

BETTENHAUSEN, K. L., & MURNIGHAN, J. K. (1985). The emergence of norms in competitive decision-making groups. *Administrative Science Quarterly, 30,* 350-372.

BEYERLEIN, M. M., JOHNSON, D. A., & BEYERLEIN, S. T. (Eds.). (1997). *Advances in interdisciplinary studies of work teams: Vol 4. Team implementation issues.* Greenwich, CT: JAI.

BION, W. R. (1961). *Experiences in groups and other papers.* New York: Basic Books.

BLAKE, R. R., & MOUTON, J. S. (1961). Reactions to intergroup competition under win-lose conditions. *Management Science, 7,* 420-435.

BOHM, D. (1980). *Wholeness and the implicate order.* London: Routledge & Kegan Paul.

BORGATTA, E. F. (1962). A systematic study of interaction process scores, peer and self-assessments, personality and other variables. *Genetic Psychology Monographs, 65,* 219-291.

BORGATTA, E. F., & BALES, R. F. (1953). Interaction of individuals in reconstituted groups. *Sociometry, 16,* 302-320.

BORGATTA, E. F., COUCH, A. S., & BALES, R. F. (1954). Some findings relevant to the great man theory of leadership. *American Sociological Review, 19,* 755-758.

BOUAS, K. S., & ARROW, H. (1996).The development of group identity in face-to-face and computer-mediated groups with membership change. *Computer Supported Cooperative Work, 4,* 153-178.

BOULDING, K. (1953). Toward a general theory of growth. *Canadian Journal of Economics and Political Science, 19,* 326-340.

BOURDIEU, P. (1977). *Outline of a theory of practice.* Cambridge, UK: Cambridge University Press.

BREWER, M. B., & GARDNER, W. (1996). Who is this "we?" Levels of collective identity and self-representation. *Journal of Personality and Social Psychology, 71,* 83-93.

BREWER, M. B., & KRAMER, R. (1986). Choice behavior in social dilemmas: Effects of social identity, group size, and decision framing. *Journal of Personality and Social Psychology, 50,* 543-547.

BRINBERG, D., & McGRATH, J. E. (1985). *Validity and the research process.* Beverly Hills, CA: Sage.

BRISMAN, J., & SIEGAL, M. (1985). The bulimia workshop: A unique integration of group treatment approaches. *International Journal of Group Psychotherapy, 35,* 585-601.

BROWN, R. J. (1978). Divided we fall: An analysis of relations between sections of a factory workforce. In H. Tajfel (Ed.), *Differentiation between social groups* (pp. 395-429). London: Academic Press.

BROWN, R. J., CONDOR, S., MATTHEWS, A., WADE, G., & WILLIAMS, J. A. (1986). Explaining intergroup differentiation in an industrial organization. *Journal of Occupational Psychology, 59,* 273-286.

BRUDERER, E., & SINGH, J. V. (1996). Organizational evolution, learning, and selection: A genetic-algorithm-based model. *Academy of Management Journal, 39,* 1322-1349.

BUCHANAN, J. (1965). An economic theory of clubs. *Economica, 32,* 1-14.

BUTTERWORTH, T. (1990). Detroit string quartet. In J. R. Hackman (Ed.), *Groups that work (and those that don't)* (pp. 207-224). San Francisco: Jossey-Bass.

CAMERON, K. S., SUTTON, R. I., & WHETTEN, D. A. (Eds.). (1988). *Readings in organizational decline: Frameworks, research, and prescriptions.* Cambridge, MA: Ballinger.

CAMPBELL, D. T., & STANLEY, J. C. (1966). *Experimental and quasi-experimental designs for research.* Chicago: Rand-McNally.

CAMPION, M. A., & LORD, R. G. (1982). A control system conceptualization of the goal-setting and changing process. *Organizational Behavior and Human Performance, 30,* 265-287.

CARLEY, K. M. (1991). A theory of group stability. *American Sociological Review, 56,* 331-354.

CARLEY, K. M., & SVOBODA, D. M. (1996). Modeling organizational adaptation as a simulated annealing process. *Sociological Methods and Research, 25,* 138-168.

CARRON, A. V. (1988). *Group dynamics in sports.* London, Ontario, Canada: Spodym.

CARRON, A. V., WIDMEYER, W. N., & BRAWLEY, L. R. (1985). The development of an instrument to assess cohesiveness in sports teams: The Group Environment Questionnaire. *Journal of Sport and Exercise Psychology, 10,* 127-138.

CARTER, L. F. (1950). *Group structures and interaction as a function of task, personality, and goal* (Contract No. 171-342). Rochester, NY: University of Rochester.

CARTER, L. F., HAYTHORN, W. W., & HOWELL, M. (1950). A further investigation of the criteria of leadership. *Journal of Abnormal and Social Psychology, 45,* 350-358.

CARTWRIGHT, D. (1968). The nature of group cohesiveness. In D. Cartwright & A. Zander (Eds.), *Group dynamics: Research and theory* (3rd ed., pp. 91-109). New York: Harper & Row.

CARTWRIGHT, D., & ZANDER, A. (Eds.). (1953). *Group dynamics: Research and theory* (1st ed.). Evanston, IL: Row, Peterson.

CARTWRIGHT, D., & ZANDER, A. (Eds.). (1960). *Group dynamics: Research and theory* (2nd ed.). Evanston, IL: Row, Peterson.

CARTWRIGHT, D., & ZANDER, A. (Eds.). (1968). *Group dynamics: Research and theory* (3rd ed.). New York: Harper & Row.

CASTI, L. (1994). Recent developments and future perspectives in dynamical systems theory. *SEAM Review, 24,* 302-331.

CHAPIN, F. S. (1957). The optimum size of institutions: A theory of the large group. *American Journal of Sociology, 62,* 449-460.

CHRISTENSEN, E. W. (1983). Study circles: Learning in small groups. *Journal for Specialists in Group Work, 8,* 211-217.

CISSNA, K. N. (1984). Phases in group development: The negative evidence. *Small Group Research, 15,* 3-32.

CLARK, N. K., & STEPHENSON, G. M. (1989). Group remembering. In P. B. Paulus (Ed.), *Psychology of group influence* (2nd ed., pp. 357-391). Hillsdale, NJ: Lawrence Erlbaum.

COCH, L., & FRENCH, J. R. P. (1948). Overcoming resistance to change. *Human Relations, 1,* 512-532.

COHEN, S. G., & DENISON, D. R. (1990). Flight attendant teams. In J. R. Hackman (Ed.), *Groups that work (and those that don't)* (pp. 361-397). San Francisco: Jossey-Bass.

CONGER, J. A., & KANUNGO, R. A. (1987). Towards a balanced theory of charismatic leadership in organizational settings. *Academy of Management Review, 12,* 637-647.

COOK, T. D., & CAMPBELL, D. T. (1979). *Design and analysis of quasi-experiments for field settings.* Chicago: Rand-McNally.

COREY, M. S., & COREY, G. (1992). *Groups: Process and practice* (4th ed.). Pacific Grove, CA: Brooks/Cole.

COWAN, G. A., PINES, D., & MELTZER, D. (Eds.). (1994). *Complexity: Metaphors, models, and reality.* Reading, MA: Addison-Wesley.

CROCKER, J., & McGRAW, K. M. (1994). What's good for the goose is not good for the gander. *American Behavioral Scientist, 27,* 357-369.

CUMMINGS, A., SCHLOSSER, A., & ARROW, H. (1996). Developing complex group products: Idea contribution in computer-mediated and face-to-face groups. *Computer Supported Cooperative Work, 4,* 229-251.

CURTIS, J. E., GRABB, E. G., & BAER, D. E. (1992). Voluntary association membership in fifteen countries: A comparative analysis. *American Sociological Review, 57,* 139-152.

DAFT, R. L., & LENGEL, R. H. (1984). Information richness: A new approach to managerial behavior and organizational design. In B. Staw & L. L. Cummings (Eds.), *Research in organizational behavior* (Vol. 6, pp. 191-233). Greenwich, CT: JAI.

DASHIELL, J. F. (1930). An experimental analysis of some group effects. *Journal of Abnormal and Social Psychology, 25,* 190-199.

DAVIS, J. H. (1973). Group decisions and social interaction: A theory of social decision schemes. *Psychological Review, 80,* 97-125.

DAVIS, J. H. (1982). Social interaction as a combinatorial process in group decisions. In H. Brandstatter, J. H. Davis, & G. Stocker-Kreichgauer (Eds.), *Group decision making* (pp. 27-58). London: Academic Press.

DAVIS, J. H., KAMEDA, T., PARKS, C., STASSON, M., & ZIMMERMAN, S. (1989). Some social mechanics of group decision making: The distribution of opinion, polling sequence, and implications for consensus. *Journal of Personality and Social Psychology, 57,* 1000-1012.

DAVIS, J. H., LAUGHLIN, P. R., & KOMORITA, S. S. (1976). The social psychology of small groups: Cooperative and mixed-motive interaction. *Annual Review of Psychology, 27,* 501-541.

DAVIS, J. H., & RESTLE, F. (1963). The analysis of problems and prediction of group problem-solving. *Journal of Abnormal and Social Psychology, 66,* 103-106.

DENISON, D. R. (1990). Airline maintenance group. In J. R. Hackman (Ed.), *Groups that work (and those that don't)* (pp. 293-308). San Francisco: Jossey-Bass.

DENISON, D. R., & SUTTON, R. I. (1990). Operating room nurses. In J. R. Hackman (Ed.), *Groups that work (and those that don't)* (pp. 293-308). San Francisco: Jossey-Bass.

DEUTSCH, M. (1949a). An experimental study of the effects of cooperation and competition upon group process. *Human Relations, 2,* 199-231.

DEUTSCH, M. (1949b). A theory of cooperation and competition. *Human Relations, 2,* 129-152.

DEUTSCH, M., & KRAUSS, R. M. (1962). Studies of interpersonal bargaining. *Journal of Conflict Resolution, 6*(1), 52-76.

DIEHL, M., & STROEBE, W. (1987). Productivity loss in brainstorming groups: Toward the solution of a riddle. *Journal of Personality and Social Psychology, 53,* 497-509.

DROGOUL, A., & FERBER, J. (1994). Multi-agent simulation as a tool for studying emergent processes in societies. In N. Gilbert & J. Doran (Eds.), *Simulating societies: The computer simulation of social phenomena* (pp. 127-142). London: University College of London Press.

DUNBAR, R. I. M., DUNCAN, N. D. C., & NETTLE, D. (1995). Size and structure of freely forming conversational groups. *Human Nature, 6,* 67-78.

DUNCAN, J. A., & GUMAER, J. (Eds.). (1980). *Developmental groups for children.* Springfield, IL: Charles C Thomas.

DUNPHY, D. (1968). Phases, roles, and myths in self-analytic groups. *Journal of Applied Behavioral Science, 4,* 195-225.

DYER, J. L. (1985). *Annotated bibliography and state-of-the-art review of the field of team training as it relates to military teams.* Fort Benning, GA: U.S. Army Research Institute for the Behavioral and Social Sciences.

EAGLY, A. H. (1987). *Sex differences in social behavior: A social-role analysis.* Hillsdale, NJ: Lawrence Earlbaum.

EAGLY, A. H., & KARAU, S. J. (1991). Gender and the emergence of leaders: A meta-analysis. *Journal of Personality and Social Psychology, 60,* 685-710.

EISENSTAT, R. A. (1990). Compressor team start-up. In J. R. Hackman (Ed.), *Groups that work (and those that don't)* (pp. 411-426). San Francisco: Jossey-Bass.

EMERY, F. E., & TRIST, E. L. (1965). The causal texture of organizational environments. *Human Relations, 18,* 21-32.

EMERY, F. E., & TRIST, E. L. (1973). Socio-technical systems. In F. Baker (Ed.), *Organizational systems: General systems approaches to complex organizations.* Homewood, IL: Richard D. Irwin.

ETTIN, M. F., FIDLER, J. W., & COHEN, B. D. (Eds.). (1995). *Group process and political dynamics.* Madison, CT: International Universities Press.

FESTINGER, L. (1954). Theory of social comparison processes. *Human Relations, 7,* 117-140.

FESTINGER, L. (1957). *A theory of cognitive dissonance.* New York: Harper & Row.

FESTINGER, L., SCHACHTER, S., & BACK, K. (1950). *Social pressures in informal groups: A study of human factors in housing.* New York: Harper Bros.

FIEDLER, F. (1964). A contingency model of leadership effectiveness. *Advances in Experimental Social Psychology, 1,* 149-190.

FISKE, A. P. (1991). *Structures of social life: The four elementary forms of human relations.* New York: Free Press.

FISKE, A. P. (1992). The four elementary forms of sociality: Framework for a unified theory of social relations. *Psychological Bulletin, 99,* 689-723.

FREEMAN, J., CARROLL, G. R., & HANNAN, M. T. (1983). The liability of newness: Age-dependence in organizational death rates. *American Sociological Review, 48,* 692-710.

FRENCH, J. R. P., Jr. (1956). A formal theory of social power. *Psychological Review, 63,* 181-194.

FRENCH, J. R. P., Jr., & RAVEN, B. (1959). The bases of social power. In D. Cartwright & A. Zander (Eds.), *Studies in social power* (pp. 150-167). Ann Arbor: University of Michigan Press.

FRESE, M., & ZAPF, D. (1994). Action as the core of work psychology: A German approach. In H. C. Triandis, M. D. Dunnette, & L. D. Hough (Eds.), *Handbook of organizational and industrial psychology* (Vol. 2, 2nd ed., pp. 271-340). Palo Alto, CA: Consulting Psychologists Press.

FUHRIMAN, A., & BURLINGAME, G. M. (1994). Measuring small group process: A methodological application of chaos theory. *Small Group Research, 25,* 502-519.

GELL-MANN, M. (1994). *The quark and the jaguar.* New York: W. H. Freeman.

GERSICK, C. J. G. (1988). Time and transition in work teams: Toward a new model of group development. *Academy of Management Journal, 31,* 9-41.

GERSICK, C. J. G. (1989). Marking time: Predictable transitions in task groups. *Academy of Management Journal, 32,* 274-309.

GERSICK, C. J. G. (1990). The bankers. In J. R. Hackman (Ed.), *Groups that work (and those that don't)* (pp. 112-125). San Francisco: Jossey-Bass.

GERSICK, C. J. G., & HACKMAN, J. R. (1990). Habitual routines in task-performing groups. *Organizational Behavior and Human Decision Processes, 47,* 65-97.

GILLETTE, J., & McCOLLOM, M. (Eds.). (1995). *Groups in context: A new perspective on group dynamics.* Lanham, MD: University Press of America.

GINNETT, R. C. (1987). *First encounters of the close kind: The first meetings of airline flight crews.* Unpublished doctoral dissertation, Yale University.

GINNETT, R. C. (1990). Airline cockpit crew. In J. R. Hackman (Ed.), *Groups that work (and those that don't)* (pp. 427-448). San Francisco: Jossey-Bass.

GLANZER, M., & GLASER, R. (1959). Techniques for the study of group structure and behavior: I. Analysis of structure. *Psychological Bulletin, 56,* 317-322.

GLANZER, M., & GLASER, R. (1961). Techniques for the study of group structure and behavior: II. Empirical studies of the effects of structure in small groups. *Psychological Bulletin, 58,* 1-27.

GOERNER, S. (1994). *Chaos and the evolving ecological universe.* Langhorne, PA: Gordon & Breach.

GOODACRE, D. M., III. (1953). Group characteristics of good and poor performance combat units. *Sociometry, 16,* 168-178.

GOODMAN, P. S. (1986). Impact of task and technology on group performance. In P. S. Goodman & Associates (Eds.), *Designing effective work groups* (pp. 120-167). San Francisco: Jossey-Bass.

GOODMAN, P. S., DEVADAS, R., & HUGHSON, T. L. (1988). Groups and productivity: Analyzing the effectiveness of self-managing teams. In J. P. Campbell & R. J. Campbell (Eds.), *Productivity in organizations.* San Francisco: Jossey-Bass.

GOODMAN, P. S., & LEYDEN, D. P. (1991). Familiarity and group productivity. *Journal of Applied Psychology, 76,* 578-586.

GORDON, D. M., GOODWIN, B. C., & TRAINOR, L. E. H. (1992). A parallel distributed model of the behavior of ant colonies. *Journal of Theoretical Biology, 156,* 293-307.

GREER, F. L., GALANTER, E., & NORDLIE, P. G. (1954). Interpersonal knowledge and individual and group effectiveness. *Journal of Abnormal and Social Psychology, 49,* 411-414.

GRUENFELD, D. H (1995). Status, ideology, and integrative complexity on the U.S. Supreme Court: Rethinking the politics of political decision making. *Journal of Personality and Social Psychology, 68,* 5-20.

GRUENFELD, D. H, & FAN, E. T. (1996). Integrative complexity through boundary spanning: The untold potential of minority status. In J. Levine, D. Messick, & L. Thompson (Eds.), *Cognition in organizations: The management of knowledge.* Hillsdale, NJ: Lawrence Erlbaum.

GRUENFELD, D. H, & HOLLINGSHEAD, A. B. (1993). Sociocognition in work groups: The evolution of group integrative complexity and its relation to task performance. *Small Group Research, 24,* 383-405.

GRUENFELD, D. H, MANNIX, E. A., WILLIAMS, K. Y., & NEALE, M. A. (1996). Group composition and decision making: How member familiarity and information distribution affect process and performance. *Organizational Behavior and Human Decision Processes, 67,* 1-15.

GRUSZNSKI, R., & BANKOVICS, G. (1990). Treating men who batter: A group approach. In D. Moore & F. Leafgren (Eds.), *Problem solving strategies and interventions for men in con-*

flict (pp. 201-212). Alexandria, VA: American Association for Counseling and Development.

GUETZKOW, H., & SIMON, H. (1955). The impact of certain communication nets upon organization and performance in task-oriented groups. *Management Science, 1,* 233-250.

GUZZO, R. A., & DICKSON, M. W. (1996). Teams in organizations: Recent research on performance and effectiveness. *Annual Review of Psychology, 47,* 307-338.

GUZZO, R. A., & SALAS, E. (Eds.). (1995). *Team effectiveness and decision making in organizations.* San Francisco: Jossey-Bass.

HACKER, W. (1985). Activity: A fruitful concept in industrial psychology. In M. Frese & J. Sabini (Eds.), *Goal directed behavior* (pp. 262-285). Hillsdale, NJ: Lawrence Erlbaum.

HACKMAN, J. R. (1986). The psychology of self-management in organizations. In M. S. Pallak & R. O. Perloff (Eds.), *Psychology and work: Productivity, change, and employment.* Washington, DC: American Psychological Association.

HACKMAN, J. R. (Ed.). (1990). *Groups that work (and those that don't).* San Francisco: Jossey-Bass.

HACKMAN, J. R., & MORRIS, C. G. (1975). Group tasks, group interaction process, and group performance effectiveness: A review and proposed integration. In L. Berkowitz (Ed.), *Advances in experimental social psychology* (Vol. 8, pp. 45-99). New York: Academic Press.

HACKMAN, J. R., & MORRIS, C. G. (1978). Group process and group effectiveness: A reappraisal. In L. Berkowitz (Ed.), *Group processes.* New York: Academic Press.

HALLINAN, M. T. (1979). The process of friendship formation. *Social Networks, 1,* 193-210.

HAMILTON, D. L., & BISHOP, G. D. (1976). Attitudinal and behavioral effects of initial integration of white suburban neighborhoods. *Journal of Social Issues, 32,* 47-67.

HANEY, C., BANKS, C., & ZIMBARDO, P. (1973). Interpersonal dynamics in a simulated prison. *International Journal of Criminology and Penology, 1,* 69-97.

HANNAN, M. T., & FREEMAN, J. (1977). The population ecology of organizations. *American Journal of Sociology, 82,* 929-964.

HANNAN, M. T., & FREEMAN, J. (1984). Structural inertia and organizational change. *American Sociological Review, 4,* 149-164.

HANSEN, C. H., & HANSEN, R. D. (1988). Finding the face in the crowd: An anger superiority effect. *Journal of Personality and Social Psychology, 54,* 917-924.

HANSEN, R. D., & DONOGHUE, J. (1977). The power of consensus: Information derived from one's own and other's behavior. *Journal of Personality and Social Psychology, 35,* 294-302.

HARE, A. P., BLUMBERG, H. H., DAVIES, M. F., & KENT, M. V. (1996). *Small groups: An introduction.* Westport, CT: Praeger.

HARRIS, S. G., & SUTTON, R. I. (1986). Functions of parting ceremonies in dying organizations. *Academy of Management Journal, 29,* 5-30.

HARRISON, A. A., & CONNORS, M. M. (1984). Groups in exotic environments. In L. Berkowitz (Ed.), *Advances in experimental social psychology* (Vol. 18, pp. 49-87). Orlando, FL: Academic Press.

HARRISON, J. R. (1998, September). *The concept of simulation in organizational research.* Paper presented at the SCANCOR Conference, Samples of the Future, Stamford, CT.

HARTWICK, J., SHEPPARD, B. L., & DAVIS, J. H. (1982). Group remembering: Research and implications. In R. A. Guzzo (Ed.), *Improving group decision making in organizations* (pp. 41-72). London: Academic Press.

HAVEMAN, H. A. (1992). Between a rock and a hard place: Organizational change and performance under conditions of fundamental environmental transformation. *Administrative Science Quarterly, 37,* 48-75.

HAVRON, M. D., FAY, R. J., & GOODACRE, D. M., III. (1951). *Research on the effectiveness of small military units* (PRS Rep. No. 885). Washington, DC: Adjutant General Department.

HAVRON, M. D., & McGRATH, J. E. (1961). The contribution of the leader to the effectiveness of small military groups. In L. Petrullo & B. M. Bass (Eds.), *Leadership and interpersonal behavior* (pp. 167-178). New York: Holt, Rinehart & Winston.

HEIDER, F. (1946). Attitudes and cognitive organization. *Journal of Psychology, 21,* 107-112.

HENDREN, R. L., ATKINS, D. M., SUMNER, C. R., & BARBER, J. K. (1987). Model for the group treatment of eating disorders. *International Journal of Group Psychotherapy, 37,* 589-602.

HENRY, K. B., ARROW, H., & CARINI, B. (1998, April). *Theoretical extensions and organizational applications of the tripartite model of group identification.* Paper presented at the annual meeting of the Society for Industrial and Organizational Psychology, Dallas, TX.

HERMAN, J., & SCHATZOW, E. (1984). Time-limited group therapy for women with a history of incest. *International Journal of Group Psychotherapy, 34,* 605-616.

HILL, W. F., & GRUNER, L. (1973). A study of development in open and closed groups. *Small Group Behavior, 4,* 355-381.

HINSZ, V. (1990). Cognitive and consensus processes in group recognition memory performance. *Journal of Personality and Social Psychology, 59,* 705-718.

HINSZ, V. B., TINDALE, R. S., & VOLLRATH, D. A. (1997). The emerging conceptualization of groups as information processors. *Psychological Bulletin, 121,* 41-64.

HOFSTEDE, G. (1980). *Culture's consequences.* Beverly Hills, CA: Sage.

HOFSTEDE, G. (1983, Fall). The cultural relativity of organizational practices and theories. *Journal of International Business Studies,* pp. 75-89.

HOGG, M. A. (1987). Social identity and group cohesiveness. In J. C. Turner, M. A. Hogg, P. J. Oakes, S. D. Reicher, & M. Wetherall (Eds.), *Rediscovering the social group: A self-categorization theory* (pp. 89-116). Oxford, UK: Basil Blackwell.

HOGG, M. (1996). Social identity, self-categorization, and the small group. In E. Witte & J. H. Davis (Eds.), *Understanding group behavior: Vol 2. Small group processes and interpersonal relations* (pp. 227-254). Mahwah, NJ: Lawrence Erlbaum.

HOGG, M. A., & HARDIE, E. A. (1991). Social attraction, personal attraction, and self-categorization: A field study. *Personality and Social Psychology Bulletin, 17,* 175-180.

HOLLINGSHEAD, A. B. (1998). Retrieval processes in transactive memory systems. *Journal of Personality and Social Psychology, 74,* 659-671.

HOLLINGSHEAD, A. B., & McGRATH, J. E. (1995). Computer-assisted groups: A critical review of the empirical research. In R. L. Guzzo & E. Salas (Eds.), *Team effectiveness and decision-making in organizations* (pp. 46-78). San Francisco: Jossey-Bass.

HOLLINGSHEAD, A. B., McGRATH, J. E., & O'CONNOR, K. M. (1993). Group task performance and computer technology: A longitudinal study of computer-mediated versus face-to-face work groups. *Small Group Research, 24,* 307-333.

HOMANS, G. C. (1950). *The human group.* New York: Harcourt, Brace & World.

HORGAN, J. (1995, June). From complexity to perplexity. *Scientific American,* pp. 104-109.

ILGEN, D. R., MAJOR, D. A., HOLLENBECK, J. R., & SEGO, D. J. (1995). Team research in the 1990's. In M. M. Chemers & R. Ayman (Eds.), *Leadership theory and research: Perspectives and directions* (pp. 245-270). New York: Academic Press.

JANIS, I. L. (1972). *Victims of groupthink: A psychological study of foreign policy decisions and fiascoes.* Boston: Houghton Mifflin.

JANIS, I. L. (1982). *Groupthink.* Boston: Houghton Mifflin.

JEHN, K. A. (1995). A multimethod examination of the benefits and detriments of intragroup conflict. *Administrative Science Quarterly, 40,* 256-282.

JEHN, K. A. (1997). A qualitative analysis of conflict types and dimensions in organizational groups. *Administrative Science Quarterly, 42,* 520-557.

JOHNSON, D. W., JOHNSON, R. T., & MARUYAMA, G. (1984). Goal interdependence and interpersonal attraction in heterogeneous classrooms: A meta-analysis. In N. Miller & M. Brewer (Eds.), *Groups in contact: The psychology of desegregation* (pp. 187-212). New York: Academic Press.

KAHN, R. L., & KATZ, D. (1953). Leadership practices in relation to productivity and morale. In D. Cartwright & A. Zander (Eds.), *Group dynamics: Research and theory* (2nd ed., pp. 554-570). Evanston, IL: Row, Peterson.

KANTER, R. M. (1977a). *Men and women of the corporation.* New York: Basic Books.

KANTER, R. M. (1977b). Some effects of proportions on group life: Skewed sex ratios and responses to token women. *American Journal of Sociology, 82,* 965-990.

KANTER, R. M. (1983). Organizational effectiveness. In D. Perlman & P. C. Cozby (Eds.), *Social psychology.* New York: CBS College Publishing.

KAPLAN, H. L., & SADOCK, B. J. (Eds.). (1993). *Comprehensive group psychotherapy.* Baltimore: Williams & Wilkins.

KARAU, S. J., & KELLY, J. R. (1992). The effect of time scarcity and time abundance on group performance quality and interaction process. *Journal of Experimental Social Psychology, 28,* 542-571.

KAST, F. E., & ROSENZWEIG, J. E. (1972, December). General systems theory: Applications for organization and management. *Academy of Management Journal,* pp. 447-465.

KATZ, D., & KAHN, R. L. (1978). *The social psychology of organizations* (2nd ed.). New York: John Wiley.

KATZ, R. (1982). The effects of group longevity on project communication and performance. *Administrative Science Quarterly, 27,* 81-104.

KAUFFMAN, S. A. (1993). *The origins of order: Self-organization and selection in evolution.* New York: Oxford University Press.

KELLY, J. R. (1988). Entrainment in individual and group behavior. In J. E. McGrath (Ed.), *The social psychology of time: New perspectives* (pp. 89-110). Newbury Park, CA: Sage.

KELLY, J. R., JACKSON, J. W., & HUTSON-COMEAUX, S. L. (1997). The effect of time pressure and task differences on influence modes and accuracy in problem-solving groups. *Personality and Social Psychology Bulletin, 23,* 10-22.

KELLY, J. R., & McGRATH, J. E. (1985). Effects of time limits and task types on task performance and interaction of four-person groups. *Journal of Personality and Social Psychology 49,* 395-407.

KELLY, J. R., & McGRATH, J. E. (1988). *On time and method.* Newbury Park, CA: Sage.

KELSO, J. A. S. (1995). *Dynamic patterns: The self-organization of brain and behavior.* Cambridge: MIT Press.

KENT, R. N., & McGRATH, J. E. (1969). Task and group characteristics as factors influencing group performance. *Journal of Experimental Social Psychology, 5,* 429-440.

KIRKPATRICK, S., GELATT, C. D., & VECCHI, M. P. (1983). Optimization by simulated annealing. *Science, 220,* 671-680.

KLEIN, K. J., TOSI, H., & CANNELLA, A. A. (1999). Multilevel theory building: Benefits, barriers, and new developments. *Academy of Management Review, 24,* 243-248.

KOLODNY, H. F., & KIGGUNDU, M. N. (1980). Towards the development of a sociotechnical systems model in woodlands mechanical harvesting. *Human Relations, 33,* 623-645.

KOMORITA, S. S. (1973). Concession making and conflict resolution. *Journal of Conflict Resolution, 17,* 745-762.

KOMORITA, S. S. (1974). A weighted probability model of coalition formation. *Psychological Review, 8,* 242-256.

KOMORITA, S. S. (1979). An equal excess model of coalition formation. *Behavioral Science, 24,* 369-381.

KRACKHARDT, D., & PORTER, L. W. (1985). When friends leave: A structural analysis of the relationship between turnover and stayers' attitudes. *Administrative Science Quarterly, 30,* 242-261.

KRAMER, S. (1990). *Positive endings in psychotherapy: Bringing meaningful closure to therapeutic relationships.* San Francisco: Jossey-Bass.

KRANTZ, J. (1985). Group process under conditions of organizational decline. *Journal of Applied Behavioral Science, 21,* 1-17.

LaCOURSIERE, R. B. (1974). A group method to facilitate learning during the stages of a psychiatric affiliation. *International Journal of Group Psychotherapy, 24,* 342-351.

LaCOURSIERE, R. B. (1980). *The life cycle of groups: Group developmental stage theory.* New York: Human Sciences Press.

LAKATOS, I. (1970). Falsification and the methodology of scientific research programmes. In I. Lakatos & A. Musgrave (Eds.), *Criticism and the growth of knowledge.* Cambridge, UK: Cambridge University Press.

LARSON, J. R., FOSTER-FISHMAN, P. G., & KEYS, C. B. (1994). Discussion of shared and unshared information in decision making groups. *Journal of Personality and Social Psychology, 67,* 446-451.

LATANÉ, B. (1981). The psychology of social impact. *American Psychologist, 36,* 343-356.

LATANÉ, B., & BOURGEOIS, M. J. (1996). Experimental evidence for dynamic social impact: The emergence of subcultures in electronic groups. *Journal of Communication, 46*(4), 25-47.

LATANÉ, B., & L'HERROU, T. (1996). Spatial clustering in the conformity game: Dynamic social impact in electronic groups. *Journal of Personality and Social Psychology, 70,* 1218-1230.

LATANÉ, B., & NOWAK, A. (1994). Attitudes as catastrophes: From dimensions to categories with increasing involvement. In R. R. Vallacher & A. Nowak (Eds.), *Dynamical systems in social psychology* (pp. 219-249). New York: Academic Press.

LATANÉ, B., WILLIAMS, K., & HARKINS, S. (1979). Many hands make light the work: The causes and consequences of social loafing. *Journal of Personality and Social Psychology, 37,* 822-832.

LAUGHLIN, P. R., & ADAMOPOULOS, J. (1982). Social decision schemes on intellective tasks. In H. Brandstatter, J. H. Davis, & C. Stocker-Kreichgauer (Eds.), *Group decision making* (pp. 81-94). London: Academic Press.

LAUGHLIN, P. R., & ELLIS, A. L. (1986). Demonstrability and social combination processes on mathematical inductive tasks. *Journal of Experimental Social Psychology, 22,* 177-189.

LAUGHLIN, P. L., & SHIPPY, T. A. (1983). Collective induction. *Journal of Personality and Social Psychology, 45,* 94-100.

LAUGHLIN, P. L., VANDERSTOEP, S. W., & HOLLINGSHEAD, A. B. (1991). Collective versus individual induction: Recognition of truth, rejection of error, and collective information processing. *Journal of Personality and Social Psychology, 61,* 50-67.

LAWRENCE, P. R., & LORSCH, J. W. (1967). *Organization and environment.* Boston: Harvard Graduate School of Business Administration.

LEBIE, L., RHOADES, J. A., & McGRATH, J. E. (1996). Interaction process in computer-mediated and face-to-face groups. *Computer Supported Cooperative Work, 4,* 127-152.

LEVINE, J. M., & MORELAND, R. L. (1985). Innovation and socialization in small groups. In S. Moscovici, G. Mugny, & E. Van Abermaet (Eds.), *Perspectives on minority influence* (pp. 143-169). Cambridge, UK: Cambridge University Press.

LEVINE, J. M., & MORELAND, R. L. (1990). Progress in small group research. *Annual Review of Psychology, 41,* 585-634.

LEVINE, J. M., & MORELAND, R. L. (1991). Culture and socialization in work groups. In L. Resnick, J. Levine, & S. Behrend (Eds.), *Perspectives on socially shared cognition* (pp. 257-279). Washington, DC: American Psychological Association.

LEWIN, K. (1948). *Resolving social conflict: Selected papers on group dynamics.* New York: Harper.

LEWIN, K. (1953). Studies in group decision. In D. Cartwright & A. Zander (Eds.), *Group dynamics: Research and theory.* Evanston, IL: Row, Peterson.

LEWIN, K., LIPPETT, R., & WHITE, R. (1939). Patterns of aggressive behavior in experimentally created "social climates." *Journal of Social Psychology, 10,* 271-299.

LORD, R. G., & MAHER, K. J. (1990). Leader perceptions and leader performance: Two distinct but interrelated processes. In J. Carroll (Ed.), *Advances in applied social psychology: Vol. 4. Business setting.* Hillsdale, NJ: Lawrence Erlbaum.

LORGE, I., & SOLOMON, H. (1955). Two models of group behavior in the solution of Eureka-type problems. *Psychometrika, 20,* 139-148.

MANTOVANI, G. (1996). *New communication environments: From everyday to virtual.* London: Taylor & Francis.

MARKOVSKY, B., & CHAFFEE, M. (1995). Social identification and solidarity: A reformulation. *Advances in Group Processes, 12,* 249-270.

MARKOVSKY, B., & LAWLER, E. J. (1994). A new theory of group solidarity. *Advances in Group Processes, 11,* 113-137.

MARSHALL, S. L. A. (1947). *Men against fire: The problem of battle command in future war.* New York: William Morrow.

MASLOW, A. H. (1943). A theory of human motivation. *Psychological Review, 1,* 370-396.

McARTHUR, L. Z., & BARON, R. M. (1983). Toward an ecological theory of social perception. *Psychological Review, 90,* 215-238.

McCLELLAND, D. C. (1985). How motives, skills, and values determine what people do. *American Psychologist, 40,* 812-825.

McCOLLOM, M. (1995a). Group formation: Boundaries, leadership, and culture. In J. Gillette & M. McCollum (Eds.), *Groups in context: A new perspective on group dynamics* (pp. 34-48). Lanham, MD: University Press of America.

McCOLLOM, M. (1995b). Reevaluating group development: A critique of familiar models. In J. Gillette & M. McCollom (Eds.), *Groups in context: A new perspective on group dynamics* (pp. 133-154). Lanham, MD: University Press of America.

McGRATH, J. E. (1984). *Groups: Interaction and performance.* Englewood Cliffs, NJ: Prentice Hall.

McGRATH, J. E. (1991). Time, interaction, and performance (TIP): A theory of groups. *Small Group Research, 22,* 147-174.

McGRATH, J. E. (1993). Introduction: The JEMCO workshop: Description of a longitudinal study. *Small Group Research, 24,* 285-306.

McGRATH, J. E. (1997). Small group research, that once and future field: An interpretation of the past with an eye to the future. *Group Dynamics: Theory, Research, and Practice, 1,* 1-27.

McGRATH, J. E., & ALTMAN, I. (1966). *Small group research: A synthesis and critique of the field.* New York: Holt, Rinehart & Winston.

McGRATH, J. E., & ARROW, H. (1996). Introduction: The JEMCO-2 study of time, technology, and groups. *Computer Supported Cooperative Work, 4,* 107-126.

McGRATH, J. E., ARROW, H., GRUENFELD, D. H, HOLLINGSHEAD, A. B., & O'CONNOR, K. M. (1993). Groups, tasks, and technology: The effects of experience and change. *Small Group Research, 24,* 406-420.

McGRATH, J. E., & BEEHR, T. A. (1990). Time and the stress process: Some temporal issues in the conceptualization and measurement of stress. *Stress Medicine, 6,* 95-104.

McGRATH, J. E., & BERDAHL, J. L. (1998). Groups, technology, and time: Use of computers for collaborative work. In R. S. Tindale, L. Heath, J. Edwards, E. J. Posavac, F. B. Bryant, Y. Suarez-Balcazar, E. Henderson-King, & J. Myers (Eds.), *Social psychological applications to social issues: Vol. 4. Theory and research on small groups* (pp. 205-228). New York: Plenum.

McGRATH, J. E., BERDAHL, J. L., & ARROW, H. (1995). Traits, expectations, culture and clout: The dynamics of diversity in work groups. In S. E. Jackson & M. N. Ruderman (Eds.), *Diversity in work teams: Research paradigms for a changing workplace* (pp. 17-45). Washington, DC: American Psychological Association.

McGRATH, J. E., & KELLY, J. R. (1986). *Time and human interaction: Toward a social psychology of time.* New York: Guilford.

McGRATH, J. E., & KELLY, J. R. (1991). Temporal context and temporal patterning: Toward a time-centered perspective for social psychology. *Time and Society, 1,* 399-420.

McGRATH, J. E., & KRAVITZ, D. (1982). Group research. *Annual Review of Psychology, 33,* 195-230.

McGRATH, J. E., & O'CONNOR, K. M. (1996). Temporal issues in work groups. In M. A. West (Ed.), *Handbook of work group psychology* (pp. 25-52). New York: John Wiley.

McKNIGHT, D. H., CUMMINGS, L. L., & CHERVANY, N. L. (1998). Initial trust formation in new organizational relationships. *Academy of Management Review, 23,* 473-490.

McPHERSON, M. J. (1990). Evolution in communities of voluntary organizations. In J. V. Singh (Ed.), *Organizational evolution: New directions* (pp. 224-245). Newbury Park, CA: Sage.

MENNECKE, B. E., HOFFER, J. A., & WYNNE, B. E. (1992). The implications of group development and history for group support system theory and practice. *Small Group Research, 23,* 524-572.

MICHAELSEN, L. K., WATSON, W. E., & SCHRADER, C. B. (1985). Informative testing: A practical approach for tutoring with groups. *Organizational Behavior Teaching Review, 9*(4), 18-33.

MILARDO, R. M. (1986). Personal choice and social constraint in close relationships: Applications of network analysis. In V. J. Derluga & R. A. Winstead (Eds.), *Friendship and social interaction* (pp. 145-166). New York: Springer-Verlag.

MILLER, D., & FRIESEN, P. H. (1980). Momentum and revolution in organizational adaptation. *Academy of Management Journal, 23,* 591-614.

MILLS, T. M. (1964). *Group transformation: An analysis of a learning group.* Englewood Cliffs, NJ: Prentice Hall.

MOORE-EDE, M. C., SULZMAN, F. M., & FULLER, C. A. (1982). *The clocks that time us.* Cambridge, MA: Harvard University Press.

MORELAND, R. L. (1987). The formation of small groups. *Group Processes: Review of Personality and Social Psychology, 8,* 80-110.

MORELAND, R. L. (1996). Lewin's legacy for small-groups research. *Systems Practice, 9,* 7-26.

MORELAND, R. L., HOGG, M. A., & HAINS, S. C. (1994). Back to the future: Social psychological research on groups. *Journal of Experimental Social Psychology, 30,* 527-555.

MORELAND, R. L., & LEVINE, J. M. (1982). Socialization in small groups: Temporal changes in individual-group relations. *Advances in Experimental Social Psychology, 15,* 137-192.

MORELAND, R. L., & LEVINE, J. M. (1984). Role transitions in small groups. In V. Allen & E. Van de Vliert (Eds.), *Role transitions: Explorations and explanations* (pp. 181-195). New York: Plenum.

MORELAND, R. L., & LEVINE, J. M. (1988). Group dynamics over time: Development and socialization in small groups. In J. E. McGrath (Ed.), *The social psychology of time: New perspectives* (pp. 151-181). Newbury Park, CA: Sage.

MORELAND, R. L., LEVINE, J. M., & WINGERT, M. L. (1996). Creating the ideal group: Composition effects at work. In E. Witte & J. H. Davis (Eds.), *Understanding group behavior: Small group processes and interpersonal relations* (Vol. 2, pp. 11-35). Mahwah, NJ: Lawrence Erlbaum.

MOSCOVICI, S. (1985). Social influence and conformity. In G. Lindzey & E. Aronson (Eds.), *The handbook of social psychology* (Vol. 2, pp. 347-412). New York: Random House.

MOSCOVICI, S., MUGNY, G., & VAN AVERMAET, E. (Eds.). (1985). *Perspectives on minority influence.* Cambridge, UK: Cambridge University Press.

MUDRACK, P. E. (1989). Defining group cohesiveness: A legacy of confusion? *Small Group Research, 20,* 37-49.

MURNIGHAN, J. K., & CONLON, D. E. (1991). The dynamics of intense work groups: A study of British string quartets. *Administrative Science Quarterly, 36,* 165-186.

MYERS, D. G., & LAMM, H. (1976). The group polarization phenomenon. *Psychological Bulletin, 83,* 602-627.

NEMETH, C. J. (1986). Differential contributions of majority and minority influence. *Psychological Review, 93,* 23-32.

NEWCOMB, T. M. (1943). *Personality and social change.* New York: Drysden.

NEWCOMB, T. M. (1953). An approach to the study of communicative acts. *Psychological Review, 4,* 183-214.

NEWCOMB, T. M. (1961). *The acquaintance process.* New York: Holt, Rinehart & Winston.

NEWCOMB, T. M. (1981). Heiderian balance as a group phenomenon. *Journal of Personality and Social Psychology, 40,* 862-867.

NOWAK, A., & LEWENSTEIN, M. (1994). Dynamical systems: A tool for social psychology. In R. R. Vallacher & A. Nowak (Eds.), *Dynamical systems in social psychology* (pp. 17-54). New York: Academic Press.

NOWAK, A., LEWENSTEIN, M., & VALLACHER, R. R. (1994). Toward a dynamical social psychology. In R. R. Vallacher & A. Nowak (Eds.), *Dynamical systems in social psychology* (pp. 279-287). New York: Academic Press.

NOWAK, A., SZAMREJ, J., & LATANÉ, B. (1990). From private attitude to public opinion: A dynamic theory of social impact. *Psychological Review, 97,* 367-376.

O'CONNOR, K. M. (1998). Experiential diversity in groups: Conceptualizing and measuring variation among teammates. In M. A. Neale, E. A. Mannix, & D. H Gruenfeld (Eds.), *Research on managing groups and teams* (Vol. 1, pp. 167-182). Stamford, CT: JAI.

O'CONNOR, K. M., GRUENFELD, D. H., & McGRATH, J. E. (1993). The experience and effects of conflict in continuing work groups. *Small Group Research, 24,* 362-382.

ORBELL, J., & DAWES, R. (1981). Social dilemmas. In G. M. Stevenson & J. H. Davis (Eds.), *Progress in applied social psychology* (Vol. 1, pp. 37-65). New York: John Wiley.

OSTROM, T. M. (1988). Computer simulation: The third symbol system. *Journal of Experimental Social Psychology, 24,* 381-392.

PELTO, P. J. (1968, April). The difference between "tight" and "loose" societies. *Transaction: Social Science and Modern Society,* pp. 37-40.

PFEFFER, J., & SALANCIK, G. R. (1978). *The external control of organizations: A resource dependence perspective.* New York: Harper & Row.

PITTENDREIGH, C. S. (1972). On temporal organization in living systems. In H. Yukor, H. Osmond, & F. Clark (Eds.), *The future of time* (pp. 179-218). New York: Doubleday.

POLLEY, R. B. (1988). Group field dynamics and effective mediation. *International Journal of Small Group Research, 4*(1), 55-75.

POLLEY, R. B. (1989). Operationalizing Lewinian field theory. *Advances in Group Processes, 6,* 205-227.

POOLE, M. S. (1981). Decision development in small groups I: A test of two models. *Communication Monographs, 48,* 1-24.

POOLE, M. S. (1983). Decision development in small groups III. A multiple sequence model of group decision making. *Communication Monographs, 50,* 321-344.

POOLE, M. S., & DeSANCTIS, G. (1989). Use of group decision support systems as an appropriation process. *Proceedings of the 22nd Annual Hawaii International Conference on System Sciences, 4,* 149-157.

POOLE, M. S., & DeSANCTIS, G. (1990). Understanding the use of decision support systems: The theory of adaptive structuration. In J. Fulk & C. Steinfield (Eds.), *Organizations and communication technology* (pp. 175-195). Newbury Park, CA: Sage.

POOLE, M. S., & ROTH, J. (1989a). Decision development in small groups IV: A typology of decision paths. *Human Communication Research, 15,* 323-356.

POOLE, M. S., & ROTH, J. (1989b). Decision development in small groups V: Test of a contingency model. *Human Communication Research, 15,* 549-589.

POWERS, W. T. (1998). *Making sense of behavior: The meaning of control.* New Canaan, CT: Benchmark.

PRIGOGINE, I., & STENGERS, I. (1984). *Order out of chaos.* New York: Bantam.

PRUITT, D. G., & KIMMEL, M. J. (1977). Twenty years of experimental gaming: Critique, synthesis, and suggestions for the future. *Annual Review of Psychology, 28,* 363-392.

PSATHAS, G. (1960). Phase movement and equilibrium tendencies in interaction process in psychotherapy groups. *Sociometry, 23,* 177-194.

RABBIE, J. M., & HORWITZ, M. (1969). Arousal of ingroup-outgroup bias by a chance win or loss. *Journal of Personality and Social Psychology, 13,* 269-277.

RABBIE, J. M., & LODEWIJKX, F. M. (1996). A behavioral interaction model: Toward an integrative theoretical framework for studying intra- and intergroup dynamics. In E. Witte & J. H. Davis (Eds.), *Understanding group behavior: Vol 2. Small group processes and interpersonal relations* (pp. 255-294). Mahwah, NJ: Lawrence Erlbaum.

RANTILLA, A. K. (1996). *Attributions for collective and individual performance.* Unpublished master's thesis, University of Illinois at Urbana-Champaign.

RAVEN, B. (1993). The origins of power: Origins and recent development. *Journal of Social Issues, 49,* 227-251.

READ, P. P. (1974). *Alive.* New York: Avon.

RHOADES, J. A., & O'CONNOR, K. M. (1996). Affect in computer-mediated and face-to-face work groups: The construction and testing of a general model. *Computer Supported Cooperative Work, 4,* 203-228.

RIDGEWAY, C. L., & BERGER, J. (1986). Expectations, legitimization, and dominance behavior in task groups. *American Sociological Review, 51,* 603-617.

ROBY, T. B., & LANZETTA, J. T. (1956). Work group structure, communication, and performance. *Sociometry, 19,* 105-113.

ROBY, T. B., & LANZETTA, J. T. (1957). *A laboratory task for the study of individuals or groups* (Rep. No. AFPTRC-TN-57-124). San Antonio, TX: Randolph Air Force Base, Operator Laboratory.

ROBY, T. B., & LANZETTA, J. T. (1958). Considerations in the analysis of group tasks. *Psychological Bulletin, 55,* 88-101.

ROETHLISBERGER, F. J., & DICKSON, W. J. (1939). *Management and the worker.* Cambridge, MA: Harvard University Press.

ROSENTHAL, R., & ROSNOW, R. (1969). *Artifact in behavioral research.* New York: Academic Press.

RUNKEL, P. J. (1990). *Casting nets and testing specimens: Two grand methods of psychology.* New York: Praeger.

RUNKEL, P. J., & McGRATH, J. E. (1972). *Research on human behavior: A systematic guide to method.* New York: Holt, Rinehart & Winston.

SADOCK, V. A. (1983). Group psychotherapy with rape victims and battered women. In H. I. Kaplan & B. J. Sadock (Eds.), *Comprehensive group psychotherapy* (2nd ed., pp. 282-285). Baltimore: Williams & Kilkins.

SALAS, E., BLAIWES, A. R., REYNOLDS, R. E., GLICKMAN, A. S., & MORGAN, B. B., Jr. (1985). Teamwork from team training: New directions. In *Proceedings of the 7th Interservice/Industry Training Equipment Conference and Exhibition.* Orlando, FL: American Defense Preparedness Association.

SALAS, E., DICKINSON, T. L., CONVERSE, S. A., & TANNENBAUM, S. I. (1992). Toward an understanding of team performance and training. In R. W. Swezey & E. Salas (Eds.), *Teams: Their training and performance.* Norwood, NJ: Ablex.

SANNA, L. J., & PARKS, C. D. (1997). Group research trends in social and organizational psychology: Whatever happened to intragroup research? *Psychological Science, 8,* 261-267.

SASHKIN, M. (1988). The visionary leaders. In J. A. Conger & R. A. Kanungo (Eds.), *Charismatic leadership: The elusive factor in organizational effectiveness* (pp. 122-160). San Francisco: Jossey-Bass.

SCHEIDLINGER, S. (1984). Short-term group psychotherapy for children: An overview. *International Journal of Group Psychotherapy, 34,* 573-585.

SCHEIN, E. H. (1983, Summer). The role of the founder in creating organizational culture. *Organizational Dynamics,* pp. 13-28.

SCHOFIELD, J. W. (1978). School desegregation and intergroup relations. In D. Bar-Tal & L. Saxe (Eds.), *The social psychology of education.* Washington, DC: Halstead.

SCHUTZ, W. C. (1958). *FIRO: A three-dimensional theory of interpersonal behavior.* New York: Holt, Rinehart & Winston.

SHAW, M. E. (1932). Comparisons of individuals and small groups in the rational solution of complex problems. *American Journal of Psychology, 44,* 491-504.

SHAW, M. E. (1954). Some effects of problem complexity upon problem solution efficiency in different communication nets. *Journal of Experimental Psychology, 48,* 211-217.

SHAW, M. E. (1958). Some effects of irrelevant information upon problem solving by small groups. *Journal of Social Psychology, 47,* 33-37.

SHERIF, M., HARVEY, O. J., WHITE, B. J., HOOD, W. R., & SHERIF, C. W. (1961). *Intergroup conflict and cooperation: The Robbers Cave experiment.* Norman, OK: Institute of Social Relations.

SHIFFRIN, R. M., & SCHNEIDER, W. (1977). Controlled and automatic human information processing: II. Perceptual learning, automatic attending, and a general theory. *Psychological Review, 84,* 127-190.

SIMMEL, G. (1902). The number of members as determining the sociological form of the group. *American Journal of Sociology, 8,* 1-46, 158-196.

SITKIN, S. B. (1992). Learning through failure: The strategy of small losses. *Research in Organizational Behavior, 14*, 231-266.

SPITZ, H., & SADOCK, B. (1973, June 1). Psychiatric training of graduate nursing students. *New York State Journal of Medicine*, pp. 1334-1338.

STASSER, G., STEWART, D. D., & WITTENBAUM, G. M. (1995). Expert roles and information exchange during discussion: The importance of knowing who knows what. *Journal of Experimental Social Psychology, 31*, 244-265.

STASSER, G., TAYLOR, L., & HANNA, C. (1989). Information sampling in structured and unstructured discussions of three- and six-person groups. *Journal of Personality and Social Psychology, 57*, 67-78.

STASSER, G., & TITUS, W. (1985). Pooling of unshared information in group decision making: Biased information sampling during discussion. *Journal of Personality and Social Psychology, 48*, 1467-1478.

STASSER, G., & TITUS, W. (1987). Effects of information load and percentages of shared information on the dissemination of unshared information during group discussion. *Journal of Personality and Social Psychology, 53*, 81-93.

STAUB, E. (1989). *The roots of evil: The origins of genocide and other group violence*. New York: Cambridge University Press.

STAW, B. M. (1976). Knee-deep in the big muddy: A study of escalating commitment to a chosen course of action. *Organizational Behavior and Human Performance, 16*, 27-44.

STAW, B. M., SANDELANDS, L. E., & DUTTON, J. E. (1981). Threat-rigidity effects in organizational behavior: A multi-level analysis. *Administrative Science Quarterly, 26*, 501-524.

STEINER, I. D. (1972). *Group process and productivity*. New York: Academic Press.

STINCHCOMBE, A. S. (1965). Social structure and organizations. In J. G. March (Ed.), *Handbook of organizations* (pp. 153-193). Chicago: Rand-McNally.

STOCK, D., & THELEN, H. A. (1958). *Emotional dynamics and group culture: Experimental studies of individual and group behavior*. New York: New York University Press.

STRAUS, S. G. (1996). Getting a clue: The effects of communication media and information distribution on participation and performance in computer-mediated and face-to-face groups. *Small Group Research, 27*, 115-142.

SUNDSTROM, E., De MEUSE, K. P., & FUTRELL, D. (1990). Work teams: Applications and effectiveness. *American Psychologist, 45*, 120-133.

SUTTON, R. I. (1988). Managing organizational death. In K. S. Cameron, R. I. Sutton, & D. A. Whetten (Eds.), *Readings in organizational design: Frameworks, research, and prescriptions* (pp. 381-396). Cambridge, MA: Ballinger.

TAJFEL, H. (1974). Social identity and intergroup behavior. *Social Science Information, 13*, 65-93.

TAJFEL, H. (1978). *Differentiation between social groups: Studies in the social psychology of intergroup relations*. London: Academic Press.

TAJFEL, H., BILLIG, M., BUNDY, R., & FLAMENT, C. (1971). Social categorization and intergroup behavior. *European Journal of Social Psychology, 1*, 149-177.

TAJFEL, H., & TURNER, J. C. (1979). An integrative theory of intergroup behavior. In S. Worchel & W. G. Austin (Eds.), *The social psychology of intergroup relations*. Monterey, CA: Brooks/Cole.

TALLAND, G. A. (1955). Tasks and interaction process: Some characteristics of therapeutic group discussion. *Journal of Abnormal and Social Psychology, 50*, 105-109.

TAYLOR, D. M., & MCKIRNAN, D. J. (1984). A five-stage model of intergroup relations. *British Journal of Social Psychology, 23*, 291-300.

TAYLOR, D. W., & FAUST, W. L. (1952). Twenty questions: Efficiency in problem solving as a function of size of group. *Journal of Experimental Psychology, 44*, 360-368.

THELEN, H. A. (1956). Emotionality of work in groups. In L. D. White (Ed.), *The state of the social sciences.* Chicago: University of Chicago Press.

THELEN, H. A., STOCK, D., & ASSOCIATES. (1954). *Methods for studying work and emotionality in group operation.* Chicago: University of Chicago, Hyman Dynamics Laboratory.

THIBAUT, J. W., & KELLEY, H. H. (1959). *The social psychology of groups.* New York: John Wiley.

TINDALE, R. S. (1989). Group versus individual information processing: The effects of outcome feedback on decision making. *Organizational Behavior and Human Decision Making, 44,* 454-471.

TRIANDIS, H. C. (1994). *Culture and social behavior.* New York: McGraw-Hill.

TRIPLETT, N. (1898). The dynamogenic factors in pace-making and competition. *American Journal of Psychology, 9,* 507-533.

TRIST, E., & BAMFORTH, D. (1951). Some social and psychological consequences of the long-wall method of coal getting. *Human Relations, 4,* 3-38.

TSCHAN, F. (1995). Communication enhances small group performance if it conforms to task requirements: The concept of ideal communication cycles. *Basic and Applied Social Psychology, 17,* 371-393.

TSCHAN, F., & VON CRANACH, M. (1996). Group task structure, processes, and outcome. In M. A. West (Ed.), *Handbook of work group psychology* (pp. 92-121). New York: John Wiley.

TUCKMAN, B. W. (1965). Developmental sequences in small groups. *Psychological Bulletin, 65,* 384-399.

TUCKMAN, B. W., & JENSEN, M. A. C. (1977). Stages of small-group development revisited. *Group and Organizational Studies, 2,* 419-427.

TUSHMAN, M. L., & ROMANELLI, E. (1985). Organizational evolution: A metamorphosis model of convergence and reorientation. *Research in Organizational Behavior, 7,* 171-222.

TURNER, J. C. (1985). Social categorization and the self-concept: A social cognitive theory of group behaviour. *Advances in Group Processes, 2,* 77-122.

TURNER, J. C., HOGG, M., OAKES, P., REICHER, S., & WETHERALL, M. (1987). *Rediscovering the social group: A self-categorization theory.* Oxford, UK: Basil Blackwell.

TURNER, J. C., SACHDEV, I., & HOGG, M. A. (1983). Social categorization, interpersonal attraction, and group formation. *British Journal of Social Psychology, 22,* 227-239.

VALLACHER, R. R., & NOWAK, A. (Eds.). (1994). *Dynamical systems in social psychology.* New York: Academic Press.

VALLACHER, R. R., & WEGNER, D. M. (1987). What do people think they're doing? Action identification and human behavior. *Psychological Review, 94,* 3-15.

VAN de VEN, A. B., & POOLE, M. S. (1995). Explaining development and change in organizations. *Academy of Management Review, 20,* 510-540.

VAN KNIPPENBERG, A., & ELLEMERS, N. (1993). Strategies in intergroup relations. In M. A. Hogg & D. Abrams (Eds.), *Group motivation: Social psychological perspectives* (pp. 17-32). London: Harvester Wheatsheaf.

VAN STEENBERG LaFARGE, V. (1995). Termination in groups. In J. Gillette & M. McCollom (Eds.), *Groups in context: A new perspective on group dynamics* (pp. 171-185). Lanham, MD: University Press of America.

VERDI, A. F., & WHEELAN, S. A. (1992). Developmental patterns in same sex and mixed sex groups. *Small Group Research, 23,* 356-378.

VIDMAR, N., & McGRATH, J. E. (1970). Forces affecting success in negotiation groups. *Behavioral Science, 15,* 154-163.

VON BERTALANFFY, L. (1968). *General systems theory* (Rev. ed.). New York: George Braziller.

WALDROP, M. M. (1992). *Complexity: The emerging science at the edge of order and chaos.* New York: Touchstone.

WALLER, M. J. (1997). Keeping the pins in the air: How work groups juggle multiple tasks. In M. M. Beyerlein, D. A. Johnson, & S. T. Beyerlein (Eds.), *Advances in interdisciplinary studies of work teams* (Vol. 4, pp. 217-247). Greenwich, CT: JAI.

WALTON, R. E., & HACKMAN, J. R. (1986). Groups under contrasting management strategies. In P. S. Goodman (Ed.), *Designing effective work groups* (pp. 168-201). San Francisco: Jossey-Bass.

WANOUS, J. P., REICHERS, A. E., & MALIK, S. D. (1984). Organizational socialization and group development: Toward an integrative perspective. *Academy of Management Review, 9,* 670-683.

WARNER, R. M. (1979). Periodic rhythms in conversational speech. *Language and Speech, 22,* 381-396.

WARNER, R. M. (1988). Rhythms in social interaction. In J. E. McGrath (Ed.), *The social psychology of time: New perspectives* (pp. 63-88). Newbury Park, CA: Sage.

WATSON, R., DeSANCTIS, G., & POOLE, M. S. (1988, September). Using a GDSS to facilitate group consensus: Some intended and unintended consequences. *MIS Quarterly,* pp. 463-478.

WATSON, W. E., KUMAR, K., & MICHAELSEN, L. K. (1993). Cultural diversity's impact on interaction process and performance: Comparing homogeneous and diverse task groups. *Academy of Management Journal, 36,* 590-602.

WEGNER, D. M. (1987). Transactive memory: A contemporary analysis of the group mind. In B. Mullen & G. R. Goethals (Eds.), *Theories of group behavior.* New York: Springer-Verlag.

WEGNER, D. M., ERBER, R., & RAYMOND, P. (1991). Transactive memory in close relationships. *Journal of Personality and Social Psychology, 61,* 923-929.

WEICK, K. E. (1995). *Sensemaking in organizations.* Thousand Oaks, CA: Sage.

WEINER, N. (1948). *Cybernetics.* Cambridge, MA: Technology Press.

WEISS, H. A., & ILGEN, D. R. (1985). Routinized behavior in organizations. *Journal of Behavioral Economics, 14,* 57-67.

WHEELAN, S. A. (1994). *Group processes: A developmental perspective.* Sydney, Australia: Allyn & Bacon.

WHEELAN, S. A., & McKEAGE, R. L. (1993). Developmental patterns in small and large groups. *Small Group Research, 24,* 60-83.

WHITE, R. K. (1969). Three not-so-obvious contributions of psychology to peace. *Journal of Social Issues, 25*(4), 23-29.

WICKER, A. W., KIRMEYER, S. L., HANSON, L., & ALEXANDER, D. (1976). Effects of manning levels on subjective experiences, performance, and verbal interaction in groups. *Organizational Behavior and Human Performance, 17,* 251-274.

WILLIAMS, J. E., & BEST, D. L. (1990). *Sex and psyche: Gender and self viewed cross-culturally.* Newbury Park, CA: Sage.

WITTENBAUM, G. M., & STASSER, G. (1996). Management of information in small groups. In J. L. Nye & A. M. Brower (Eds.), *What's social about social cognition? Social cognition research in small groups* (pp. 3-28). Thousand Oaks, CA: Sage.

WOOD, W., LUNDGREN, S., OUELLETTE, J. A., BUSCERNE, S., & BLACKSTONE, T. (1994). Minority influence: A meta-analytic review of social influence processes. *Psychological Bulletin, 115,* 323-345.

WORCHEL, S. (1994). You can go home again: Returning group research to the group context with an eye on developmental issues. *Small Group Research, 25,* 205-223.

WORCHEL, S. (1996). Emphasizing the social nature of groups in a developmental framework. In J. L. Nye & A. M. Brower (Eds.), *What's social about social cognition? Research on socially shared cognition in small groups* (pp. 261-282). Thousand Oaks, CA: Sage.

WRIGHT, S. (1932). The roles of mutation, inbreeding, crossbreeding and selection in evolution. *Proceedings of the Sixth International Congress on Genetics, 1,* 356.

YALOM, I. D. (1995). *The theory and practice of group psychotherapy* (4th ed.). New York: Basic Books.

ZACCARO, S. J., & BURKE, C. S. (1998, April). Team versus crew leadership: Differences and similarities. In R. J. Klimoski (Chair), *When is a team a crew—and does it matter?* Symposium conducted at the annual meeting of the Society for Industrial and Organizational Psychology, Dallas, TX.

ZEGGELINK, E. (1993). *Strangers into friends: The evolution of friendship networks using an individual oriented modeling approach.* Amsterdam: Thesis Publishers.

ZEGGELINK, E. (1995). Evolving friendship networks: An individual-oriented approach implementing similarity. *Social Networks, 17,* 83-110.

ZILLER, R. C. (1965). Toward a theory of open and closed groups. *Psychological Bulletin, 64,* 164-182.

Name Index

Subject Index

About the Authors

Holly Arrow is Assistant Professor of Psychology at the University of Oregon and a member of the Institute of Cognitive and Decision Sciences at that university. She is interested in the formation and development of small groups whose membership changes over time. She studies how the perceptions, decisions, and actions of group members shape the evolution of group structure, including norms, group identity, and patterns of social influence. She received a PhD in social and organizational psychology from the University of Illinois at Urbana-Champaign.

Joseph E. McGrath is Professor Emeritus of Psychology and Women's Studies at the University of Illinois, Urbana-Champaign. He received an MA in psychology from the University of Maryland and a PhD in social psychology from University of Michigan. His research interests include small group interaction and task performance; collaborative work in groups using computer-mediated communication systems; social psychological factors in human stress; research methodology; the social psychology of time; and gender issues in social psychological processes.

Jennifer L. Berdahl is Assistant Professor of Organizational Behavior and Industrial Relations at the Haas School of Business, University of California, Berkeley. She received an MA in industrial relations and a PhD in social psychology from the University of Illinois at Urbana-

Champaign. She has researched sexual harassment in organizations, gender and leadership dynamics in small groups, and the effects of resource power on social influence and memory. She has also developed a computational model of small groups to examine the effects of demographic diversity on group performance, member commitment, member learning, and status structures over time.